COMICS
1964-2024

This book was published to accompany the exhibition 'Bande dessinée, 1964–2024'
at the Centre Pompidou, Paris, Galerie 2, from 29 May to 4 November 2024.

In partnership with the Bibliothèque Publique d'Information and Ircam
and the Fonds Hélène & Édouard Leclerc pour la Culture

FONDS
HÉLÈNE&ÉDOUARD LECLERC
POUR LA CULTURE

With the support of Indosuez Wealth Management
and the Japanese Friends of the Centre Pompidou

COMICS
1964-2024

Edited by
Thierry Groensteen
Lucas Hureau
Anne Lemonnier
Emmanuèle Payen

Centre Pompidou
T&H

ACKNOWLEDGMENTS

First and foremost, we would like to thank all the artists who are part of this exhibition. This project could not have come to fruition without their involvement, and they have provided valuable information and insights throughout the preparation stage. Thanks also to those who kindly agreed to make their works available for the duration of the exhibition.

In addition, we would like to express our thanks to all the institutions and individuals whose generous loans made this exhibition possible:
Pietro Alligo
Bibliothèque Nationale de France, Paris
Bibliothèque Patrimoniale de la CIBDI, Angoulême
Bernadette Bienfait
Mariano and Silvana Buscaglia
Fondation Boon pour les Arts Graphiques Narratifs
Fondation Hergé
Fujiko F. Fujio Pro Co., Ltd.
Fujio Productions Ltd.
Furari Co., Ltd.
Galerie Anne Barrault, Paris
Galerie de la Bande Dessinée, Brussels
Galerie Georges-Philippe & Nathalie Vallois, Paris
Galerie Martel, Paris
Peter Janda
Hiroshima Peace Memorial Museum, Hiroshima
KAWS
Claude Leblanc
Michel-Édouard Leclerc
Michel Lieuré
Bernard Mahé
9e Art Références Collection, Paris
Thierry Mallet
MEL Compagnie des Arts
MEL Publisher
The Morris family
Musée de la Bande Dessinée, CIBDI, Angoulême
Ulrich Schröder
Philippe Simay
Thierry Smolderen
The Ohio State University Billy Ireland Cartoon Library & Museum, Columbus, Ohio
Marina Vlady
and all those who wished to remain anonymous.

Finally, we would like to thank all the teams at the Centre Pompidou whose work made this project a reality, and to all of those who, in a variety of ways, contributed to the exhibition and this book, in particular: Charline Bailot, Jean-Baptiste Barbier, Anne Barrault, Vincent Bernière, Fanny Blanckaert, Philippe Boon, Martin Bretécher, Laurent Bruel, Kae Byoga, Bernard de Choisy, Jean Chung, Antonio Crepax, Philippe Cruvellier, Leopold Dahan, Myriam Dartois, Olivier Delflas, Marguerite Demoëte, Clémentine Deroudille, Alexandre Devaux, Stéphane Duval, Vincent Eches, Serge Ewenczyk, Catherine Ferreyrolle, Joan Fontaine, Léo Frezel, Arthur Fuchs, Tristan Garcia, Clémentine Gasque, Anette Gehrig, Laurent Gerbier, Isabelle Giraud, Nausicaa Giraud, Daniele Gradella, Paul Gravett, Jim Halperin, Alain Huberty, Manon Kalbez, Robert Kirkman, Ronan Lancelot, Nelly Lavaure, Christophe Ledannois, Michel Lieuré, Frédéric Lorge, Bernard Mahé, Simone Mattotti, Benoît Maurer, Kim Minchan, Benoît Mouchart, Yuta Nabatame, Amélie Payan, Benoît Peeters, Vincent Petit, Wendy Pflug, Lisa Portejoie, Dominique Radrizzani, Thomas Ragon, Michèle Reiser, Jenny Robb, Nick Rodwell, Johanna Schipper, Ulrich Schröder, Thomas Sirdey, Miyako Slocombe, Silenn Thomas, Nadège Vainas, Saveria de Valence, Patrizia Zanotti, Rina Zavagli.

A spectacular celebration of comics, the season 'La BD à tous les étages' brings the full diversity of *la bande dessinée* to the Centre Pompidou. With major exhibitions such as 'Bande dessinée et vie quotidienne' in 1977–78 and 'Hergé' in 2006, the Centre Pompidou has long been a pioneering institution in recognizing comics as a major artform. The Bibliothèque Publique d'Information plays a proactive role in this, staging retrospectives dedicated to Jean-Marc Reiser (2003), Willem (2006), Art Spiegelman (2012), Claire Bretécher (2015), André Franquin (2016), Riad Sattouf (2018), Catherine Meurisse (2020), and more recently, Chris Ware (2022) and Posy Simmonds (2023).

Continuing in the same spirit of innovation and collaboration, the Centre Pompidou, the Bibliothèque Publique d'Information and Ircam now come together to shine a light on the world of comics as a whole.

The exhibition 'Bande dessinée, 1964–2024', produced in partnership with the Fonds Hélène & Édouard Leclerc pour la Culture, uses twelve themed sections to explore the many imaginary worlds of comics, the emotions they rouse and the huge range of techniques they employ. Presenting a lavish cross-section of comics past and present, it invites visitors to explore its ongoing evolution over the decades, from the swinging sixties underground to the contemporary cutting edge.

We begin the story in the 1960s with the rise of the counterculture. Around the world, at a time when the medium was still viewed as entertainment for children, publishing pioneers began to produce comics for an adult audience. In France, *Hara-Kiri* broke new ground for visual humour, while the adventures of *Barbarella* were created by Jean-Claude Forest and published by Éric Losfeld. In Japan, the avant-garde monthly magazine *Garo* showcased the many different forms that auteur comics could take. In 1968, Robert Crumb's *Zap Comix* made him the figurehead for underground comics in the USA. This graphic revolution laid the groundwork for the many multifaceted worlds of contemporary comics.

Throughout the exhibition, unexpected connections between artists are allowed to emerge. These echoes are emphasized by the chosen themes of each section, which include dreams, humour, science fiction, personal stories, and history and memory. The exhibited works include iconic original artwork, page sequences that reflect a range of storytelling techniques, and digital art. These are accompanied by a selection of notebooks, documents and brand new interviews with artists. The exhibition opens and closes with specially created wall art by two great comics artists, Blutch and Chris Ware.

This exhibition and the book that accompanies it would not have been possible without the joint efforts of the two curators, Anne Lemonnier, assistant curator at the Musée National d'Art Moderne, and Emmanuèle Payen, head curator at the Bibliothèque Publique d'Information. We would also like to thank the two specialist advisors who worked on this project, Thierry Groensteen, comics historian and theorist, and Lucas Hureau, director of MEL Compagnie des Arts and MEL Publisher. Our warmest thanks to all the teams whose work made this exhibition a reality.

For their support and encouragement, our special thanks go to Michel-Édouard Leclerc and Marie-Pierre Bathany, respectively the president and the director of the Fonds Hélène & Édouard Leclerc pour la Culture.

Lastly, we would like to express our gratitude to all the lenders and most of all to the artists who agreed to loan us their art for five months. It's thanks to them that this exhibition has been possible, bringing together three major branches of the artform – *bandes dessinées* from Europe, manga from Asia, and comics from the USA – for the first time in France.

Laurent Le Bon
President of the Centre Pompidou

Xavier Rey
Director of the Musée National d'Art Moderne – Centre de Création Industrielle

Christine Carrier
Director of the Bibliothèque Publique d'Information

Frank Madlener
Director of Ircam

At last, comics have gained the status that is their due. For many years, the world of art and culture relegated comics to a corner for children who wanted to read about adventurous boy scouts and mischievous schoolgirls. But by the early 1970s, comics creators had broken free, becoming politicized, liberated from the rather outdated visual stereotypes that were imposed on them from outside, and ready to join the burgeoning cultural revolution. In France, newsstands were packed with a varied range of publications such as *Pilote*, *Hara-Kiri*, *Métal hurlant*, *L'Écho des savanes*, *Fluide glacial* and *(À suivre)*. They built up big readerships and their fans now fill the halls at French comics festivals from Angoulême and Saint-Malo to Bastia, Lyon and Amiens. This public recognition is well deserved.

In Europe, Asia and the USA, comics are now no longer just a publishing phenomenon. They fuel the worlds of films, licensed toys and merchandise, not to mention theme parks and the thriving fields of animation and video games. But amid this commercial boom, it makes sense to emphasize the artistic legitimacy of those who can compete with the best artists working in other media.

Major exhibitions, organized by leading curators, are another reflection of the huge talents working in this field. These have included 'VRAOUM! Trésors de la bande dessinée et art contemporain' (La Maison Rouge – Fondation Antoine de Galbert, Paris, 2009), 'Archi & BD, la ville dessinée' (Cité de l'Architecture et du Patrimoine, Paris, 2010), and monograph exhibitions such as Robert Crumb (Musée d'Art Moderne de la Ville de Paris, 2012), Miyazaki and Mœbius (Monnaie de Paris, 2004–2005) and Art Spiegelman (Bibliothèque Publique d'Information-Centre Pompidou, Paris, 2012). Elsewhere in Europe, the exhibitions 'Manga' (British Museum, London, 2019) and 'Cómic. Sueños e historia' (CaixaForum, Spain, 2022–2024) have drawn massive crowds. Parallel to these events, the Cité Internationale de la Bande Dessinée et de l'Image in Angoulême (CIBDI) and the Bibliothèque Nationale de France have made comics part of their collections.

Impetus also came from the Fonds Hélène & Édouard Leclerc pour la Culture, based in Landerneau. Between exhibitions on Gérard Fromanger, Joan Miró, Henry Moore and Marc Chagall, I thought a lot about comics, in the light of a seventeen-year partnership with the Angoulême Festival that enabled me to forge firm friendships with artists such as André Juillard, Régis Loisel, Florence Cestac, Philippe Druillet and many others. They convinced me to create a collection, in order to conserve and publish their works – it was then that I launched MEL Publisher. But there was also a need to tell their stories and exhibit their work. At the Fonds Leclerc, we staged a celebration of the artists featured in the magazines *Métal hurlant* and *(À suivre)*: Mœbius, Paul Gillon, Chantal Montellier, Jacques Tardi, José Muñoz, Comès, Hugo Pratt, François Boucq and Nicole Claveloux, among others. The exhibition was then shown in Angoulême (CIBDI, 2014) and Liège (2017). We also hosted the first retrospectives dedicated to the work of Lorenzo Mattotti and, more recently, Enki Bilal. More than two hundred artists have been shown in our gallery in Landerneau.

In recent years, comics creation has grown more diverse, bringing us work from artists such as Brecht Evens, Fanny Michaëlis, Marion Fayolle and Riad Sattouf. A new generation is now forging its own path, in the face of the manga boom and the flood of Marvel and DC comics properties on TV and cinema screens. Notably, there has been a wave of comics telling more intimate, personal stories. Female comics creators are being rightfully celebrated, including Aline Kominsky-Crumb, Julie Doucet, Claire Bretécher and Kuniko Tsurita. Alongside the achievements of Marjane Satrapi, Pénélope Bagieu and Camille Jourdy, another memorable event occurred in France: Catherine Meurisse was made a member of the Académie des Beaux-Arts in 2022.

The Fonds Leclerc could not resist joining the adventure that the Centre Pompidou has planned. Alongside its teams, we encourage you to discover the glittering host of artists and writers who fill every floor of this major Paris landmark. Instead of following a chronological path through comics history, this exhibition offers visitors a series of themes, some familiar ('Humour', 'Science Fiction'), others less so ('Fear', 'Geometry'), creating a dialogue between the greatest artists from three great comics traditions of the world: Europe, Asia, and the USA.

Michel-Édouard Leclerc
President of the Fonds Hélène & Édouard Leclerc pour la Culture

A New 'Golden Age' Realized

The past sixty years have brought unprecedented changes in the form, medium, industry and status of comics. This period is only the last part of some three centuries of international creativity by earlier pioneers exploring the possibilities of storytelling in sequential images, with or without words, as audacious and authorial narratives. But as this book demonstrates – as well as the accompanying exhibition over the summer of 2024 in France's Musée National d'Art Moderne at the Centre Pompidou in Paris – the recent transformations over less than a lifetime have accelerated and exceeded expectations. The current digital era has already radically changed so much worldwide and shows no signs of slowing down, but the focus here is exploring how we have got to now, through one-off, physical, hand-made artworks, predominantly from American, Franco-Belgian and Japanese creators.

Comics have long been peculiar for being disdained or dismissed entirely by many aesthetic arbiters and cultural gatekeepers in both literary and artistic circles. Tellingly, in the wake of the skewed inclusion of comics as source materials in the Museum of Modern Art's divisive *High and Low* exhibition in 1990–91 in New York and, a year later, MoMA's modest, six-week exhibit of the complete artworks for *Maus*, Art Spiegelman convened top museum luminaries to his studio to learn more from his 'Comics 101' lecture. Most were entirely unfamiliar with this rich history. During the Q&A that followed, Robert Storr, curator in the Department of Painting and Sculpture who had organized the *Maus* exhibit, recalled how MoMA set up its Film Department as early as 1935, and proposed that they now might establish a Comics Department. Spiegelman later learned that a top director at MoMA had told curators there afterward that a major comics exhibition, let alone a department, would happen only over his dead body. Luckily, as the Pompidou exhibition proves, institutions can outlast individuals, so sometimes one individual can introduce lasting change.

What we come to call something new is often indicative of our attitudes about it. Think of the 'novel', based on initially being derided as a sensationalist novelty, which then became prized in literary circles. In the case of comics, their name derives from their comical origins and suggests either amusing fripperies or, more alarmingly to those in authority, subversive satire. Through the 20th century, the English-language term was spread by the aggressive export of comics, especially by America's newspaper strip syndicates and comic book publishers, so that it was soon adopted or adapted elsewhere, for example into 'komiks' in Poland and the Philippines, or 'komikkusu' in Japan.

Different names were invented or repurposed for comics in other languages and are revealing, often carrying humorous, diminutive and/or childish connotations. In Japanese, they are more commonly called *manga* or 'pictures let loose', a neologism pre-dating Hokusai's famous 19th-century non-narrative sketchbooks, which shifted meanings after the arrival and imitation of European and American caricatures and comics. Italians call them *fumetti* or 'little smokes', referring to their distinctive speech balloons. In Spanish *tebeos* comes from their early children's weekly *TBO*, short for 'I see you', while *historietas* or 'small stories' is common across much of South America. *Gibi* was Brazil's first name for comics, derived from a 19th-century slur for a black person, and later referring to racist caricatures of them in early periodicals and to the youngsters who sold them on the street. These unacceptable origins became forgotten, as *gibi* continues to be used in magazine titles today and since the 1970s in *gibitecas*, popular free spaces in Brazil's public libraries to read their comics collections.

The French-language term for a comic as a printed periodical used to be the broader term of an *illustré*, meaning illustrated. But already in the 1930s in French, a refreshingly neutral description – *bande dessinée* or 'drawn strip'– entered circulation, inspired by the influx of America's addictive serialized daily and Sunday strips aggressively exported into France and Belgium. This term, abbreviated to BD, or sometimes *bédé*, swiftly caught on for Franco-Belgian productions.

France stands out, however, as the first and to date the only country in the world to decide that comics, in the singular, is also an art. This was achieved not by simply lumping in comics within one or more of the other historically acknowledged arts, but by identifying it as an entirely separate and distinct art with properties and possibilities all its own. This unique cultural shift was heralded sixty years ago in March 1964, when Claude Beylie (1932–2001), the French cinema critic and historian and an aficionado of comics, notably American strips, declared his proposal that comics is an art in an essay in *Lettres et médecins*, a literary supplement of *La Vie médicale*, and suggested it be considered the '9th Art'.

It was the German philosopher Hegel (1770–1831), who had distinguished and ranked the five arts as architecture, sculpture, painting, music and poetry, in that order. So Beylie's suggestion of this apparently low 9th position for comics was not based on the importance, quality or date of origin of comics, but on the order it was to be accepted. By then, cinema, which postdates comics, had already been declared the 7th Art, and television and photography were competing for the 8th spot. So comics came in 9th, because that was the next unallocated position available. Beylie noted also that this would serve as a tribute to one of his favourite strips, *Secret Agent X-9*, originated by writer Dashiell Hammett and illustrator Alex Raymond.

Beylie's proposal was quickly seized upon by two Flemish Belgians, Morris, pen-name of Maurice De Bevere, the knowledgable cartoonist of the comedy cowboy 'Lucky Luke' in the children's weekly *Spirou*. With Pierre Vankeer, a collector and activist, they began a wide-ranging feature for *Spirou* in December 1964 entitled *9th Art, Museum of Bande Dessinée*, presenting the medium's rich international heritage to their impressionable young readers.

Building up to May 1968, something was definitely in the air in France. Revolutions were brewing in politics, society and culture, 'high' and 'low'. It was in this zeitgeist, as well as amid the rise in fine art circles of 'Pop Art', whose practitioners often appropriated imagery from comics, that the Musée des Arts Décoratifs in Paris opened a landmark exhibition on 7 April 1967 entitled 'Bande dessinée et figuration narrative'. This marked the first time any major art museum had presented comics. The guest curators, members of a lobbying society of comics enthusiasts, intended to fill the museum's whole gallery and cover a very broad history going back to cave paintings. Sadly, in the end they were allowed only part of the gallery space, because the Museum wanted also to present parallel contemporary works by assorted fine artists, grouped under the label 'figuration narrative' for their break from abstraction and embrace of other influences, including comics.

The majority of the works on show came from American newspaper strips, highly appreciated in this era by their French fans who had read them since their childhood. There were no original artworks from them on display, but printed enlargements of masterly single panels from the greatest strips, partly to counter Lichtenstein's ironic focus on romance and war comic books. These blow-ups amazed Katherine Collins, then budding Canadian cartoonist Arn Saba, aged 19, who stumbled across this exhibition on holiday. 'These were up to 6 × 8 feet! Their size recalibrated my standards of appreciation for comics,' she recalled in 'I Was There!' in *CONUNDRUM: An Annual Catazine of the Comic Arts* #4 (Conundrum Press, Canada, 2023). 'And the lengthy texts posted on the walls gave intelligent voice to the analysis and appreciation of the comics; this was something I had been lacking for my whole life. From then on, worldwide, a respectful and unafraid archiving of comics began to grow.' The exhibition had a wider impact through its catalogue, and informed further first exhibitions of comics in art institutions in Antwerp, Brussels, Berlin, Vienna, Nuremberg, London, Rotterdam, Seville and elsewhere.

Improved respect has also been accorded, none too soon, to those who make comics. While the historical model of properties and franchises persists, often owned by the publishers, and perpetuated by expendable workers-for-hire, sometimes brilliantly, there are also greater opportunities for a writer and artist working in collaboration, or a doubly-talented or 'amphivalent' solo creator, as in the majority of those chosen in this book and exhibition, to tell their tale complete in a single volume or across several, conveying their vision in the way only they can, and retaining their authorial rights.

It was also in 1964 that the term 'graphic novel' was coined in English by the American enthusiast and historian Richard Kyle. Already aware of advances in Europe and Japan, he concluded his essay on 'The Future of the Comics', mailed out in the November 1964 issue of *Capa-Alpha* to his fellow members of the comics amateur press association, by proposing 'the terms "graphic story" and "graphic novel" to denote the artistically serious "comic book strip".' He advocated the concept widely and in 1976 published America's first graphic novel to be billed as such, *Beyond Time and Again* by George Metzger. Kyle's editorial to his first *Graphic Story World* newsletter in May 1971 speaks to us across the years: 'There is nothing more powerful, it is said, than an idea whose time has come. The time has come for the graphic story, and the great promise of the first "Golden Age" of comic books is about to be realized.'

Paul Gravett

IF WE SINK TO THE MOON THOSE GIANTS WILL GET US!
THEY'LL NOT GET US IF I NAIL THIS BIRD! WE'LL MAKE HIM TOW US TO MARS! AH! I'VE GOT HIM!
OH! WE ARE TRAVELING THROUGH THE AIR LIKE A COMET. WE OUGHT TO BE NEAR MARS BY NEXT WEEK!
WE'LL BE ON MARS NEXT SUNDAY SURE AND SEE THE MOST WONDERFUL SIGHTS IMAGINABLE! I SEE SOME OF THEM NOW!

Winsor McCay (1869–1934, USA)
Little Nemo in Slumberland
Strip for 17 April 1910 (detail)
Private collection, courtesy MEL Publisher

AN EVOLVING ARTFORM

Benoît Peeters

Since the days of Rodolphe Töpffer, an early master of the form, comics have constantly reinvented themselves. They have moved from the world of books to the news press, then back to book form. They were originally aimed at adults, then at children, then acquired an adult readership once again. And while the biggest developments have occurred in the USA, in Japan (as manga), and in the French-speaking world (as the *bande dessinée*[1]), there are few countries that have produced no comics at all.

For many years, the richness and diversity of comics history went unacknowledged. This was partly because, before the digital era, the formats in which they were published were easily damaged or lost, but it was also because comics were not respected, especially in the academic world. Fortunately, works by pioneers of the genre, from Caran d'Ache to Lyonel Feininger, as well as masterpieces by creators on the outskirts of the field, from Frans Masereel to Martin Vaughn-James and Charlotte Salomon, have been discovered or rediscovered around the world, and gateways can be perceived between these remarkable works and more recent creations.

So what is a comic?

If we are trying to agree on the basic features of a comic, we could define it, very broadly, as a sequence of drawings, almost always printed, and usually accompanied by text. Thierry Groensteen highlights the importance of what he calls 'iconic solidarity':[2] the pictures do not simply co-exist, but are interconnected to an extent that makes them inseparable. Comics writer and theorist Jean-Christophe Menu deems that comics 'must be made up of a series of at least two panels separated by a blank space called a gutter, which can also be the margin of the page or simply the act of turning the page'.[3] They generally include far more than two panels, although over the years the average number has tended to decrease.

One of the key features of a comic is the creation of connections between these images, within their sequence and across the space of the pages. This means transforming contiguity into continuity, guiding the reader's gaze from one panel to the next, from one strip to the next and from one page to the next. In the elegant words of Art Spiegelman, 'comics are time turned into space'.

Unlike in cinema, where each frame appears and disappears in sequence, the panels in a comic are initially viewed simultaneously, as the reader looks at the page or double-page spread: before they start reading, they get an overall sense of the atmosphere and notice the most striking images. Creating a comic means making a series of texts and images work together, playing with negative space and its effects, adding surprises, often choosing to avoid flashy panels that might overpower those next to them. In this sense, comics are also an art of performance.

One of the most obvious differences between western comics and manga is their approach to what is included and what is left out. Most *mangaka* break down actions into smaller pieces than their western counterparts, prioritizing a visual reading. They include more panels, with less text in each speech bubble, so that every panel can be read almost instantly. In western comics, each panel tends to be a synthesis: it depicts both the start of an action and its outcome, and often includes a number of lines of dialogue. But in both systems, the way each sequence flows is fundamental. Rather than simply placing images side by side, the art of comics is about bringing together the visual and narrative elements into a dynamic whole.

Claire Bretécher (1940–2020, France)
Les Frustrés (*Frustration*), 'Fantasia', 1976

It is not important whether the space between the panels is in the form of a white gutter (the most traditional approach), black or coloured bands (as in some US comics), a simple line (as in the work of Rodolphe Töpffer and Claire Bretécher), or whether there is no frame around the space at all (as in many graphic novels). This issue, like many others, has many possible solutions, showing that the language of comics remains highly fluid.

From page to book

The vertical grid of panels that is so familiar today is by no means the only way of presenting a comic. In the 1830s and 1840s, Töpffer presented his stories in a horizontal format, in a single strip: *Monsieur Crépin*, *Monsieur Pencil* and *Le Docteur Festus* could be displayed in the form of a frieze, as a long band of images.

Full-page comics were first published in the second half of the nineteenth century, in the French and wider European press. Gustave Doré, Wilhelm Busch, Albert Robida, Théophile Alexandre Steinlen and a few others displayed their originality and inventiveness, as did cartoonist Marie Duval, British-born to French parents, who was the first female comics writer.

In the USA, at the turn of the twentieth century, comics started to break new ground. In the spectacular Sunday comics by Richard Outcault, Winsor McCay, George Herriman and a few others, page layouts combined image and narrative into an inextricable design. The aim was to catch the reader's eye straight away, and then hold on to it. The visual power of these pages depended on the fact that they could be enjoyed in isolation. Of course, sometimes the story was carried over from one week to the next, as in *Little Nemo in Slumberland*, but often the narrative connections were little more than a pretext.

By contrast, in the adventure comics that flourished in the US and Europe in the 1920s, the page layouts are generally less spectacular: their primary function is to serve to tell a much longer story. To fit the constraints of newspaper publication, many stories were first created in strip form before being reworked in other formats. But even in the most traditional of comics, great creators, ranging from Milton Caniff to Edgar P. Jacobs, from Maurice Tillieux to Naoki Urasawa, place huge importance on the overall page design. They take care to guide the reader's gaze horizontally and vertically across the page, and they make playful use of panel positioning, as well as variations in scale, the arrangement of key elements and the effects of light.

In the late 1960s, many comics creators started using a regular grid arrangement for their pages, aptly described by André Franquin as the 'waffle iron'. In the series *Lone Sloane*, Philippe Druillet's bold baroque style, his huge panels teeming with details and his symmetrical compositions influenced a number of artists, including Mœbius. Equally impressive was the way in which bodies and panels are sliced up in Guido Crepax's *Valentina*: embracing voyeurism and fetishism, the Italian master isolates details to create a style of erotica that is inextricably linked to the language

Winsor McCay (1869–1934, USA)
Little Nemo in Slumberland
Strip for 17 April 1910
Private collection, courtesy MEL Publisher

Fred (1931–2013, France)
Philémon, vol. 14: *L'Enfer des épouvantails*, 1983
Page 11
Private collection, courtesy MEL Publisher

of comics. In Japan, the tireless, constantly innovative Osamu Tezuka often used playful page layouts, for example in the *Phoenix* series, which was first published in 1954 and ran for many years.

Exploring the possibilities of the medium was also an important feature of Fred's series *Philémon*, first published in 1965. In the book *Simbabbad de Batbad*, one scene shows Philémon climbing all over the body of an enormous dog. As in *Gasoline Alley*, a wonderful series by Frank King, which ran from 1918 to 1959, but which Fred probably never saw, this page design creates a paradoxical space that is both two-dimensional and three-dimensional at the same time. In *L'île des brigadiers*, Fred pushes his experimentation even further. One of the first pages has a blank panel in the centre, presenting the reader with the perfect trap. Like us, Philémon travels from left to right, from the first panel to the second. But someone calls out to him: 'No! Not that way! For goodness' sake! The reader has got everything out of order! This page should be read from top to bottom, then from bottom to top. Oh dear! ... You'll have to start again!' There is nothing else to do but return to the first picture, go down a ladder, then climb back up using an enchanted rope.

In the 1990s and 2000s, some comics began to take these visual games even further: in series such as *Julius Corentin Acquefacques* and *3"*, Marc-Antoine Mathieu expanded the labyrinth so that it filled the entire book.

The author who pioneered the most radical innovations may well be Chris Ware. In *Jimmy Corrigan: The Smartest Kid on Earth* and *Rusty Brown*, the reader is confronted with complex spaces that make use of all the visual elements of comics. The page is both sequential and simultaneous, representational and symbolic. And every part of the book as a physical object is used, including the cover and flyleaves. *Building Stories* goes even further. A large box contains fourteen printed works of different sizes, with no instructions as to the correct order in which to read them: pieces of a puzzle that each reader puts together in their own way. The mixture of linguistic and visual elements, with a narrative that is smashed to smithereens and pieced back together, creates a reading experience that is similar to a mind map. The close-ups and wide shots, texts and images are all interlinked, reflecting the way our brain works.

In *Here*, Richard McGuire creates a similarly powerful reading experience, embracing an innovative approach to expand the potential of the medium. In this book, every double-page spread shows a place containing many layers of time, diving into the distant memories of a family, a house, a landscape, and the people and animals that once inhabited

it. The use of inset panels, which act as windows onto different periods, allows multiple time periods to inhabit the same double-page spread, with the background image showing the same primary location. We find ourselves in 1372, 2005 and 2126 all at the same time, in prehistory and in an uncertain future, inside the minds and personal lives of a few fragile characters. It is a world that is both comforting and dangerous, miniature and cosmic, looking both backwards and forwards.

Overwritten timelines

Classic comics characters exist in a strange kind of temporal suspension. They may go on a number of adventures, but they remain unchanging. Whatever happens to them, Asterix and Obelix will always be fighting Caesar's troops; Lucky Luke will always be a poor lonesome cowboy; Iznogoud still wants to be Caliph instead of the Caliph; and Gaston Lagaffe will never be a competent employee.

Tintin and his friends have a strange relationship with time, built around a number of paradoxes. The timeline of their adventures can easily be pieced together: there are the comics before and after the introduction of Captain Haddock, and before and after the first appearance of Professor Calculus. And there is a sense of memory at work, as the characters often refer to their past adventures. But between the moment when Tintin leaves Chang at the end of *The Blue Lotus* and the moment when he finds him again in a cave in Tibet, the time that has passed cannot be measured chronologically. Neither Tintin nor Chang seems to have aged, but the world around them has changed considerably. They live in timelines that are layered on top of each other, like a palimpsest that's overwritten again and again, made up of a network of allusions and footnotes.

The gang of children in *Peanuts* never grow up, although they sometimes have birthdays. Characters such as Mafalda or Calvin and Hobbes don't change either. Although these characters are drawn with just a few lines, they are deeply etched in our memories. The mechanics of publication – mainly in the form of daily comic strips, which were so important for decades – played a pivotal role. For young readers, and for adults revisiting them, this sense of being almost frozen in time creates the impression of a lost paradise. No matter what happens to them, the characters do not change and never come any closer to death.

This paradoxical relationship with time seems to me to be a key element of comics. Despite the major transformations

Chris Ware (born 1967, USA)
Jimmy Corrigan: The Smartest Kid on Earth, 2000
Page 16

that the genre has undergone over the past half-century, there is still something old-fashioned about comics that appeals to their most avid readers. We would like our favourite characters to keep going on more adventures, to know that we can always find them again, no matter what happens. We might call this the principle of familiarity, a sense of reassurance that is a vital part of the magic of these series.

I have also been struck by the widespread demand for heroes, such as Blake and Mortimer, Lucky Luke and Astro Boy, to be brought back to life after their creators have died. It is as if those people who had loved these heroes since their childhood could not reconcile themselves to seeing them disappear and therefore sought to keep them alive, even if they are no longer quite the real thing. This phenomenon of reviving or rebooting classic characters, born out of a mixture of commercial considerations and nostalgia, does not mean there cannot be success stories, such as Émile Bravo's wonderful *Spirou* series, which managed to imbue the titular bell-boy with greater psychological depth by pitting him against the chaos of the Second World War.

The slow evolution that, from the 1960s onwards, saw comics move away from unchanging characters and embrace novelistic characters should not necessarily be interpreted as progress, but as the exploration of new narrative possibilities. In works such as Jean Giraud and Jean-Michel Charlier's *Blueberry*, Hugo Pratt's *Corto Maltese* or Frank Miller's *The Dark Knight Returns*, comic book characters find themselves living within a temporality that affects and changes them: friendships are formed and come to an end, injuries start to have an impact, and even death becomes a possibility. The protagonists have left behind the world of the eternal present and now have to face historical time; they have abandoned the world of myth and entered the world of novels.

Towards graphic novels

From the 1980s onwards, this new relationship with time came to lie at the heart of graphic novels, and the touchstone for the genre is undoubtedly *Maus*. Art Spiegelman's story is not only about the Holocaust and its survivors; it also explores questions of time in a number of ways: father-son relationships, diving into history and memory, the slow unfolding of the book itself.

Embracing a very different tone, Alan Moore and Dave Gibbons' *Watchmen* series was a major landmark in the history of the graphic novel. In one long, perfectly constructed narrative, the authors reimagined the archetypes of comic books: what might superheroes become in a world that no longer needs them?

Katsuhiro Ōtomo's *Akira* had an equally significant influence, first in Japan and then around the world. With its epic feel, its apocalyptic aesthetic and its visual energy, this story, which is over 2,000 pages in total, has captivated many generations of readers.

Beyond all questions about black and white versus colour, about format or binding, graphic novels are characterized by their ambitious narratives and themes, and by the freedom with which they are written. Today they are a major area of growth. Although it is impossible to draw a clear distinction between graphic novels and comics, and although we should be wary of imposing any kind of hierarchy, this new genre has captivated many new readers – especially female readers.

The switch from magazines to books has had huge consequences, both financial and aesthetic. When stories appeared as series in daily or weekly magazines, every strip or page had to include enough detail to hold the reader's attention. In monthly magazines, chapters began to become the narrative unit, creating an entirely different rhythm. The graphic novel, which often has an extensive page count, has allowed creators to play around with space and time. What seemed inconceivable at the time of publishing comics in periodicals has become natural now that authors are working in book form.

In graphic novels such as Craig Thompson's *Blankets* and *Habibi*, an entire sequence can be made up of decorative motifs and calligraphy. Kiriko Nananan's *Blue* also features scenes that have been distilled down to their purest form, suspended moments where the text and illustrations are reduced to almost nothing, making space for the subtlest feelings. In *My Favorite Thing is Monsters*, Emil Ferris uses a number of different compositions and styles, constantly changing the way in which she is telling the story. The book is presented as the illustrated diary of a ten-year-old child, and it combines the features of illustrated stories with elements drawn from comics, cartoons, academic drawing, superheroes and art history. Every double-page spread holds a new surprise.

Graphic novels in particular have embraced more personal, often autobiographical subject matter, with works such as Fabrice Neaud's *Journal*, Alison Bechdel's *Fun Home*, Marjane Satrapi's *Persepolis* and Riad Sattouf's *The Arab of the Future*. In another sense, every comic is autobiographical to some extent, no matter what kind of story it is telling, because the style of the art and lettering is individual to its creators. Their hands can be felt on every page.

We should not allow ourselves to be misled by the word *novel*, however. This category also includes many non-fiction works. Just as documentaries have found a place in the world of cinema, comics have proven that they can offer a new way of approaching reportage, biography, history, essays and popular science. These new subjects have huge potential, as long as comics are treated as more than just a tool.

The ambiguous status of original artwork

Long before any discussion of comics as an art form, comics played their part in revitalizing drawing as a discipline, at a time when many artistic movements had lost interest in it. But it was more difficult for the medium to embrace some styles because of the restrictions of the printing process. Clean lines were easiest to reproduce: this is one of the reasons why the 'clear line' style developed, as can be seen in the work of Benjamin Rabier and Yves Chaland, as well as Hergé and Joost Swarte. However, far from being

restricted to a single style, comics creators experimented with many different approaches, borrowing from realism and cartoons, from collage and painting. From George Herriman to Taiyō Matsumoto, from Claire Bretécher to Joann Sfar, from Alberto Breccia to Julie Doucet, comics artists have always embraced the flexibility of the form.

Original page art is an unusual object, with an uncertain status. For many years, most authors and publishers considered it to be nothing more than a stage in the creative process. For the publisher, the final printed page was all that mattered. Once the original artwork had been reproduced using the photoengraving process, it had fulfilled its purpose. People had no qualms about adding technical instructions or stamps. Sometimes, they forgot to return the art to the illustrator. On other occasions, it was simply thrown away. Bob McCay cut up a number of pages created by his father Winsor, trying to put together new sequences for *Little Nemo*. And original art by Franquin and Peyo was used for practice by colourists who were learning their trade. In the best case scenario, original art was considered a document, evidence of the creative process. Hergé gave away pencil sketches, and sometimes even inked pages, to some of his visitors. Other originals were lent out for exhibitions and carelessly glued to pieces of card.

Since the late 1980s, the situation has changed dramatically. We now pay close, almost obsessive attention to the artist's lines, technique and amendments. Original page art has become an important object of study that is featured in exhibitions and sold for high prices. Major auction houses have begun to show an interest in it, a number of specialist galleries have sprung up and the market value of some artists has skyrocketed, with Hergé not least among them. For some collectors, original page art now seems to represent the essence of comics, more so than the comic book itself.

In itself, there is nothing wrong with this interest. Original pages by Harold Foster and Paul Gillon are impressive with their large size, showcasing the illustrators' lines. The liveliness of the brushwork in illustrations by José Muñoz, Edmond Baudoin and Blutch is captivating, while the beauty of the bold colours in the art of Nicole Claveloux and Brecht Evens leaves a lasting impression. The fragility of the pages is also palpable: in the work of Hugo Pratt and Mœbius, the art is sometimes faded or partly rubbed away, because it was created using felt-tip or ecoline; in the work of other illustrators, the pencil marks, glued-on elements, retouches and marginal notes are a source of fascination.

Comics exhibitions

Comics have been the subject of exhibitions for many years. In France, the first major exhibition, 'Bande dessinée et figuration narrative', was held at the Musée des Arts Décoratifs in Paris in 1967; it featured enlarged copies of panels by leading American and European comics creators. Since then, there have been a number of exhibitions that have adopted different approaches: simply hanging pages on the walls, educational displays, recreating a comic book world, as well as major retrospectives like those showcasing the work of Hergé at the Grand Palais in Paris (2016–17), Hugo Pratt at the Musée des Confluences in Lyon (2018–19), Lorenzo Mattotti (2015–16) and Enki Bilal (2020–21) at the Fonds Hélène & Édouard Leclerc pour la Culture in Landerneau, and Emmanuel Guibert at the Académie des Beaux-Arts (2020). The celebration of comics now staged at the Centre Pompidou represents a major step forward in the aesthetic appreciation of the art form.

But the fetishization of original comics art, along with the speed with which specialist galleries and public auctions have sprung up, raise a number of questions. When we look

Bill Watterson (born 1958, USA)
Calvin and Hobbes
Strip for 2 May 1993

Brecht Evens (born 1986, Belgium)
Les Noceurs (The Wrong Place), 2010
Page 140

at pages drawn by Albert Uderzo or Jacques Tardi, Jirō Taniguchi or Posy Simmonds, we feel that they are infused with the energy of a narrative: they were originally designed to be read and this is an important aspect of what makes them memorable. When a page from a comic is hung on a wall in a museum or a gallery, this fundamentally changes its meaning. Removed from the narrative of which it is a part, often stripped of the colour that is meant to complete it, and sometimes with the text elements missing, the page becomes more of a decorative object than a narrative one.

If selling original comics art becomes more lucrative for authors than selling comic books themselves, that could mean a fundamental change to the nature of comics. As the market for original artwork grows, some illustrators might be tempted to create more splash pages with immediate appeal – fewer, more spectacular images, preferably without speech bubbles – to the detriment of other, subtler forms of page layout, which are more difficult to separate out from the narrative as a whole. Comics may risk becoming an imitation of themselves, in a similar way to the changes in street art that occurred when that genre hit the art market.

This change is by no means inevitable. For many authors and readers, the main attraction of comics is not the original art, but their unique way of telling a story that is read but also seen, the way a group of images can coexist harmoniously on the same page, and how the process of reproducing these images is embraced, viewed not as a limitation, but as an integral part of the work.

Of course, the medium will continue to change, especially with new technologies being developed. The majority of comics creators now use digital illustration tools. Digital comics publishing is also growing, especially in Asia. However, although new formats may take the place of paper, it seems to me that comics are a robust and unique art form that can change without falling apart. While it has already created a number of masterpieces, the 'invisible art',[4] as Scott McCloud called it, has by no means reached its final page.

1. In French-speaking countries, the term *bande dessinée*, often shortened to BD, can refer to both a comic strip, i.e. a short row of panels published in a newspaper or magazine, and a comic book, i.e. a separate publication.
2. Thierry Groensteen, *Système de la bande dessinée*, Paris: P.U.F., 1999; English edition: *The System of Comics*, trans. Bart Beaty and Nick Nguyen, Jackson, MS: University Press of Mississippi, 2007.
3. Jean-Christophe Menu, *La Bande dessinée et son double*, Paris: L'Association, 2011.
4. Scott McCloud, *Understanding Comics: The Invisible Art*, New York: HarperCollins, 1993.

Jean-Claude Forest (1930–98, France)
Barbarella (detail)
Le Terrain Vague, Paris, 1964

THE DECADE THAT REINVENTED COMICS

Thierry Groensteen

'Being a comics artist in the 1950s and 1960s meant, at best, having a career that wasn't worthy of the name, earning a living through childish things or not earning a living at all, and at worst, corrupting children.' This is how Jessica Kohn sums up the lack of respect accorded to comics creators in her study of the social history of the *bande dessinée* in France and Belgium in the post-war period.[1] At the time, comics were considered nothing more than a form of entertainment for children, viewed with suspicion by teachers and ignored by the cultural elite.

In the USA, newspaper comic strips were often known as 'the funnies', reflecting what was originally the medium's only aim: to entertain, to amuse, to make the reader laugh or smile. When we think of *Peanuts* (written and illustrated by Charles Schulz from 1950 until his death in 2000), it is often Snoopy's antics that come to mind first, rather than the psychological musings and metaphysical questions pondered by Charlie Brown and his friends. In the French-speaking world, the works of Hergé, André Franquin, Edgar P. Jacobs, Morris and Maurice Tillieux were similarly seen as little more than fun for children; there was no critical analysis to recognize and celebrate their immense talents.

However, within the space of the 1960s, a series of events and publishing projects around the world would open up new horizons for comics. The medium began to embrace different ambitions, find new audiences and gain the respect it deserved. And nothing would ever be the same again. That is why this decade offers an ideal starting point for an account of the great adventure of modern comics. The changes that were set in motion during that decade would lead, step by step, to the foundation of the Musée de la Bande Dessinée in Angoulême in 1990, to the Bibliothèque Nationale in Paris staging its first major exhibition dedicated to comics in 2000, to Catherine Meurisse and Emmanuel Guibert being made members of the prestigious Académie des Beaux-Arts in France, and to the present exhibition, with comics being showcased in all their glory at the Centre Pompidou, whose public library has already held a number of exhibitions dedicated to individual comics artists.[2]

The *bande dessinée* comes of age

In 1959, a new comic book, *Pilote*, was launched in France, founded by Jean-Michel Charlier and René Goscinny. Goscinny would go on to revolutionize the way comics were viewed, not only as the writer of the hugely successful *Asterix* series (whose star appeared the cover of French news magazine *L'Express* in 1966), but also by fighting for comics writers to be given recognition for their craft. Little by little, this comic for children transformed into a magazine for teenagers and young adults, featuring the work of innovative artists (from Claire Bretécher to Philippe Druillet, from Reiser to Gotlib) and exploring serious social issues, particularly in the aftermath of the civil unrest that took place across France in May 1968.

At around the same time, the first French associations for comics lovers were starting to form – first the Centre d'Études de Littératures d'Expression Graphique (Celeg), then the Société Civile d'Études et de Recherches des Littératures Dessinées (Socerlid). Their members were activists, working to rescue the BD from the status of a minor art form aimed solely at children, showcase the genre's rich history and set up institutions and infrastructure (scholarly journals, festivals, exhibitions).

However, a year after *Pilote* was launched, a significant change came from an unexpected direction, on the periphery of the comics industry. The monthly magazine *Hara-Kiri* was born out of a meeting between two colourful personalities, François Cavanna and Georges Bernier, known by the name of 'Professor Choron'. Its first issue, sold only by street vendors, was published in September 1960 and featured a cover by Fred (opposite below). Reclaiming one reader's disparaging description, the publication began to proudly call itself 'a silly, nasty magazine'. The team working with the two founders included the illustrators Roland Topor, Cabu, Gébé, Georges Wolinski, Reiser and Pierre Fournier. One famous image (published in issue 27 in 1963) is Topor's literal depiction of Cavanna's belief that 'humour is a fist in the face' (opposite above). In the words of Cavanna, future author of *Les Ritals* and *Les Russkoffs*, 'Nothing is taboo, nothing is respectable, not even your own mother, not even the Jewish martyrs, not even those who are dying of hunger... [We must] laugh at everything, fiercely, bitterly, to exorcise the old monsters.'[3] *Hara-Kiri* did not only contain comic strips, but they were a regular feature alongside articles, parody ads, photo stories and witty cartoons, as another way of expressing the magazine's transgressive, libertarian ethos – although Fred's wonderful series *Le petit cirque* struck a different note, infused with a more melancholy, poetic feel. The magazine was accused of being 'indecent' and 'pornographic' and it was banned in July 1961 and May 1966. It was certainly a shocking, radical voice in the France of General de Gaulle.

February 1969 saw the launch of a weekly version of the magazine, *Hara-Kiri Hebdo*, which was replaced the following year by *Charlie Hebdo*, featuring work by Willem, who had moved to France from the Netherlands. Here the content had a greater focus on current events. Cabu made a name for himself with his news reports in comic strip form, decades before the genre came to prominence through the work of illustrators such as Joe Sacco and Étienne Davodeau and magazines such as *XXI* and *La Revue dessinée*. Cabu created comics depicting notable recent happenings such as a gathering of 35,000 Jehovah's Witnesses at the stadium in Colombes (*Hara-Kiri Hebdo*, no. 29, 18 August 1969), a number of pacifist and anti-nuclear demonstrations, as well as major jazz festivals.

Jean-Claude Forest had been drawing for children's publications since 1949. He was 32 years old when he created sci-fi heroine Barbarella in 1962 (see p. 18). Aside from the Breton housemaid Bécassine and the mischievous Espiègle Lili, who could both trace their roots back to the Belle Époque, very few BDs at the time featured female main characters. What's more, the illustrations were closely scrutinized by France's Committee for Oversight and Control of Publications for Children and Young People, who viewed any female character as a potential source of sexual content. This meant that illustrated magazines were forced to self-censor. It was therefore not in a comic but an erotic magazine, *V Magazine*, where Forest launched his new character, a voluptuous, independent space adventurer who was free with her affections. This unconventional heroine, with a body like Brigitte Bardot, would later be reimagined in a pop art style on the cover of the comic book published in 1964 by Le Terrain Vague, an imprint run by Éric Losfeld, a Belgian publisher who had moved to Paris. While Losfeld had most likely been attracted by the erotic element of Forest's work – he published the erotic novel *Emmanuelle* and reprinted the works of the Marquis de Sade – he probably also appreciated its literary merit. A reader of Lewis Carroll and the surrealists, Forest said that his imagination was inspired more by words than by images, and that he worked just as hard – perhaps even harder – on his text as on his illustrations.[4]

As Véronique Bergen has noted, although Barbarella's adventures are set in a science fiction realm, she is surely a woman of the 1960s, with her stories tackling issues such as 'ethics and eroticism, bodily and spiritual freedom, antispeciesism and transhumanism, the environmental crisis and criticism of modes of governance'.[5]

For Losfeld, *Barbarella* set the template for a collection of comics that spanned a total of nineteen titles up until 1973. She also paved the way for other 'liberated' heroines created by artists such as Guido Crepax (*Valentina*), Guy Peellaert (*The Adventures of Jodelle* and *Pravda*), Nicolas Devil (*Saga de Xam*), Robert Gigi and Claude Moliterni (*Scarlett Dream*) and Paul Cuvelier and Jean Van Hamme (*Epoxy*). These lavishly produced albums did not follow a series format and, in many cases, had not been previously published in magazines. They can therefore be considered early precursors of graphic novels.

In late 1964, Jean-Claude Forest was hired by magazine publisher Daniel Filipacchi to oversee a new kind of weekly comic. *Chouchou* was notable for its large format (56 × 40 cm), which was closer to a newspaper than a magazine. Forest published one of his own creations in the magazine, *Baby Cyanide*, and wrote the script for *Les Naufragés du temps* (*Lost In Time*), a science fiction saga illustrated by Paul Gillon that would go on to become a classic. He published Schulz's *Peanuts*, which made one of its earliest appearances in the French press, and featured stories by Hugo Pratt (the western series *Billy James*), Jacques Lob and Georges Pichard (*Tenebrax*), Raymond Poïvet, Robert Gigi, and Guy Mouminoux, also known as Dimitri. *Chouchou* laid the groundwork for the BDs of the decade that followed, even though it only lasted for fourteen issues.

Whether or not they met with success, these publishing initiatives show that perceptions of the *bande dessinée* among the intellectual elite in France were changing. Intellectuals (such as Edgar Morin, Évelyne Sullerot, Marie-José Mondzain and Pierre Couperie), book publishers (Losfeld, Francis Lacassin), magazine publishers (Pierre Lazareff, Daniel Filipacchi) and figures from the film world (critics Claude Beylie, who coined the term 'the Ninth Art' for comics in an article published in 1964, Robert Benayoun and Barthélemy Amengual, and director Alain Resnais) all began to show an interest in the genre. This growing respect for comics was pivotal in moving them out of the realm of children's entertainment and opening up new horizons.

An event of a very different kind, but one that, in hindsight, was by no means less important, took place in 1965: Jean Boullet opened the first specialist BD store in France,

Roland Topor (1938–97, France)
Untitled
Art published in *Hara-Kiri*, no. 27, April 1963

Fred (193‑–2013, France)
Tarsinge l'homme Zan, published in *Hara-Kiri*, no. 3, December 1960
Page 1

Le Kiosque, at 79 rue du Château, Paris. Unfortunately, he was forced to close the shop due to heavy debts in 1969. Boullet was a well-known socialite who moved in artistic circles; he was a painter, illustrator and cinema critic with a particular passion for horror films, and was openly gay. He made comics one of his wide range of interests from the counterculture and even the occult (sexology, magic, demonology). Other specialist BD stores sprang up over the years that followed, including Lutèce and Futuropolis in Paris, and The Skull and Pepperland in Brussels. They mainly focused on traditional *bandes dessinées* and sold their wares to a clientele of collectors. However, fanzines, independent comics, avant-garde publications and books by the stars of *Pilote* and soon *Métal hurlant* were soon added to their range, forming a tightly woven network and giving these titles the chance to reach an informed readership. Up until that point, BDs could only be found in supermarkets and newsagents. As more specialist shops sprang up, often run by passionate fans, the sector grew and built up a community of readers.

Alternative manga: made in Japan

The magazine *Garo* first appeared in Tokyo in September 1964, published by Seirindō, and it embraced a new form of manga. The contributors included Yoshihiro Tatsumi, who had already made his name in 1957 by inventing *gekiga*, a darker style of manga that was aimed at adult readers, dealing with serious subjects and employing dramatic realism. But *Garo* went a step further, refusing to bow to commercial concerns. It opened up a space in which authentic, original stories could flourish, where writers had artistic freedom and could explore philosophy, social issues, fantasy, surrealism, satire and erotic themes. Read in artistic circles, by students and intellectuals, *Garo* never had a large circulation, but it was popular with a generation of young people who held anti-establishment views. The stories reflected their hopes and demands, exploring themes such as sexual liberation, the impact of the Second World War, student demonstrations and the Vietnam War.

Garo published work by artists including Sanpei Shirato, Yoshiharu Tsuge and his younger brother Tadao, Shigeru Mizuki, Susumu Katsumata and one woman, Kuniko Tsurita. Many of these artists had already made a name for themselves in the field of *kashihon*, or rental manga, which were available to rent from a range of specialist stores. Mizuki – who would go on to write the successful manga *Kitaro*, published by Kōdansha – contributed 'short stories in which strange creatures from beyond the grave appear in people's daily lives, forcing them to face the consequences of their madness.'[6] Yoshiharu Tsuge and Yū Takita were pioneers of *watakushi manga*, an autobiographical genre with a name that literally meant 'manga about me'; Tsuge created poignant and personal depictions of his childhood, his travels, his dreams and his nightmares. In his sixth story for *Garo* (*Chīko*, March 1966; p. 22), he depicts himself as an unsuccessful manga artist who lives with a bar hostess. His most famous story, *Screw Style* (June 1968), is based on a dream and is an unsettling tale that seems to depict the meanderings of the unconscious. In *Oba's Electroplate Factory* (1973), he drew

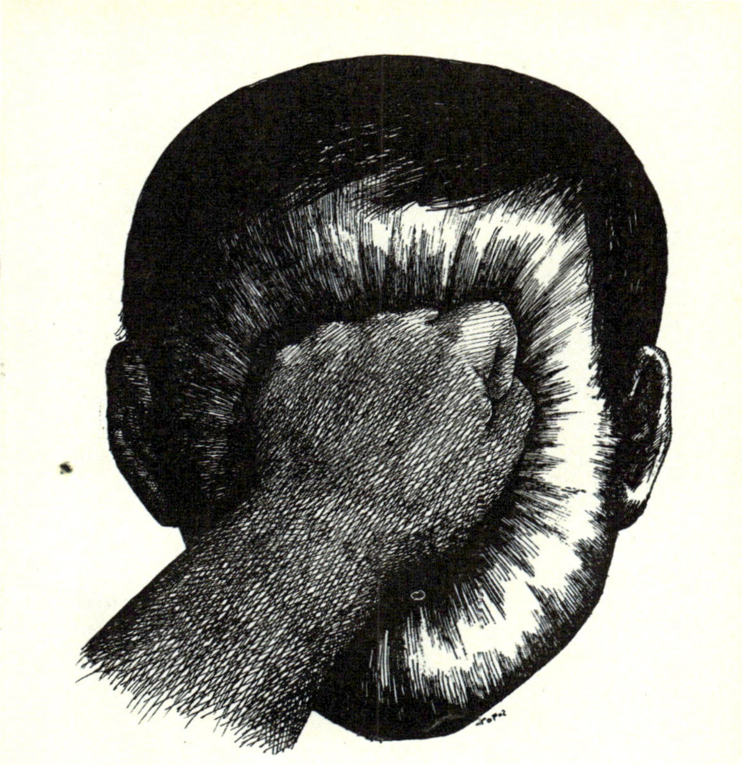

Yoshiharu Tsuge (born 1937, Japan)
Chīko, published in *Garo*, no. 14, March 1966
Page 14

Alejandro Jodorowsky (born 1929, Chile)
Fábulas pánicas (*The Panic Fables*), c. 1968
Episode 21

on his teenage years, exploring the fate of those who were left behind by the economic dream. Tsuge himself grew up in extreme poverty and sometimes had to resort to selling his blood to survive. In 1985–86 he published a graphic novel that is internationally renowned as a masterpiece of the autobiographical genre: *The Man Without Talent*.

Panic and transgression

Moving to another continent, on 4 June 1967, the cultural supplement of the weekly newspaper *El Heraldo de México* featured the first appearance of *The Panic Fables*, a series drawn and written by Alejandro Jodorowsky. Five years earlier, Jodorowsky had founded the avant-garde art collective Panic Movement with Topor and Fernando Arrabal in Paris. From this, he took the title for this series of comics, which were published every week for six and a half years, until 30 December 1973. They were coming-of-age stories, brief philosophical lessons in which the author explored a syncretic philosophy that was closely linked to Zen Buddhism. They were not collected together in a single volume until half a century after their first publication.[7] Created during the years when Jodorowsky was directing his first films, *El Topo* and *The Holy Mountain*, *The Panic Fables* testify to his remarkable artistic freedom and inventiveness. In their unique style, their self-mocking tone and their rejection of intellectualism, they reflect the American underground comics scene that was emerging at that time.

This underground scene did not appear out of thin air. In 1960, Harvey Kurtzman, who had already revolutionized the world of comics by founding *Mad* magazine in 1952, was asked by the publisher James Warren to edit *Help!*, a new monthly. Low sales meant that *Help!* had to become a quarterly and the title folded for good in September 1965. But it was in these pages that Kurtzman, with his long-term collaborator Will Elder, created the character of Goodman Beaver. The photographic covers were in a similar vein to those of *Hara-Kiri*. Future Monty Python members Terry Gilliam and John Cleese did work for the magazine, as did Woody Allen. Featured artists included names such as Robert Crumb, Gilbert Shelton, Jay Lynch and Skip Williamson. These four were some of the most iconic figures of the underground scene, with Crumb (p. 24) quickly coming to be seen as the de facto leader. Not only had his character Fritz the Cat already featured in *Help!*, but in January 1965 the magazine also published his illustrated report on Harlem, then, three months later, Kurtzman sent him to Bulgaria to report on the situation there.

The first 'head shop', which sold all the paraphernalia of a hippie lifestyle, opened in San Francisco in January 1967. Many underground comic creators were drawn to this city, which became the capital of the counterculture. February 1968 saw the publication of the first issue of *Zap*, the first in a number of self-published comics by this generation of creatives – almost three hundred in the space of five years (almost all black and white), including *Bijou Funnies* (1967–73), *Yellow Dog* (1968–73), *Gothic Blimp Works* (1969) and *Slow Death Funnies* (1970–92). Along with music, comics became one of the most important forms of expression in

FABLES PANIQUES
TEXTE DESSIN ET COULEUR DE
ALEJANDRO JODOROWSKY
MAÎTRE: JE VAIS TRÈS MAL!
QUELLE POSITION DÉSAGRÉABLE
J'AI LE CORPS PLEIN DE CHAIR!
QUAND JE MARCHE...
JE BOUGE MES JAMBES!
DÈS QUE J'OUVRE LA BOUCHE...
UN TROU APPARAÎT SUR MON VISAGE!
J'AI LE NEZ TROUÉ...
ET LES COURANTS D'AIR S'ENGOUFFRENT.
ATCHOUM!
JE DOIS TOUJOURS AVOIR LA LANGUE PLEINE DE SALIVE DANS LA BOUCHE
J'AI BEAU ME SECOUER LA TÊTE...
ELLE EST PLEINE DE CHEVEUX!
COMME J'AIMERAIS PRENDRE MES PIEDS ET LES METTRE DANS MES POCHES!
MES BRAS PENDENT DE MES ÉPAULES!
TOUT CE QUE JE ME METS DANS LA BOUCHE ET MASTIQUE DISPARAÎT
J'A HONTE DE TOUT REGARDER AVEC MES YEUX
TOUJOURS LE MÊME VISAGE
DÈS QUE JE BOUGE IL SE COUVRE DE GRIMACES
DES BRUITS ENTRENT DANS MES OREILLES
FUU
BOING
CLAR
SOCK
BAROOM
QUE MES SOURCILS SONT LOURDS
ON M'APPELLE "LE 20 ONGLES"
ICI MÊME JE ME CRÈVE UN ŒIL ET JE ME COUPE UNE OREILLE...
PARCE QUE JE LES AI EN DOUBLE!
...CEPENDANT JE N'AI PAS DE SEINS
J'ÉCHANGE UNE OREILL CONTRE UN SEIN!
J'ÉCHANGE UNE OREILLE CONTRE UN SEI....N!
IMBÉCILE. IL SE PLAINT CAR IL CROIT QUE SON CORPS LUI APPARTIENT

Robert Crumb (born 1943, USA)
Your Hytone Comix, 'Stoned Agin!', 1971
Inside back cover

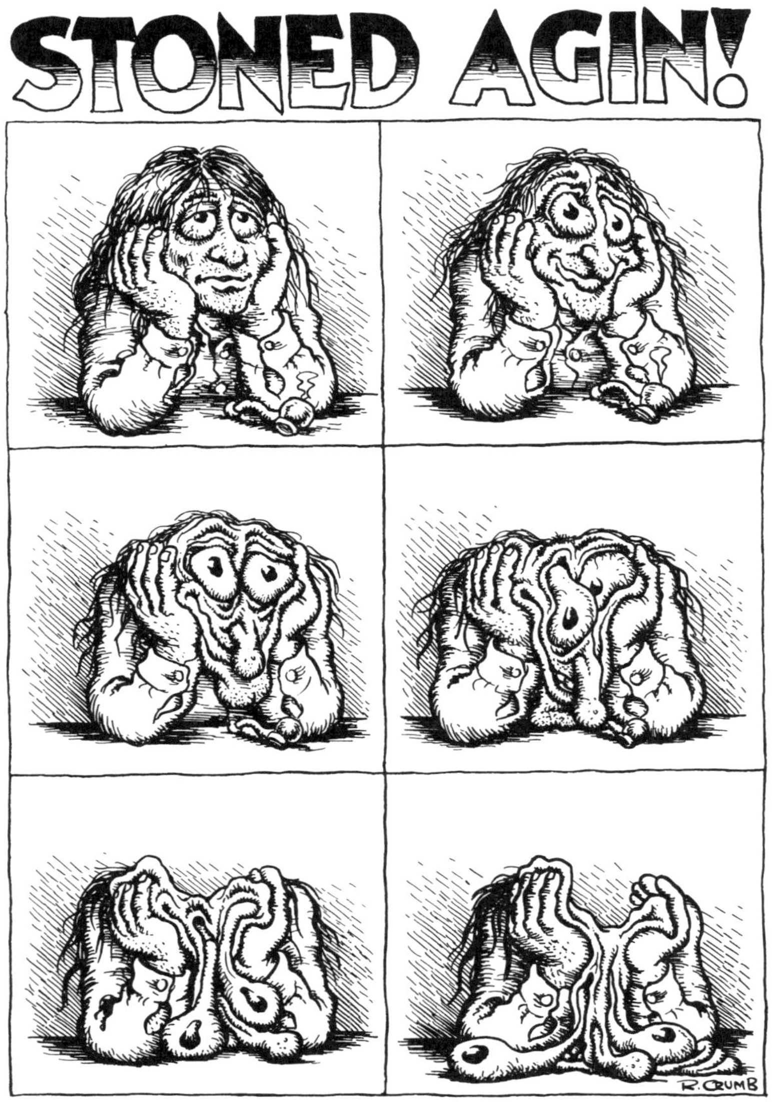

this era, their content shaped by the young generation's opposition to the Vietnam War, as well as psychedelic art, free love and access to drugs of all kinds, from marijuana to LSD. The underground scene was not a homogenous movement: it included elements of the grotesque, obscenity and provocative works, but also social commentary, poetry, formal experimentation and political engagement. With the groundbreaking works of Justin Green (*Binky Brown Meets the Holy Virgin Mary*, 1972) and, appearing almost immediately afterwards, Art Spiegelman and Crumb, it was also the crucible in which American autobiographical comics were originally formed.

Women were also involved in the movement. The first comic book created by an all-female team, which referenced women's liberation on the cover, was *It Ain't Me Babe*, published in July 1970 by Last Gasp Eco-Funnies, with Trina Robbins as editor-in-chief. Two years later, Robbins was part of a collective of illustrators, including Michele Brand, Lora Fountain, Sharon Rudahl and Aline Kominsky, who launched *Wimmen's Comix*, while another all-female team (Chin Lyvely and Joyce Farmer) launched *Tits & Clits*. Aline Kominsky – who later married Crumb – mainly published autobiographical tales shot through with typically Jewish humour and self-mockery. Diane Noomin, who co-founded *Twisted Sisters* with Kominsky, created an alter ego known as Didi Glitz. Gay comics also began to appear, including Rand Holmes's *Harold Hedd* (1972) and Howard Cruse's *Barefootz* (1971–80).

Comic-book adventures and beyond

Although *Hara-Kiri*, *Garo* and underground comics were created on the margins of the comic industry and broke with tradition, it should also be acknowledged that some prominent mainstream comics writers in the 1960s were aware of the changes taking place and so seized the opportunity to develop their own practice, producing works that showed they were pursuing new ambitions. Hergé and Hugo Pratt were two of these figures.

Pratt started in comics in 1945 and tried his hand at a number of different genres: war stories (*Ernie Pike*), westerns (*Sergeant Kirk, Fort Wheeling*), jungle adventures (*Ann of the Jungle*) and superheroes (*Ace of Spades*). In 1967, with financial support from the wealthy property developer Florenzo Ivaldi, he launched a magazine called *Sgt. Kirk* (in which the character's adventures were reprinted), with a print run of 3,000 copies. The magazine had a more luxurious feel than the BDs that had come before. In it, Pratt published the work that would change the course of his career: *The Ballad of the Salty Sea*, the first Corto Maltese story, published between July 1967 to February 1969.

An ensemble piece, with the action taking place in Melanesia between November 1913 and January 1915, the *Ballad* weaves together the fates of a number of different characters: the adventurous sailor Corto Maltese, alongside Rasputin, Christian Slütter, Pandora, Cain, Tarao and the Monk. While it draws on the established adventure tropes, it also evokes a broader literary heritage, including references and allusions – some subtle, others more obvious – to Louis-Antoine de Bougainville's *Voyage Around the World*, *Robinson Crusoe*, *Moby Dick*, *The Rime of the Ancient Mariner*, Rainer Maria Rilke, Mary Shelley and even Euripides. Pratt saw comics as a literary form and, in the early 1980s, he was one of the first people to speak of 'visual literature' – a term that has since been adopted by some critics – drawing, whether consciously or not, on the concept of 'graphic literature' pioneered by Rodolphe Töpffer in the 1830s.

The Ballad of the Salty Sea was reprinted in book format by Casterman in late 1975, and in January 1976 it was named the best realist comic at the third International Comics Festival, held in Angoulême. At 163 pages, the book was the equivalent of almost four ordinary BDs (48 bound pages was the French standard). When, three years later, Casterman launched the monthly magazine *(À suivre)*, one of its promoters, Didier Platteau, summed up its approach in these words: 'A monthly black and white magazine publishing long stories in chapters, in the manner of *The Ballad of the Salty Sea*, which is a kind of prototype for what we would like to do'.[8] *The Ballad* already fully embodied the idea of 'comics bursting into the world of literature' that *(À suivre)* sought to embrace.

When he published the twenty-first *Tintin* adventure, Hergé turned his readers' expectations of the series on their head. *The Castafiore Emerald* featured no globe-trotting: all of the action took place in a single location, Marlinspike Hall. There was no attempt to raise the stakes of the story: it was not all of the diva's legendary jewels that vanished, but a single emerald, and even this disappearance only took place two thirds of the way through the comic, carefully placed so as to make it a non-event. Young reporter Tintin was not even pitted against a worthy adversary: the thief turns out to be a magpie! Instead of a traditional mystery story, the Belgian illustrator created a comedy of manners whose real subject seemed to be a woman disrupting the all-male team of Tintin, Haddock, Professor Calculus and Nestor, with all the mishaps, misunderstandings and commotion that this created. *The Castafiore Emerald* could be read on many levels, and Michel Serres and Benoît Peeters have praised it for its depth and complexity.[9] It was also one of the first *bandes dessinées* to turn away from action and make daily life, lack of action, the passage of time, and human relationships its main focus, long before more personal stories had begun to be published in graphic novel form.

It is therefore clear that the seeds of everything that would come to define today's comics – the involvement of women, tackling questions about politics and society, reportage, personal life, daily life, the graphic novel format, etc. – were already present in the comics of the 1960s.

There may be no other form of expression that has undergone such a dramatic transformation, breaking away from being seen as mere entertainment and reinventing itself as a distinct form of literature that explores the contemporary world around it and is fully recognized as its own discipline within the visual arts.

1. Jessica Kohn, *Dessiner des petits Mickeys. Une histoire sociale de la bande dessinée en France et en Belgique (1945–1968)*, Paris: Éditions de la Sorbonne, 'Histoire contemporaine' series, 2022, p. 189.
2. These exhibitions were: 'Reiser!' (2003–4), 'Willem' (2006), 'Art Spiegelman: Co-Mix' (2012), 'Claire Bretécher' (2015-16), 'Gaston, au-delà de Lagaffe' (2016-17), 'Riad Sattouf. L'écriture dessinée' (2018), 'Catherine Meurisse. La vie en dessin' (2020), 'Chris Ware' (2022), 'Posy Simmonds. Dessiner la littérature' (2023–24) and 'Corto Maltese' (2024).
3. François Cavanna, quoted in *Charlie Hebdo*, special issue no. 24, 'Cavanna raconte Cavanna', November 2008, p. 39.
4. See Numa Sadoul, 'Entretien avec Jean-Claude Forest', *Schtroumpf. Les Cahiers de la bande dessinée*, no. 26, 1st issue, 1975, p. 17.
5. Véronique Bergen, *Barbarella. Une space oddity*, Brussels: Les Impressions Nouvelles, 'La Fabrique des héros', 2020.
6. Béatrice Maréchal, '*Garo*, magazine rebelle', *Neuvième art 2.0*, April 2004: http://neuviemeart.citebd.org/spip.php?article239
7. English-language edition: *The Panic Fables*, Rochester, VT: Park Street Press, 2017.
8. Didier Platteau, quoted in Nicolas Finet, *(À suivre), 1978–1997. Une aventure en bandes dessinées*, Paris: Casterman, 2004, p. 15.
9. See Michel Serres, 'Les bijoux distraits ou la cantatrice sauve', in *Hermès II. L'interférence*, Paris: Éditions de Minuit, 1972; reprinted in *Hergé mon ami. Études et portraits*, Brussels: Moulinsart, 2000. See also Benoît Peeters, *Les Bijoux ravis. Une lecture moderne de Tintin*, Brussels: Magic Strip, 1984; new edition: *Lire Tintin. Les Bijoux ravis*, Brussels: Les Impressions Nouvelles, 2007.

EL
RES

Blutch (born 1967, France)
'She looks just like you', based on *Hypocrite and the Loch Ness Monster* by Jean-Claude Forest
2024
Wall art created for this exhibition

IT'S GREAT TO
CONSUME
"EAT"
SAYS BLUDNEY PLUD
BOREDOM
ILLUSTRATED
No. 2369

Zap Comix, no. 6, March 1973
Cover by Gilbert Shelton (detail)

COUNTERCULTURE

Thierry Groensteen

The liberal, transgressive comics that were published in the 1960s in magazines such as *Hara-Kiri* in France, *Garo* in Japan and the many American underground comics – or comix – attracted a new readership of students and young adults to a medium that, up until that point, had been considered the preserve of children and teenagers. Like rock music, these comics became markers of cultural identity for a young generation with anti-establishment views, and an integral part of what would soon come to be known as the counterculture.

At its heart, the counterculture was about attacking and subverting the norms and values of mainstream culture, celebrating everything that was prohibited, condemned or censored by the authorities and so-called good taste. It popularized recreational drugs, supported free love, promoted a political interpretation of social relationships, power structures and disaffection, and challenged consumerism.

At the end of the 1960s, French cartoonist Gébé published his iconic *An 01* ('The Year 01'), a utopian manifesto with a slogan that still resonates to this day: 'We stop everything. We think about it. And it's not sad.'

The comics of the counterculture scene also broke with the earlier history of the medium itself. They defied the expectation that comics should be aimed at children, including restrictions around morality, which were enforced in France by the Act of 16 July 1949 and in the USA by the Comics Code, adopted in 1955.

This meant that, wherever possible, traditional publishers were bypassed in order to avoid censorship. The means of production had to be in the hands of the creators. This approach survived beyond the 1960s: the magazines *L'Écho des savanes* and *Métal hurlant* were founded by artists' collectives, as were alternative publishing houses such as L'Association in the 1990s.

The Bazooka group, which had links to the punk movement, was born in the graphics studios of the Académie des Beaux-Arts in Paris. It sent shockwaves through the world of *bande dessinée* in the 1970s, with its avant-garde creations that appropriated images from different sources, sometimes of a sexual or shocking nature. The group came to fame through the short-lived monthly magazine *Un regard moderne*, published by *Libération*.

Nowadays, when we look back at works born from the counterculture, a degree of ambivalence can be perceived, especially when it comes to the involvement and depiction of women. Writer and comic book 'herstorian' Trina Robbins called the underground scene a 'boys' club' and highlighted its rampant misogyny. Robert Crumb was criticized by a number of feminists. Many readers still find his unflinching depiction of his sexual obsessions – imbued with a heavy dose of self-parody – and the submissiveness of women in his fantasies disturbing. Similarly, while the prominence of eroticism in publisher Éric Losfeld's output was once seen as a form of liberation, now it feels inherently voyeuristic.

The counterculture produced the 'wrong kind' of comics in more than one sense, but the questions it raised still challenge us to this day.

Garo
No. 85, December 1970 (cover by Kuniko Tsurita)

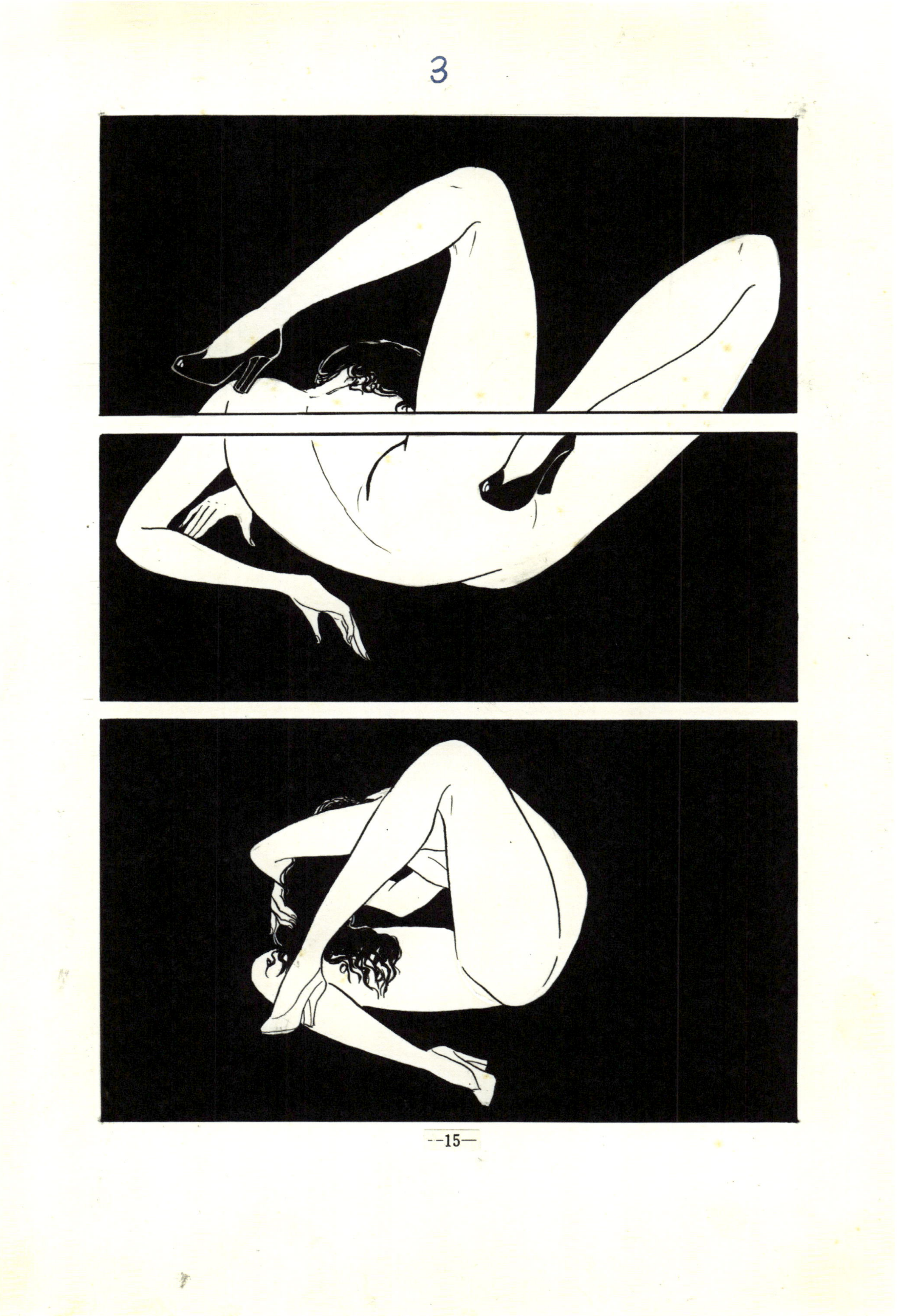

Kuniko Tsurita (1947–85, Japan)
My Wife is an Acrobat, published in *Garo*, no. 128, April 1974
Page 3

Susumu Katsumata (1943–2007, Japan)
Ghost of Spring, published in *Garo*, no. 103, March 1972
Page 14

Susumu Katsumata (1943–2007, Japan)
Ghost of Spring, published in *Garo*, no. 103, March 1972
Cover art

Shin'ichi Abe (born 1950, Japan)
That Miyoko Asagaya Feeling, published in *Garo*, no. 88, March 1971
Pages 12 & 14

Shin.
'70.11.17

Nicolas Devil (born 1943, France),
written by Jean Rollin
Saga de Xam
Éditions Éric Losfeld, Paris, 1967

Robert Gigi (1926–2007, France),
written by Claude Moliterni
Scarlett Dream
Éditions Eric Losfeld, Paris, 1967

Jean-Claude Forest (1930–98, France)
Barbarella
Le Terrain Vague, Paris, 1964

Jean-Claude Forest (1930–98, France)
Barbarella, 1964
Page 45

Georges Pichard (1920–2003, France), written by Danie Dubos
Lolly-Strip, 1967
Page 20

Nicolas Devil (born 1943, France), written by Jean Rollin
Saga de Xam, 1967
Page 80

Guido Crepax (1933–2003, Italy)
Valentina
Éditions Éric Losfeld, Paris, 1969

Caza (born 1941, France)
Kris Kool
Éditions Éric Losfeld, Paris, 1970

Guido Crepax (1933–2003, Italy)
Valentina, 'I Sotterranei' ('The Subterraneans'), 1968
Page 12

Hara-Kiri, no. 16, April 1962 (cover by Fred)

Hara-Kiri, no. 5, February 1961 (cover by Fred)

Georges Wolinski (1934, Tunisia–2015, France)
Unpublished cover design for *Hara-Kiri*, May 1967

Jean-Marc Reiser (1941–83, France)
Unpublished illustration for *Hara-Kiri*, no. 79, April 1968

Fred (1931–2013, France)
Le Petit Cirque, published in *Hara-Kiri*, no. 44, October 1964
Pages 1 & 2

C'EST MERVEILLEUX, CARMEN, ENFIN NOUS AVONS UN TRAPÉZISTE!
ESPION!
C'EST UN TRAPÉZISTE VOYAGEUR! VOYEZ, IL PORTE UNE BAGUE AVEC UN MESSAGE.
HUM!..
VOUS MÉRITERIEZ QU'ON VOUS PENDÎT POUR CELA!
PHEU!..
BOHÉMIENS, VA!
OUAIS, OUAIS!
OH! REGARDE, PAPA, DES TRAPÉZISTES!
TU VEUX UNE GIFLE?
FRED

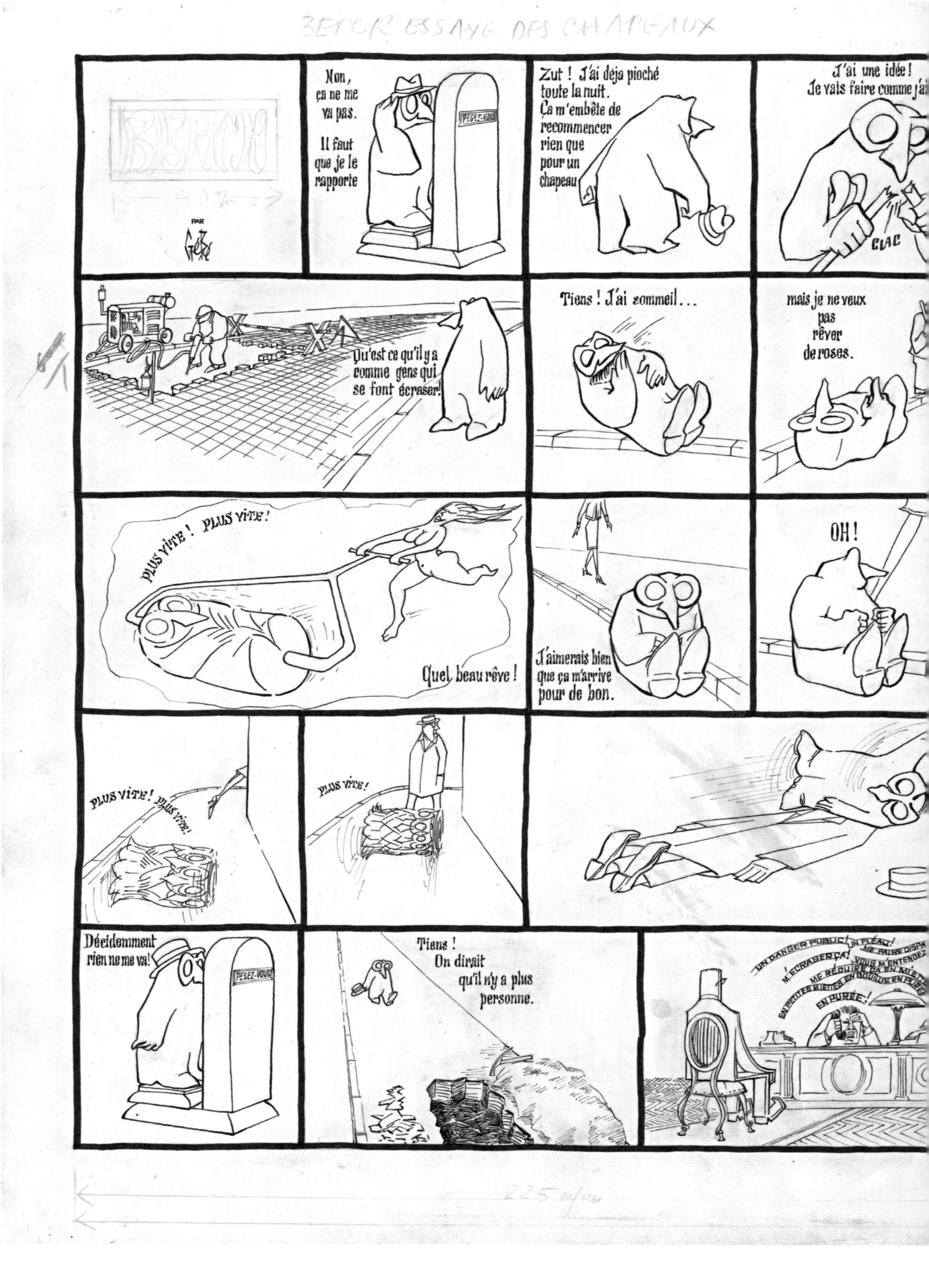

Gébé (1929–2004, France)
Berck essaie des chapeaux, published in *Hara-Kiri*, no. 48, February 1965

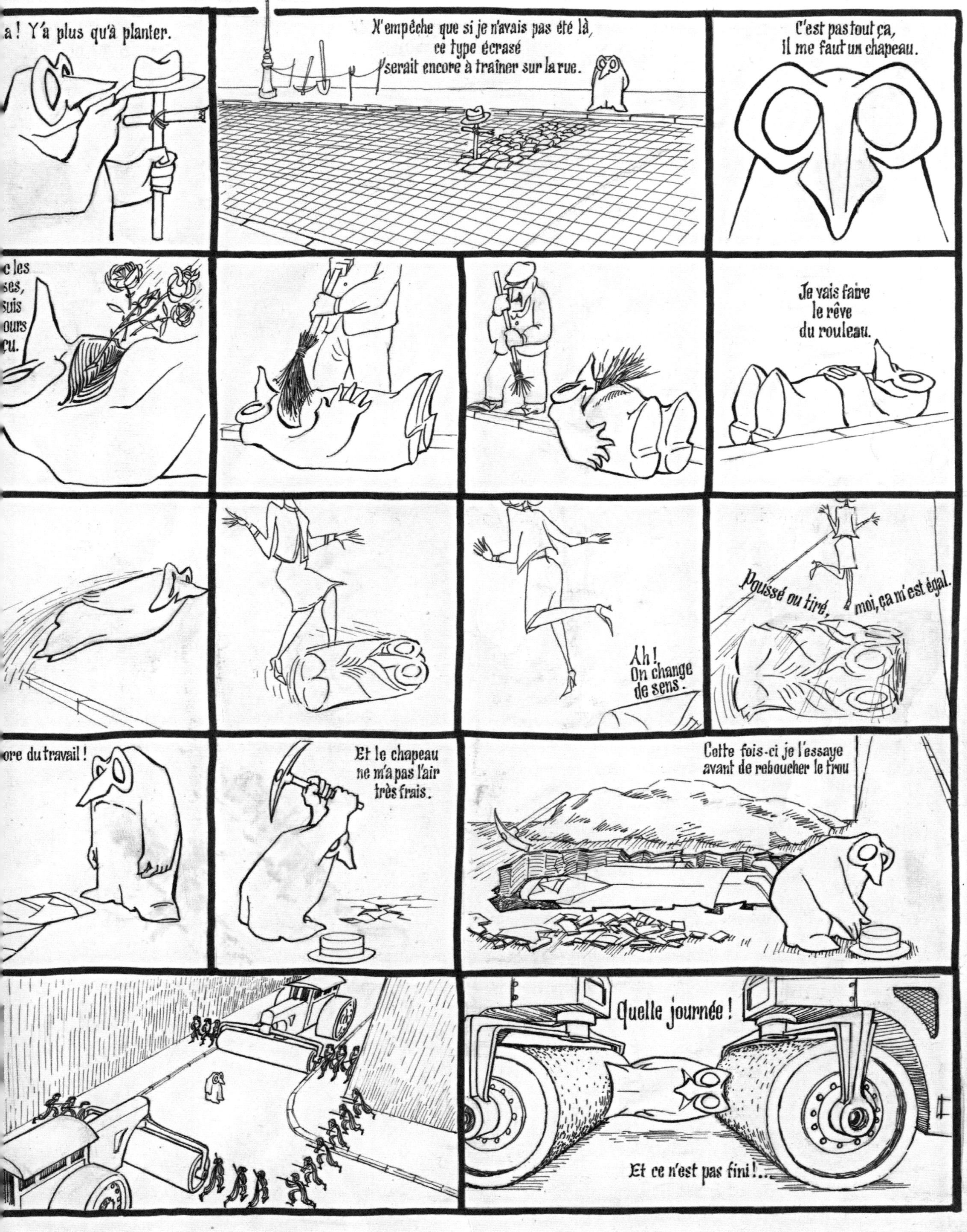

a ! Y'a plus qu'à planter.
N'empêche que si je n'avais pas été là, ce type écrasé serait encore à traîner sur la rue.
C'est pas tout ça, il me faut un chapeau.
c les
ses,
suis
ours
çu.
Je vais faire le rêve du rouleau.
Pousssé ou tiré, moi, ça m'est égal.
Ah ! On change de sens.
ore du travail !
Et le chapeau ne m'a pas l'air très frais.
Cette fois-ci je l'essaye avant de reboucher le trou
Quelle journée !
Et ce n'est pas fini !...

HARA-KIRI

Willem (born 1941, Netherlands)
Quelques fois par an..., published in *Hara-Kiri*, no. 86, November 1968
Pages 1 & 2

Scandaleux!
Cher madame, êtes-vous interessé d'acheter une esclave blanche?
Cruel!
Horrible homme!
Monstre!
Salopard!
Cette même après-midi ...
Combien coute cet homme ravissant?
Après 6 semaines....
Déjà approvisioné!
Elle est trop laide...
Beuh!
Elle n'est pas assez obscène.
Tragique, tu es invendable.
Mais je suis de la chair humaine! (n'est-ce pas?)
CHAIR HUMAINE GRATUIT! CADEAU POUR VOUS!
Apres 6 mois...
Mais hélas, même gratuit personne ne voulait avoir la femme, quelle triste histoire! Surtout il commença à pleuvoir.
Lá! Quelqu'un qui me ne refusera pas!
Hm! Ne qu'un mendiant répugnant.
Un créature de Dieu, willem!
...et elle se donnait au pauvre...
PLOF
MUET
MERCI!
Etait-il heureux avec ce présent? Personne ne pouvait le dire, il luimême de moins.
Mais moi je ne la pouvais pas oublier, je retournais le lendemain et achetais un tendre souvenir à la femme.
Cet pièce s.v.p.
NOUVEAU!
CHAIR HUMAINE EN DETAIL!
willem

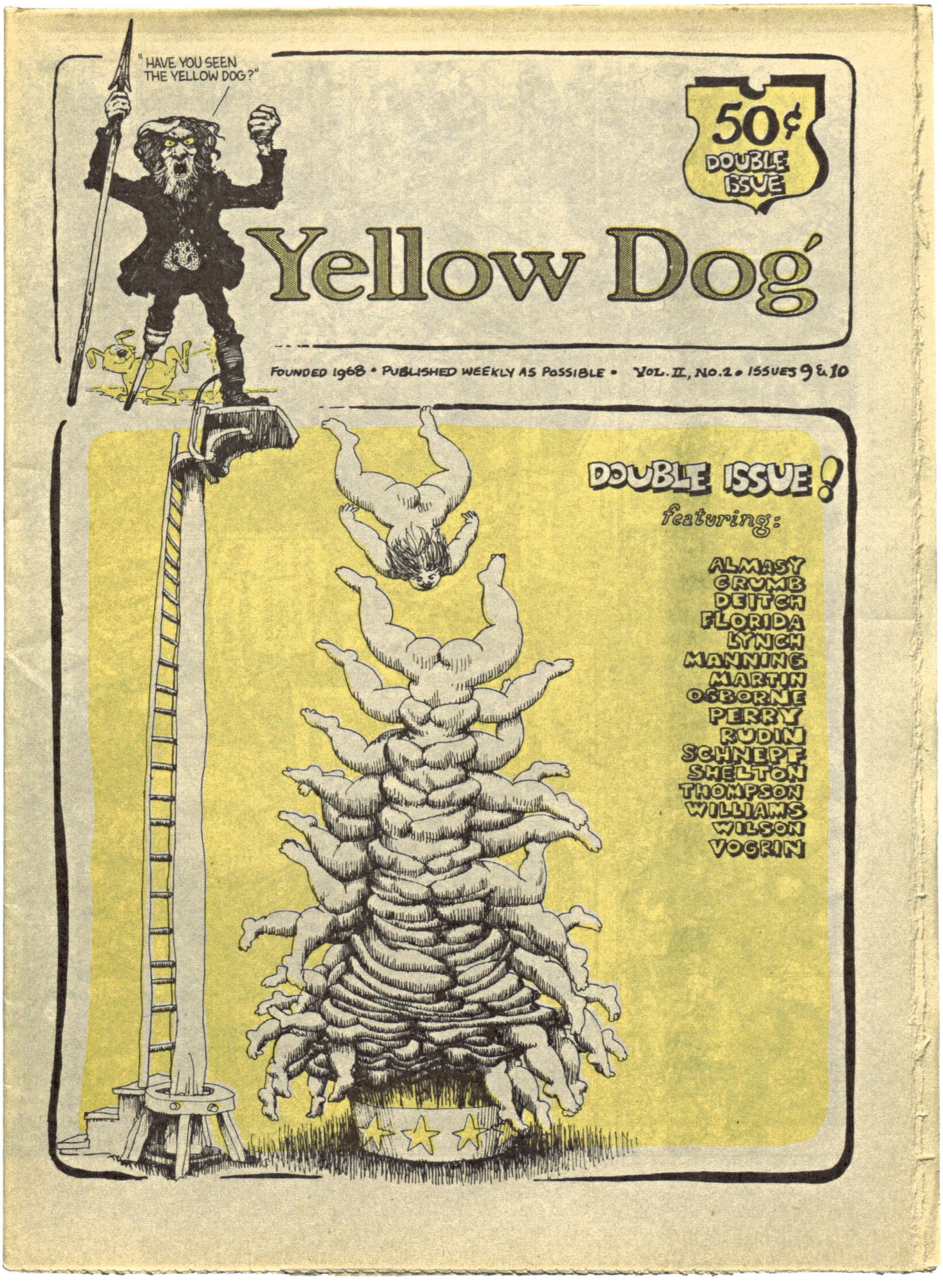

Yellow Dog, vol. 2, nos. 9 & 10, 1969
(cover by Robert Crumb)

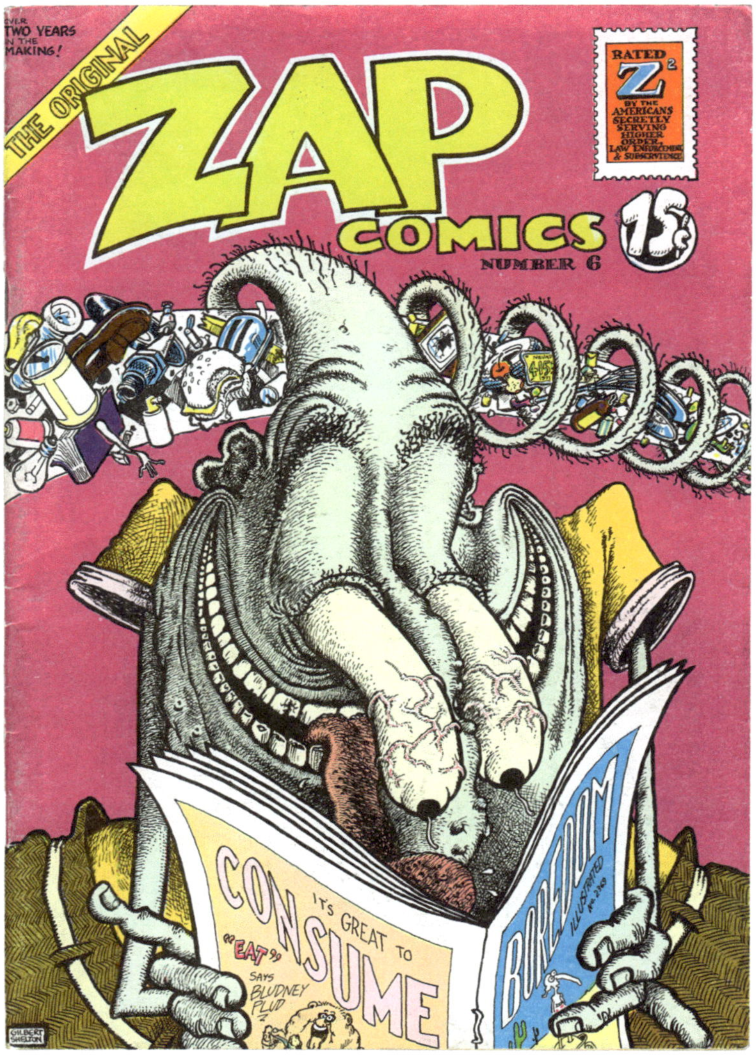

Zap Comix, no. 6, March 1973
(cover by Gilbert Shelton)

Zap Comix, no. 8 August 1975
(cover by Robert Crumb)

Gilbert Shelton (born 1940, USA)
The Fabulous Furry Freak Brothers, 1969
T-shirt design

S. Clay Wilson (1941–2021, USA)
The Nocturnal Bad Biter, 1970
Page 1

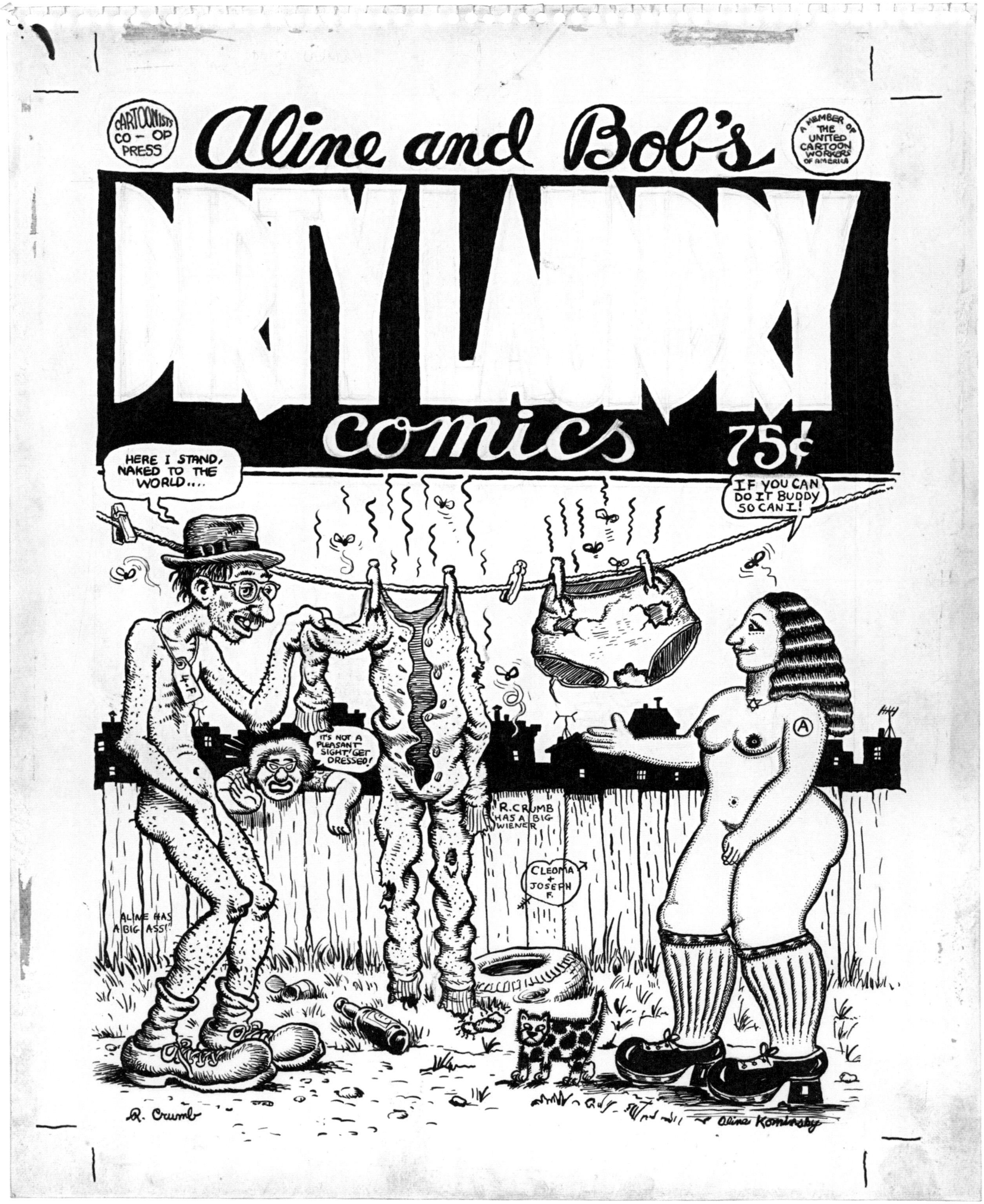

Aline Kominsky-Crumb (1948, USA–2022, France) & Robert Crumb (born 1943, USA)
Aline and Bob's Dirty Laundry Comics, 1974
Cover art

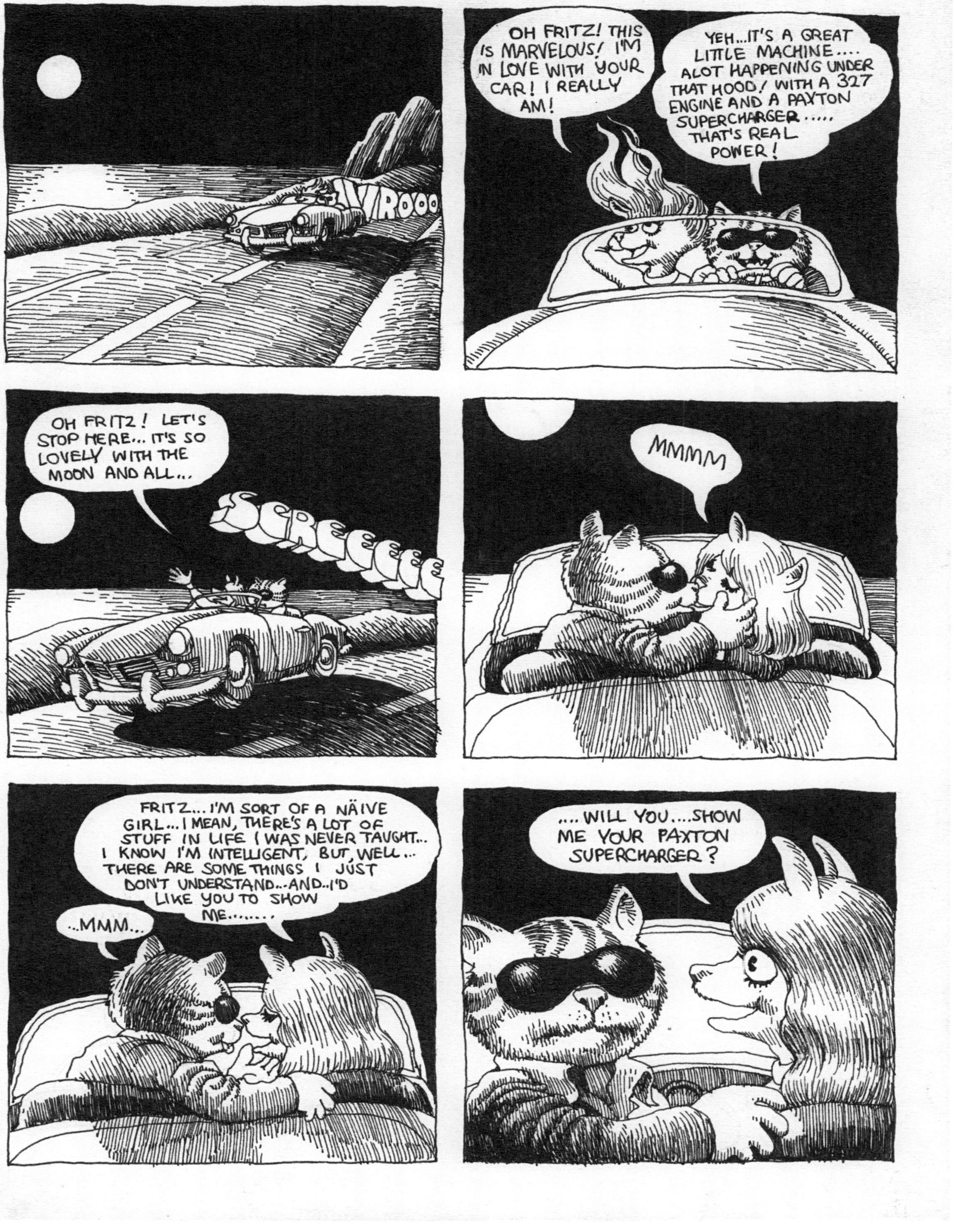

Robert Crumb (born 1943, USA)
Fritz the Cat, 'Secret Agent for the CIA', 1965
Page 16

Art Spiegelman (born 1948, Sweden)
Comics as a Medium for Self-Expression, published in *PRINT Magazine*, May–June 1981
Cover art

Jay Lynch (1945–2017, USA)
Nard n' Pat, 1974

Kiki Picasso (born 1956, France) & Loulou Picasso (born 1954, France), members of the Bazooka collective
My Grandpa's Name is Modern Art, But I Can Do Better Than Him, published in *Un regard moderne*, no. 1, March 1978
Back cover art

Olivia Clavel (born 1955, France), member of the Bazooka collective
Les Aventures de Télévision, 1980
'Télé voyage', part 2, page 1

Hideshi Hino (born 1946, China)
Hell Baby, 1982
Cover art (detail)

FEAR

Lucas Hureau

In the USA, horror comics first appeared in the 1940s. At first they were often adaptations of classic literature, but they also drew on the highly popular pulp magazines that had flourished there since the early 1920s.

In 1950, EC Comics launched *The Crypt of Terror*, which was followed by a wave of horror comics. Horror elements also crept into science fiction and police procedurals. Four years later, the rising popularity of the genre was stalled by the creation of the Comics Code Authority (CCA), which oversaw the content of comic books. Terms such as 'horror' and 'terror' were banned from titles; ghouls, vampires, werewolves and cannibals were forbidden subjects; representations of excessive violence or overt sexuality were prohibited; and good always had to triumph over evil.

It wasn't until the mid-1960s that comics such as *Creepy*, *Eerie* and *Vampirella* ushered in a horror renaissance. The most iconic artists of the day were Richard Corben and Bernie Wrightson. In 1983, Wrightson published an illustrated version of Mary Shelley's novel *Frankenstein*.

Marvel and DC Comics got involved in horror some years later, with, from 1972 onwards, the series *Tomb of Dracula* (Marvel) and *Swamp Thing* (DC). The latter was created by Len Wein and illustrated by Wrightson. Alan Moore and Stephen R. Bissette took over the reins in 1983, moving away from horror and fantasy in favour of environmental, political and social commentary. Since that point, horror has often been used as a means of reflecting on other themes, as is brilliantly demonstrated by *The Walking Dead* (2003–19), a series written by Robert Kirkman and illustrated by Tony Moore and later Charlie Adlard, which focuses on individual and collective responses to extreme situations.

Japan is another major territory for horror comics. The genre first appeared there in 1959 with Shigeru Mizuki's series *GeGeGe no Kitaro*, which featured one of the first supernatural protagonists. The series combines fantasy, mild horror, folklore and Japanese traditions with a heavy dose of comedy. In the years that followed, Kazuo Umezz became the master of pure horror, first creating scary comics for children, then, as his readership grew older, turning to a psychological approach. Although it is not as well known as *The Drifting Classroom* (1972–74) and *Baptism* (1974–76), his most terrifying creation is *God's Left Hand, Devil's Right Hand* (1986–88).

Other mangaka who took up the baton included Hideshi Hino with *Hell Baby* (1982), *The Red Snake* (1983) and *Panorama of Hell* (1984), followed by Junji Itō, the creator of *Tomie* (1987–2000) and *Uzumaki* (1998–99), while Gō Tanabe created an impressive adaptation of the works of H. P. Lovecraft.

Drawing on the literary movement Ero Guro Nansensu (focused on the 'erotic grotesque') and the work of writer Edogawa Ranpo, Suehiro Maruo created manga that combined horror, the macabre, the grotesque and the erotic. Shintarō Kago created work in a similar vein.

A tradition of comics that combined horror and fantasy to create an often unsettling atmosphere started to appear in the 1990s. In France, Stéphane Blanquet and Ludovic Debeurme followed parallel paths, with Blanquet embracing excess while Debeurme favoured a more restrained approach. Jim Woodring in the US and Imiri Sakabashira in Japan created fantasy worlds peopled by imaginary creatures, while in Charles Burns's *Black Hole*, Daniel Clowes's *Like a Velvet Glove Cast in Iron* and Atsushi Kaneko's *Soil*, the fantastical invades everyday suburban life.

Hideshi Hino (born 1946, China)
Hell Baby, 1982
Pages 20 & 21

ゴロン
あ……悪魔……!!
ゴロン
うっ……
ゴロゴロゴロ
ううう〜〜……
うわあ〜〜〜っ!!

Hideshi Hino (born 1946, China)
Hell Baby, 1982
Cover art

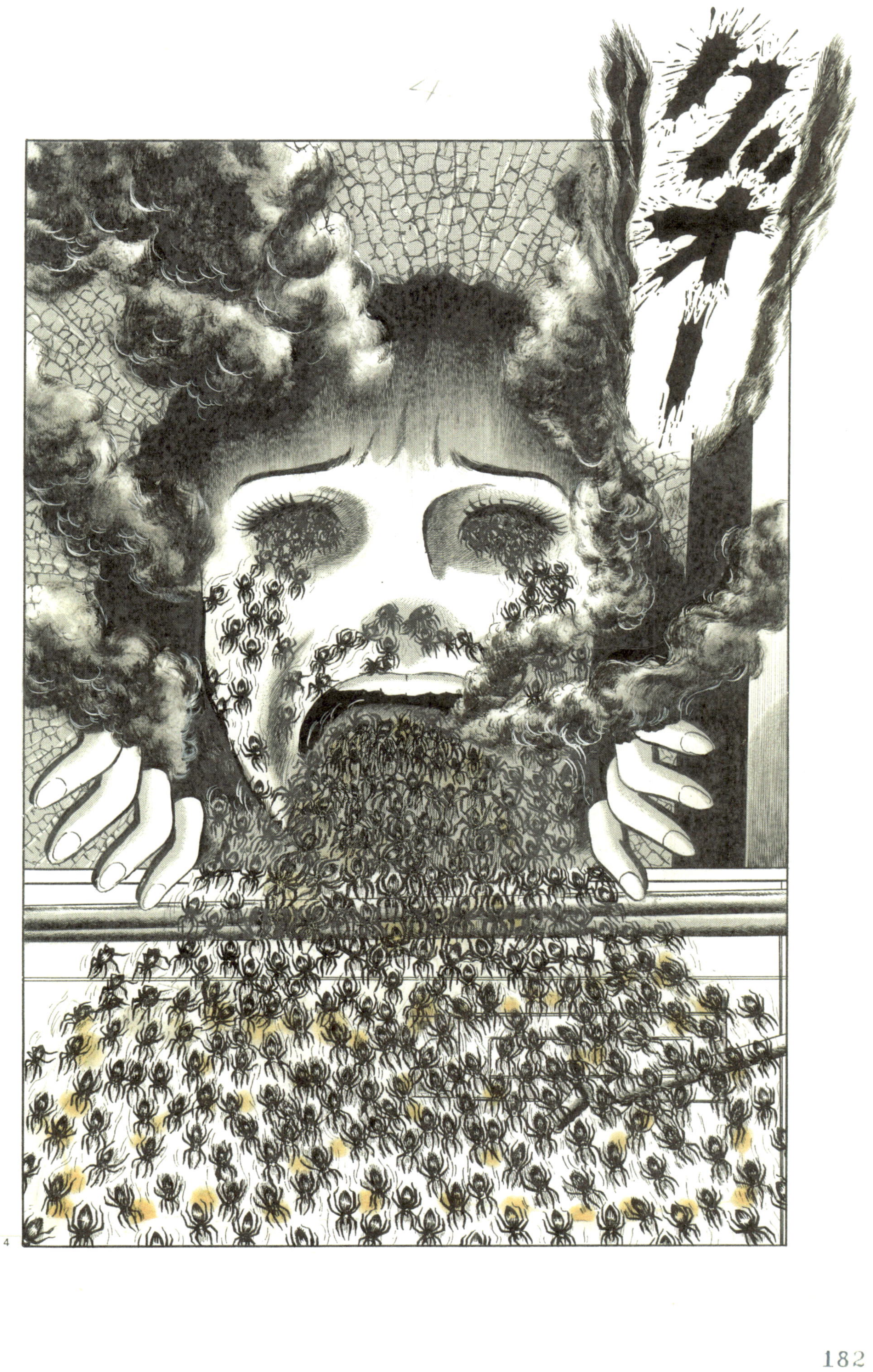

Kazuo Umezz (born 1936, Japan)
God's Left Hand, Devil's Right Hand, 1987
'Tongue of the Spider Queen', page 4

Suehiro Maruo (born 1956, Japan)
The Scream, 1988

Gō Tanabe (1975, Japan)
The Shadow over Innsmouth, vol. 2, 2020 (based on the novella by H. P. Lovecraft, 1936)
'Nightmare', pages 32–33 & 36–37

Charlie Adlard (born 1966, UK)
The Walking Dead, no. 153, 2016
Cover art

Bernie Wrightson (born 1948, USA)
Frankenstein, or The Modern Prometheus, 1977 (based on the novel by Mary Shelley, 1818)
Page 17

Gene Colan (1926–2011, USA), written by Marv Wolfman
Tomb of Dracula, no. 22: '…In Death Do We Join! Gorna… Lord of the Living Lightning!', Marvel Comics, 1974
Pages 14–15

Daniel Clowes (born 1961, USA)
Like a Velvet Glove Cast in Iron, 2017
Sketch for cover art

Charles Burns (born 1955, USA)
Black Hole, c. 1997

Joann Sfar (born 1971, France)
Grand Vampire, vol. 5: *La Communauté des magiciens*, 2004
Title page art

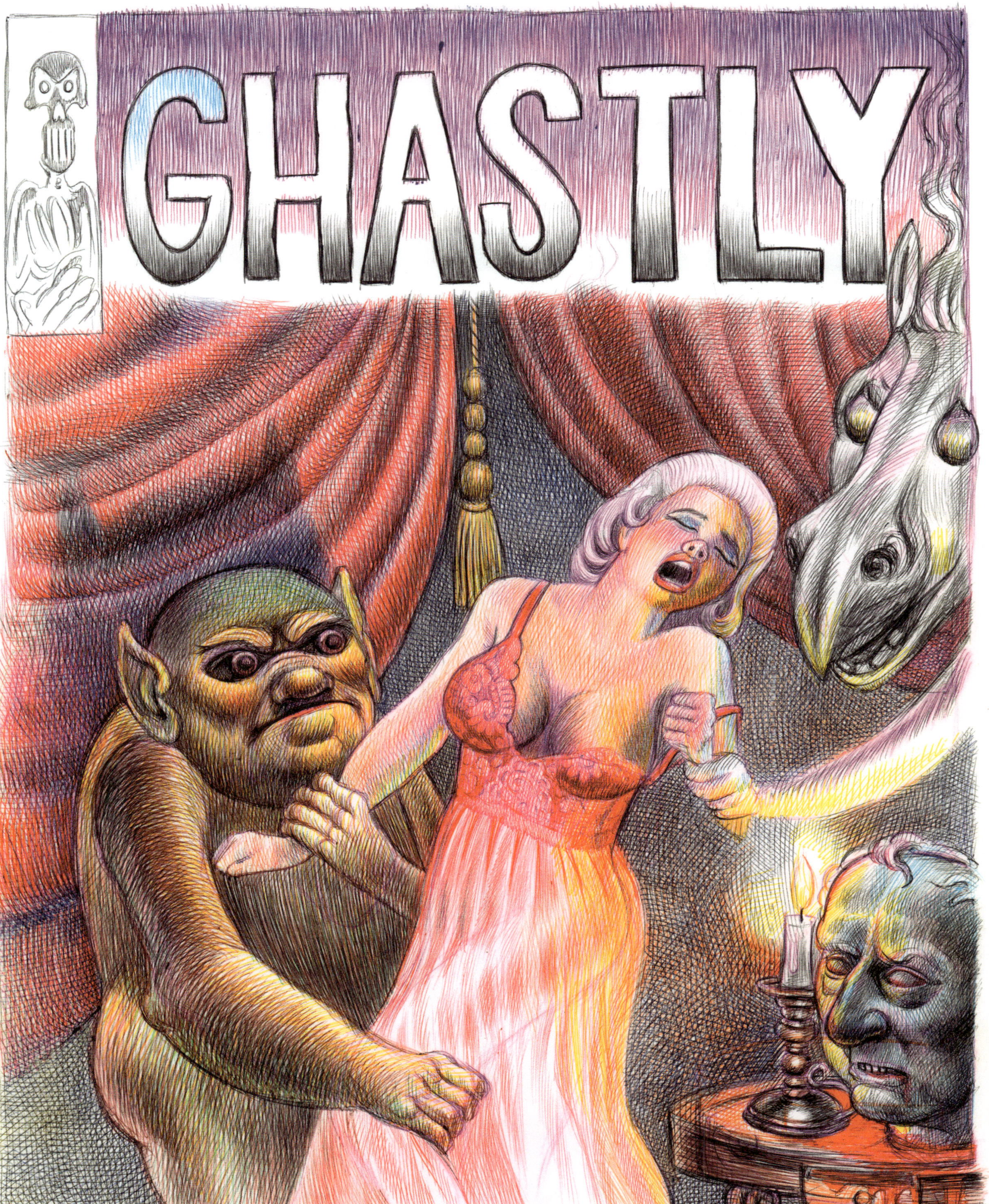

Emil Ferris (born 1962, USA)
Ghastly, 2018

Stéphane Blanquet (born 1973, France)
La Pythie face aux signes, 2015
Tapestry designed by the artist, woven by TextielLab

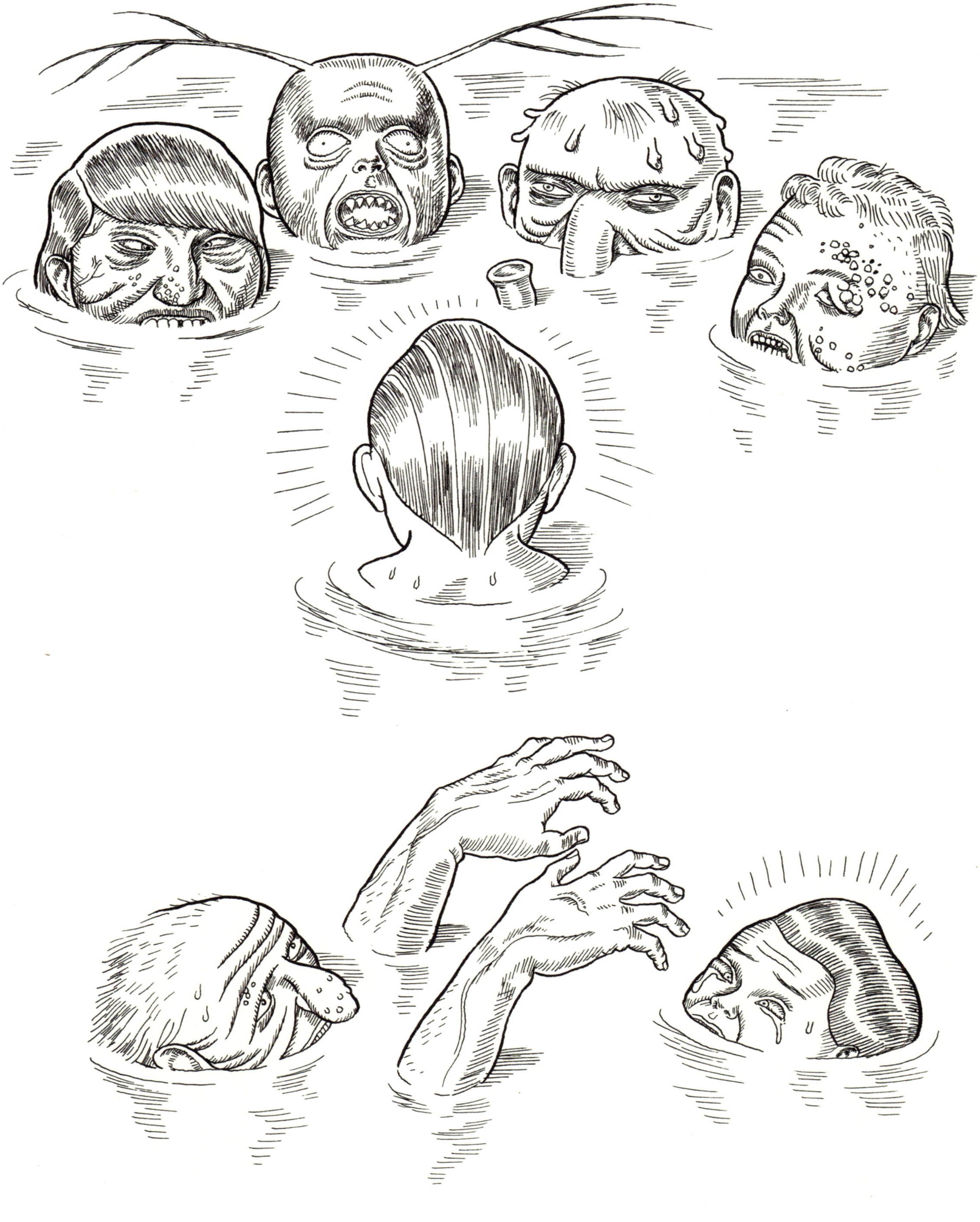

Ludovic Debeurme (born 1971, France)
Le Grand Autre, 2007
Page 78

Anke Feuchtenberger (born 1963, Germany), written by Katrin de Vries
Die Hure H wirft den Handschuh (*W the Whore*), 2007
Page 153

DORS.
DORS.

Killoffer (born 1966, France)
Les Cauchemars de l'amateur, 2016
Panel 30 (detail)

DREAMS

At the edge of reality

Johanna Schipper

'The chief characteristic of the mind
is to be constantly describing itself.'
Henri Focillon, *The Life of Forms in Art*[1]

Dream: a simple word for a universal experience. The English language has a myriad of synonyms: nightmare, daydream, chimera, illusion, fantasy, desire, wish, hope, utopia, mirage, hallucination. Contemporary comics draw on these themes in multiple ways, usually in one of two forms: 'reported dreams'[2] in illustrated form, and dream fiction. Reported dreams represent only a small proportion of comics that draw on dreams as subject matter. They most often appear in autobiographical works, and are sometimes used to create visual 'dream diaries' – the nocturnal equivalent of a daybook or journal. Far more common are comics that take inspiration from dreams, in which dream motifs are worked into a wide range of narrative forms. Meanwhile, dream fiction – such as Neil Gaiman's series *The Sandman* (1989–96) – belongs to the fantasy and supernatural genres and draws on typical tropes of those genres. But what exactly do we mean when we talk about dreams?

The strange figures of the night

From the 1970s onwards in the USA and Japan, then in the late 1980s in Europe and Quebec,[3] the rise of autobiographical comics meant that reported dreams began to feature. However, while the popularity of comics based on real life grew exponentially, the inclusion of reported dreams remained relatively rare. The main reason was the belief that dreams do not make good stories. In *Songe est mensonge* (2010), Boulet offers a witty meditation on how boring our dreams sound when we tell other people about them, comparing dream stories to the adventures of a poodle 'who is also George Clooney'. Gally explores a similar idea in a webcomic from 2015,[4] telling the story of how a joke she came up with in a dream turned out to be pointless and silly when she woke up. Therefore it seems much simpler to recycle dreams into fiction, in the same way as Federico Fellini did in his films.[5]

Unlike in literature, where the dividing line between dreamlike fiction and actual reported dreams was clearly drawn in the twentieth century,[6] the two registers often coexist side by side in comics. Depicting dreams in illustrated form accentuates the porous nature of the boundary between the two genres. David B. plays around with both approaches: in 1992 he created an iconic collection of illustrated dream diaries, *Le Cheval blême*; then, from 1996 onwards, he published *Epileptic*, an autobiography that features a number of dreams. He also published *Incidents in the Night*, a collage-style story based around recurring characters that haunt his dreams. In each of these works, dreams have a different function: they are metaphorical in *Epileptic*, they shape the action in *Incidents in the Night*, and they create a narrative and visual framework in *Le Cheval blême*. David B. went on to publish a second collection of dream diaries, *Les Complots nocturnes* (2005). For this master of black and white comics, dreams became an accent, a tone, within his diverse range of stories.

The raw material of dreams is difficult to work with. For this reason, comics creators often prefer to use dreams as inspiration for fictional stories, rather than creating visual records of their dreams without changing or adding anything. Comics such as Elene Usdin's *René·e aux bois dormants* (2021) and the works of Paz Boïra, which are narratively rich and feature stunning visuals, were first inspired by their creators' dreams. In these examples, dreams should be seen as a tangle of intertwined images that must be unravelled to form a narrative thread, which the act of fictionalization allows the author to reweave. Matthias Picard's visual retelling of a dream experienced by the musician Matthieu Chedid (also known as M) in the book *La B.O2-M-* (2015) begins with a set of instructions that tells readers to approach the work in a non-linear fashion, using the soundtrack supplied with the book as a guide. In *Haunted* (2015), Philippe Dupuy shapes the narrative around repeated elements and pathways experienced in snippets of dreams. The work can be read as a graphic poem in which the author is driven by a search for identity, a theme that is also explored in Max's *The Extended Dream of Mr. D.* (1998).

The central motif in Mœbius and Alejandro Jodorowsky's series *The Incal* (1981–88) is also a dream, although in this case it is a lucid dream. Following in the tradition of Carlos Castañeda's stories, Jodorowsky believes that the dream he had represents the essence of the *art of dreaming*.[7] Although lucid dreams are rare, we should also note that they are fairly unremarkable and we all experience them at least once in our lives. The influence of the New Age aesthetic that Mœbius *and* Jodorowsky created in *The Incal* can be seen in a special edition of the magazine *(À suivre)* in 1991, entitled *Silence, on rêve* ('Quiet, we're dreaming'), which was directed by Mœbius.

Dreams that draw on reality

The act of recreating remembered dreams in visual form brings with it a number of preconceived ideas, mainly inherited from psychoanalysis. With this in mind, it is interesting to note that David B., Julie Doucet, Aleksandar Zograf and Jean-Christophe Menu – who all kept dream diaries – never underwent analysis and were more interested in the exercise of transcribing their dreams than in interpreting them. Alison Bechdel and Rachel Deville were both exceptions to this rule. Bechdel is one of the few comics artists to invite a psychological reading of her work, in *Are You My Mother?* (2012). Rachel Deville created her work on dreams while she was undergoing psychoanalysis, and hints of this can be seen in the striking 'Psychodream', the final story in the collection *La Maison circulaire* (2015). Since the early 1950s, when Nathaniel Kleitman, Eugene Aserinsky and Michel Jouvet discovered REM sleep, psychoanalysis has not been the only discipline involved in researching dreams and sleep. Although the different disciplines disagree over the meaning and purpose of dreams, there is now a consensus that around 65% of dreams are made up of recent memories from our waking lives.[8] Therefore they don't always have a sexual meaning, unless they're referring to a recently experienced event. Artists also recognized this, which led Jean-Christophe Menu to say that a *dream* is a form of *reality* that is not very different from *real life*.[9] Telling someone about a dream is therefore like 'standing in front of them naked', as Alfred Maury described it in the nineteenth century.[10] As a publisher, Menu went on to release dream diaries from many other French-speaking creators. He broke new ground with the early experiments that appeared in the magazine *Lapin*, published by L'Association, throughout the 1990s and 2000s, then went on to publish Barthélémy Schwartz's *Le Rêveur captif* (2012) and Rachel Deville's *L'Heure du loup* (2013).

However, most dream diaries have been published in small print runs or on social media. Julie Doucet's accounts of her terrifying or funny dreams appeared in her mini-zines, then in her comic book series *Dirty Plotte* (1989–98). The author also liked to rework dream elements into her zany, punk-infused short stories. Inspired by dreams in which she had male sexual characteristics, she created a humorous leitmotif for a series of short stories on the theme of 'If I were a man'. Repurposing the content of her dreams in this way allowed her to strip it of its emotional charge. The recurring dream about half-human babies that features in *Là là, chu tanney là!!! ou le rêve récidiviste* (1995) may be linked to her account of a miscarriage in *My New York Diary* (2011).[11] The quirky, comic tone in this story plays down, in the words of Barthélémy Schwartz, the possibility of a traumatic reawakening that always lurks somewhere within the concept of sleep.

Dreams contain more content about political[12] and social issues than we would like to admit. Statistically, women are more likely to dream about being attacked, while men are more likely to dream about committing attacks.[13] But for this kind of interpretation to be applied, creators must come to a kind of 'dream agreement' with their readers, similar to Philippe Lejeune's 'autobiographical pact'.[14] Yoshiharu Tsuge never confirmed that *Screw Style*, published in *Garo* in 1968, was a reported dream, which led to much debate about what meaning readers should ascribe to the work. Meanwhile, no one would have known that Émilie Gleason's *Slapinbag* (2017) was inspired by a dream if the author hadn't stated it in her introduction. Dream sequences in autobiographical works, however, do not give rise to the same complications. Everyone knows what the dreams of being attacked in Catherine Meurisse's *Lightness* (2016) and Luz's *Catharasis* (2015) are referring to. Rediscovered identity, physical pain and emotional freedom are common themes of the dreams that appear in Camille Royer's *My First Dream in Japanese* (2019), Caroline Sury's *Cou tordu* (2010), Geneviève Castrée's *Susceptible* (2012) and Élodie Font and Carole Maurel's *Coming In* (2021).

However, these comics inspired by remembered dreams are shaped by two inherent biases: memory bias – which means that we are more likely to remember interesting dreams or nightmares – and the bias of our beliefs – which makes us interpret the content of our dreams to fit our own prejudices. Therefore, scenes of flying become a central motif in the anthology *Flock of Dreamers* (1997), edited by Saša Rakezić (known as Aleksandar Zograf) and Bob Kathman, while underground culture gives the dream diaries of Gilbert Shelton, Jim Wooding and Rick Veitch a psychedelic, hallucinatory quality.

Ambiguous objects

Patrice Killoffer has been an avid reader of Castañeda's work since he was young and is more interested in altered states of consciousness than in dreams in the strictest sense. From sleepwalking as a teenager to suffering from insomnia as an adult, the author relates a number of experiences that are similar to the hypnotic sleep state that the surrealists sought to reach. In 2017, the eight-page story 'Veilles de l'amateur de cauchemar' was published in the magazine *Pandora*; this narrative unfolds like a tale of sleep paralysis.

We see the creator's partner sleeping – a recurring motif in his work – as well as a female silhouette coming towards the couple, its shape reminiscent of an erect phallus. Is this a metaphorical representation of 'morning glory'? The author seems to have consciously imbued his art with sexual connotations. A commonplace occurrence in psychoanalysis is to link dreams to repressed desires. Blutch's *La Volupté* (2006) is a good example of this. The work is shaped by its creator's obsession with failing virility and the naked bodies of (very) young women. This suggests a dream is a pretext for Blutch's predominantly cinematic inspiration drawn from the absurdist aesthetic of Quentin Dupieux and the fetishistic style of Luis Buñuel.

Psychoanalysis also naturalized the male gaze – the objectification of the female body – starting with Sigmund Freud's concept of scopophilia (*Schaulust*, the pleasure in looking). In the early 1960s, the first publication of *Barbarella* marked the entry of comics into an adult domain. Jean-Claude Forest's iconic heroine inspired the fantasies of an entire generation, as a sexually available woman with a resemblance to Brigitte Bardot. The intergalactic adventurer navigated a universe full of phallic rockets and other erotic symbols. Ten years after the series was adapted for cinema by Roger Vadim in 1968, Forest revived *Barbarella* in an adventure entitled *The Moon Child* (1977). In this story, the heroine uses a 'dream machine' to track down a man named Browningwell, a rebellious artist who is in the process of creating a masterpiece. Barbarella is pregnant with his child and says that her baby is an even more extraordinary masterpiece. Even now, at the start of the third millennium, we can still admire Forest's virtuosity as an illustrator, while justifiably criticizing the many clichés about the wonders of motherhood and the approach to sexual liberation that never truly breaks free from gender stereotypes. However, the character of Barbarella has not entirely disappeared from pop culture: she was an inspiration behind the drag persona of US star RuPaul.

Freud wrote that dreams function in a similar way to a comic strip. In this view, a dream is a concept of another world, which is governed by its own absurd logic. This *other* world could be 'country A' in Fred's *Philémon*, 'desert B' in the work of Mœbius, or the world created by Nikita Mandryka in *Le concombre masqué*. It seems likely that the underground tunnels in Menu's *Mont Vérité* may also lead there. But isn't the same thing true of any narrative that speaks to our memories through mysterious pathways? From the twilight zones in Anke Feuchtenberger's series of short stories *Bärmi & Klett*, published in the 1990s, to Sandrine Martin's *La Montagne de sucre* (2012), the web of dreams is woven far beyond the panels of our favourite comics.

As a vital part of our subjective experience, dreams have been at the heart of comics since their invention by Rodolphe Töpffer in the nineteenth century. Whether they are dreams that the author really had or simply a pretext for a crazy adventure, they are a kind of prism through which to explore ideas and beliefs from a particular time period. They create a metanarrative, which often draws more on politics than on the imagination. Dream diaries in comics have little in common with 'false dreams' that are entirely made up – except for those inspired by real dreams, such as the ones that Hergé created for his characters. They are perfectly credible because they are based on the author's dream memories. They possess the power that dreams have, with no need to use flashy effects to move us on an emotional level. Recognizing this, Diane Obomsawin, aka Obom, adopted a minimalist approach to transcribing dreams. When we read her dream diaries in *Plus tard* (2007) or *Pink Mimi Drink* (2010), they don't match our preconceived ideas of dreams. No. They remind us of the laughter that emerges in our deepest sleep.

1. Henri Focillon, *The Life of Forms in Art*, trans. George Kubler, Princeton, NJ: Princeton University Press, 1992.
2. Here I am borrowing the term 'reported dreams', which is used by neuroscientists who specialize in the study of sleep to designate notes that are made about dreams immediately after waking.
3. Thierry Groensteen, 'Rêves de papier', in *Nocturnes. Le rêve dans la bande dessinée*, ed. Thierry Groensteen, exh. cat., Paris: Citadelles & Mazenod; Angoulême: Cité Internationale de la Bande Dessinée et de l'Image, 2013, p. 147.
4. Gally, 'Et patin couffin', 25 February 2015: https://gallybox.com/blog/?s=patin+couffin
5. Fellini's dream illustrations can be seen in Federico Fellini, *The Book of Dreams*, New York: Rizzoli, 2020.
6. See Marie Bonnot's excellent doctoral thesis, *Le Récit de rêve des surréalistes à nos jours*, supervised by Alain Schaffner at the Université de Paris III in 2020.
7. Carlos Castañeda, *The Art of Dreaming*, London: Element Books, 1994
8. Isabelle Arnulf, *Une fenêtre sur les rêves. Neurologie et pathologies du sommeil*, Paris: Odile Jacob, 2014, p. 27.
9. Jean-Christophe Menu, interviewed by Christian Rosset, in Christian Rosset, *Avis d'orage sur le rêve*, radio essay, Manoushak Fashahi (director), 'L'atelier de la création', France Culture, 28 February 2013.
10. Alfred Maury, quoted by Jacqueline Carroy, 'Archives de soi et publications oniriques au xixe siècle' (p. 12), in Claude Millet (ed.), *Les Archives au xixe siècle. Nouveaux partages, nouveaux usages*, Publications du Centre Jacques-Seebacher, 2017: http://seebacher.lac.univ-paris-diderot.fr/bibliotheque/items/show/41
11. A more detailed analysis can be found in Johanna Schipper, 'Rêver comme en plein jour: les nocturnaux graphiques de Julie Doucet', *Neuvième art 2.0*, 2022: http://neuviemeart.citebd.org/spip.php?article1415
12. Charlotte Beradt, *The Third Reich of Dreams*, trans. Bruno Bettelheim, Bexley: Aquarian Press, 1985.
13. Bernard Lahire, *La Part rêvée. L'interprétation sociologique des rêves*, vol. 2, Paris: La Découverte, 2021.
14. Philippe Lejeune, *Le Pacte autobiographique*, Paris: Seuil, 1975, quoted in Marie Bonnot, *Le Récit de rêve des surréalistes à nos jours*, 2020.

Jean-Claude Forest (1930–98, France)
Barbarella, vol. 3: *Le Semble-Lune* (*The Moon Child*), 1977
Page 26

Fred (1931–2013, France)
Philémon, vol. 14: *L'Enfer des épouvantails*, 1983
Page 25

Blutch (born 1967, France)
La Volupté, 2006
Pages 44 & 45

Blutch

David B. (born 1959, France)
Les Complots nocturnes (*Nocturnal Conspiracies*), 2005
Dream no. 17: 'The Heads', pages 1 & 2

Je sors du taxi, je suis une grande ombre.
HOTEL
RESTAU
Pour rentrer dans cet immeuble je prends la forme exacte de son ombre.

Killoffer (born 1966, France)
Les Cauchemars de l'amateur, 2016
Panels 27–30 (unpublished)

RiEN RiEN . DORS.
DORS.

Julie Doucet (born 1965, Canada)
Là là, chu tanney là!!! ou le rêve récidiviste (*My Most Secret Desire*), 1995
Panels 19–23

MAIS, C'EST UN CHAT!!!
OUI, DÉSOLÉE, ON EST EN PLEINE PÉNURIE DE BÉBÉS... UN CHAT C'EST MIEUX QUE RIEN, NON?
OH, OUI OUI!
20

RÊVE DU DIMANCHE 23 SEPTEMBRE 1994
MON DIEU! MON BÉBÉ A TELLEMENT RAPETISSÉ QU'ON DIRAIT UN TOUT PETIT INSECTE!
VU À LA LOUPE
UN CHAT!
21

RÊVE DU MERCREDI 17 AOÛT 1994
REGARDE COMME LE BÉBÉ BOUGE DANS MON VENTRE!..
22

IL BOUGE PAS MAL DIS DONC!...
OUAIS
HEY WOW C'EST PAS NORMAL ÇA!!!
EUH GLP JE SAIS PAS!
23

Claire Bretécher (1940–2020, France)
Agrippine, vol. 4: *Agrippine et les inclus*, 1993
'Au bagne' (detail)

HUMOUR

Thierry Grosteen

Drawing on the traditional art of caricature, comics have sought to make readers young and old laugh since their earliest days. Although they now embrace a much more diverse range of subject matter and approaches, they have never turned their back on their comedic origins.

René Goscinny is one of the most widely read French authors in the world. His name is indelibly linked to *Asterix* and *Lucky Luke*, witty recreations of historical periods – Roman-occupied Gaul in the former, the Wild West in the latter. The energy of the artwork by his collaborators Albert Uderzo and Morris was perfectly suited to his character-based comedy. Each series has its own tone: while wordplay and puns abound in *Asterix*, they do not appear in *Lucky Luke*, at Morris's request.

In New York, where he lived for seven years, Goscinny became friends with Harvey Kurtzman, who in 1952 launched *Mad* magazine, which took satire and subversion to a broad audience. Gotlib's series *Rubrique-à-brac* brought together two traditions: *Mad* and the Marx Brothers from the English-speaking world (parody, silliness, exaggeration) and the French tradition of Alphonse Allais and Goscinny (literary stylings, fake seriousness, quirkiness and double meanings).

Gotlib was the star of the weekly magazine *Pilote*, where he worked alongside Claire Bretécher, who also created a series that borrowed from history (the medieval princess *Cellulite*) before turning her keen gaze on her contemporaries. The mirror that she held up to readers of the *Nouvel Observateur* from 1973 onwards led Roland Barthes to dub her the 'best sociologist of the year' in 1976.

André Franquin created a softer kind of anarchy with the humour in *Gaston Lagaffe*. Then, suffering from depression, he explored shockingly dark themes in *Idées noires*. While Gaston's childlike soul was trapped in the body of an adult, Zep's *Titeuf* was descended from a long line of rogues and rascals. His kingdom was the playground, where his schoolboy humour and his fascination with the opposite sex were given free rein.

Charlie Brown, Linus, Lucy and the rest of the cast of *Peanuts* are more innocent, often pondering questions of a surprisingly metaphysical nature. Charles Schulz brought their small world to life every day for fifty years, managing to create a work with universal scope within a modest, restrained framework.

Bill Watterson built on this tradition with *Calvin and Hobbes*, in which young Calvin's toy tiger comes to life and becomes the perfect playmate. Meanwhile, little Nobita Nobi can count on the unfailing support of his robot cat Doraemon, who has been one of the most popular characters in manga since the 1970s, drawn by the two-man team known as Fujiko Fujio. One of their compatriots, Fujio Akatsuka, also created a number of funny comics.

An increasing number of female illustrators have also flexed their comedic muscles. Among the most memorable BD creations are the big-nosed figures of Florence Cestac, the quirky educational comics of Marion Montaigne and the faux naivety and absurdism of Anouk Ricard.

When Catherine Meurisse was made a member of the Académie des Beaux-Arts on 15 January 2020, it was a major step forward in the recognition of both *bande dessinée* and cartoon humour as artforms.

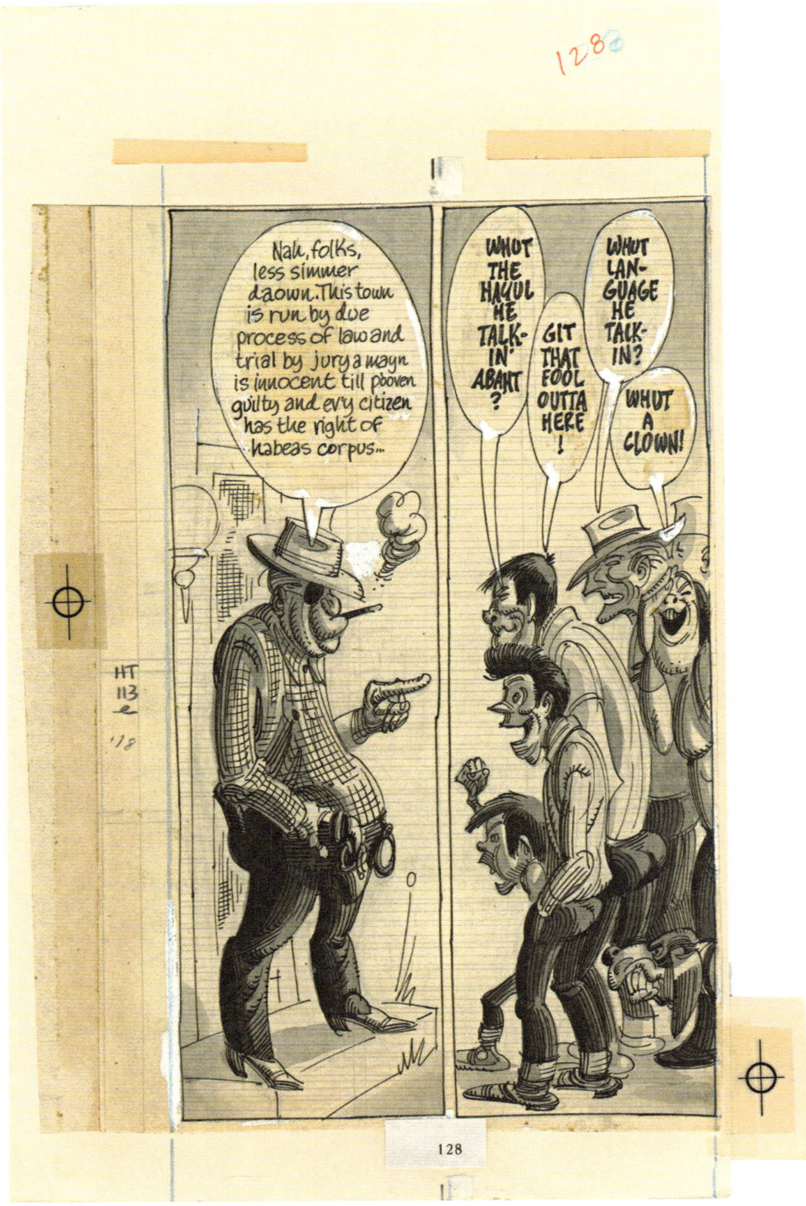

Harvey Kurtzman (1924–93, USA)
Jungle Book, 1959
'Decadence Degenerated', pages 128 & 129

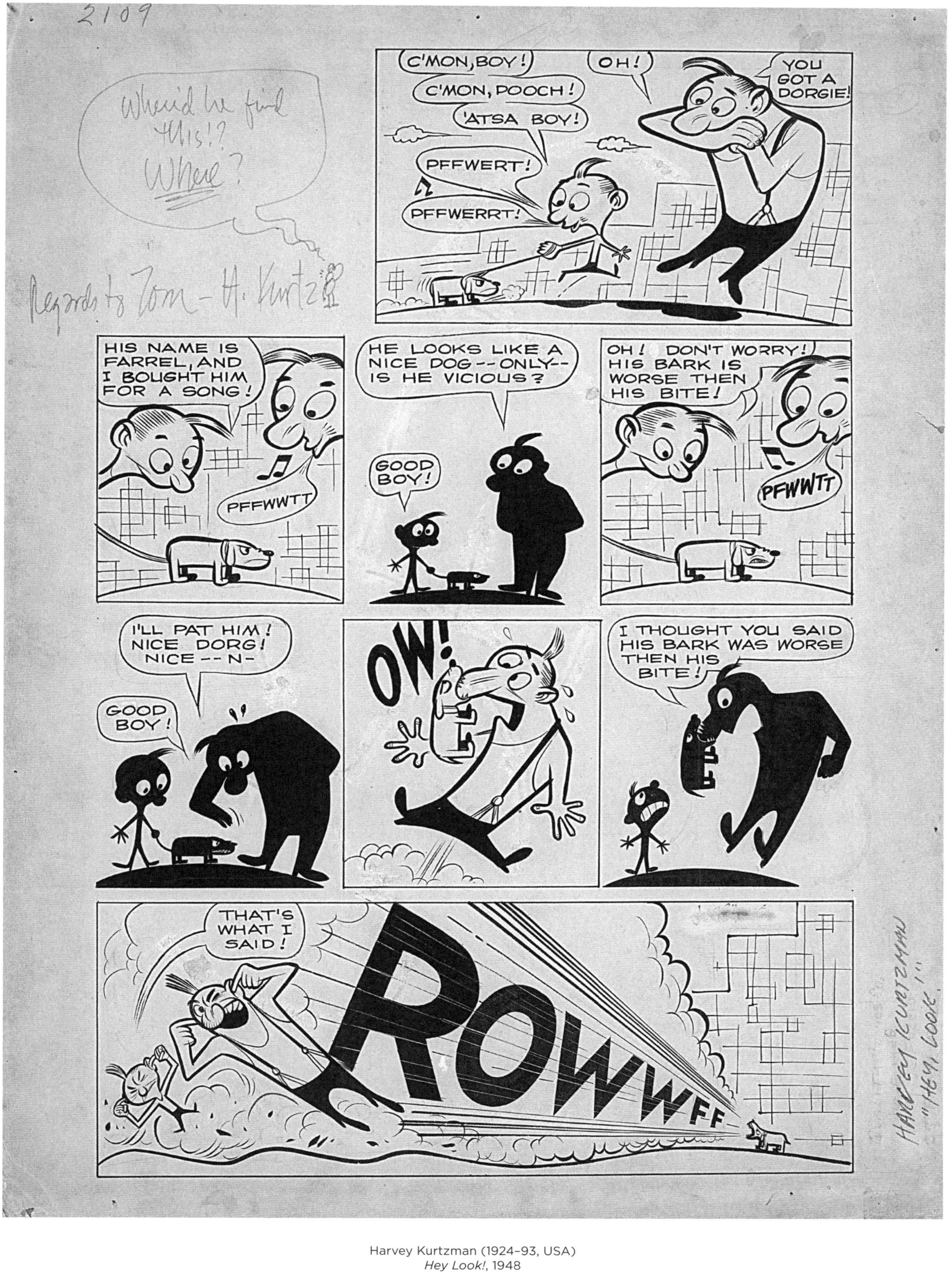

Harvey Kurtzman (1924–93, USA)
Hey Look!, 1948

Charles M. Schulz (1922–2000, USA)
Peanuts
Strip for 26 April 1964

/4 WIDE
OPY
ORLANDO
CEPEDA
. U. S. Pat Off.—All rights reserved
964 by United Feature Syndicate, Inc.
IT'S A LIVING!
SCHULZ

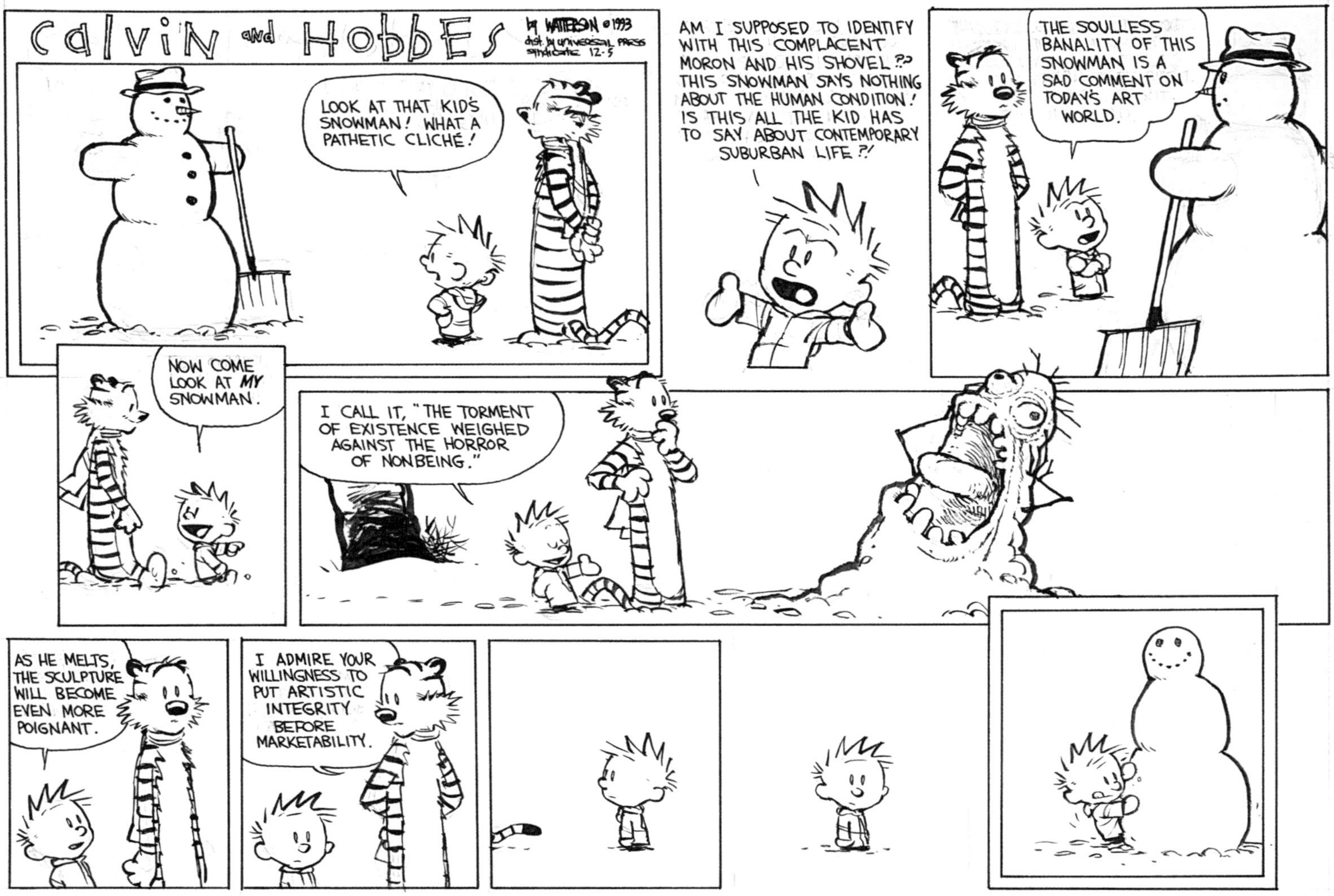

Bill Watterson (born 1958, USA)
Calvin and Hobbes
Strip for 5 December 1993

Zep (born 1967, Switzerland)
Titeuf, vol. 4: *C'est pô juste...*, 1995
'C'est pô grave'

Fujio Akatsuka (1935, China–2008, Japan)
The End of Unagi-Inu (Eel-Dog), 1973
Title page art

Fujiko F. Fujio
Doraemon, 'Fishing Indoors', 1982
Page 4

RIDETE, P
SEI STATO DAL CAPPELLAIO?
SÌ, IL PIÙ GRANDE DELLA CITTÀ
...DUNQUE... SAPETE MIAGOLARE, ABBAIARE, RUGGIRE... BENE, BENE... E, DITEMI, E NITRIRE?
OH, QUELLO È IL MIO FORTE!
IMPRESARIO
UNO DUE E...
CAMERIERE, È UN'INDECENZA! CI HO TROVATO UN CAPELLO!
SFUMATURA BASSA
COME VA VECCHIO MIO? NON CI SI VEDEVA DA ....
MEDIC
NOTAIO
HAI INDOVINATO: SUO PADRE FA IL MURATORE.
ASPETTAMI CARA, VENGO SU!
SÌ, L'HO SPOSATA!
MEGALOMANE!
TESTAMENTO: ALLORA SIAMO INTESI: NON SONO IN CASSA PER NESSUNO!
SÌ, SONO GEMELLI!
NO, NON È DI RAZZA...
L'HO CAPITO, AMORE MIO, NON STAI PIÙ IN TE DALLA GIOIA...
SVLÒNZ!
DA COME TI TOGLI I PEDALINI SI VEDE CHE SEI STATO IN UN NIGH CON LO SPOGLIARELLO...
FAI DI NUOVO IL BAGNO? NE HAI FATTO UNO STAMATTINA... E PERCHÈ QUELL'OMBRELLO?
PER NON BAGNARMI CARA. MI PARE LOGICO, VERO CARA?
POVERO AUTODIDATTA
...E POI, CARA MIA, FINO A PROVA CONTRARIA, I PANTALONI IN QUESTA CASA LI PORTO IO!
CINQUEMILA!
VEDO
VEDO
PASSO!
...È INUTILE, NON ATTACCA... QUINDI NON ALZARE LA VOCE...
PERCHÈ HA IL SEMAFORO?
...È UN INCROCIO
CIECO

Benito Jacovitti (1923–97, Italy)
Ridete, prego (*Laugh, Please*), 1964

Morris (1923–2001, Belgium), written by René Goscinny
Lucky Luke, vol. 19: *The Rivals of Painful Gulch*, 1961
Pages 1 & 2

M86/17
?
LES BRAS EN L'AIR, FISTON!
BAISSE TON FOULARD, FISTON! JE VEUX VOIR COMMENT EST FAIT TON NEZ!
?
ÇA VA, FISTON, TU PEUX PASSER TON CHEMIN!...
MAIS ENFIN, QUELLE EST CETTE MANIE QUI FAIT QUE LES NATURELS DU PAYS VOUS ARRÊTENT POUR DÉTAILLER VOTRE VISAGE ?!!...
...IL Y A UN INSTANT, UN TYPE M'A ARRÊTÉ POUR REGARDER MES OREILLES ET...
TES OREILLES, FISTON? OÙ EST-IL PASSÉ, CE TYPE QUI VOULAIT VOIR TES OREILLES?
PAR LÀ...
MERCI, FISTON!
ILS SONT TOUS FOUS DANS LE PAYS!
TU L'AS DIT, FISTON...
NOUS NE NOUS Y ATTARDERONS PAS, MAIS IL FAUT TOUT DE MÊME TROUVER UN ABRI POUR LA NUIT...
PAINFUL GULCH
GITÉ DE LA JOI ET DE LA PAIS
PAINFUL GULCH HOTEL. SALOON
TOUT CONFORT
ÉCURIES POUR CHEVAUX
CHAMBRES POUR LEURS CAVALIERS
BOUGIES À TOUS LES ÉTAGES
MORRIS & GOSCINNY

Albert Uderzo (1927–2020, France), written by René Goscinny
Astérix chez les Belges (*Asterix in Belgium*), 1978
Page 13

Gotlib (1934–2016, France)
Rubrique-à-brac, vol. 5, 1974
Cover art

Gotlib (1934–2016, France)
Rubrique-à-brac, 'Spaghetti Western', 1969
Pages 1 & 2

PTOUY
J'AI LE COUP DE POMPE
LES DUELS AU PISTOLET SE DÉROULENT COMME DES RITES ANTIQUES EXTRAORDINAIREMENT MAGNIFIÉS CETTE FOIS, À L'INVERSE DES AUTRES SCÈNES. LES ADVERSAIRES S'OBSERVENT UN LONG MOMENT TANDIS QUE S'ÉLÈVE UNE MUSIQUE QUASI-RELIGIEUSE.
ET SOUDAIN, C'EST LE SILENCE. ON SENT QU'IL VA SE PASSER DES CHOSES. NOTONS QU'À CE MOMENT, LE TRUAND A PRATIQUEMENT LA MAIN SUR LA CROSSE DE SON COLT.
TU FERAIS MIEUX DE MONTRER TES YEUX, GRINGO, AU LIEU DE PERDRE TON TEMPS EN BAVARDAGES STÉRILES !
Z
FIN DU DIALOGUE
MONTRE TES YEUX !
ALLEZ GRINGO ! MONTRE-LES, TES YEUX !
LE HÉROS, PAR CONTRE, EST CHARGÉ COMME UN BOURRICOT, ET LA PENSÉE QUI NOUS VIENT À PRIORI EST QU'IL VA LUI FALLOIR UN BON QUART D'HEURE POUR ACCÉDER À SON REVOLVER.
TES YEUX DE SALE RAT DE COYOTTE, HÉ !.. MONTRE-LES, HÉ, TES YEUX !
RITZ
HILTON TOMBSTONE
CLARIDGE HOTEL
OR, À LA STUPÉFACTION GÉNÉRALE, LE HÉROS, MALGRÉ CE HANDICAP, DESCEND TOUT DE MÊME LE TRUAND. ET MÊME, IL SE BAT PARFOIS AINSI CONTRE 4 OU 5 TRUANDS À LA FOIS, QU'IL ABAT L'UN APRÈS L'AUTRE PAREILLEMENT. (1)
PENG PENG PENG
PENG PENG
(1)_ LÀ, JE N'AI DESSINÉ QU'UN SEUL TRUAND, VU QU'UN CONTRE UN, ÇA FAIT PLUS "DUEL ANTIQUE". ET PUIS, CINQ OU SIX PERSONNAGES PAR IMAGE, ÇA VA PAS NON DES FOIS ?
ON SE DIT "CE N'EST PAS POSSIBLE !.. C'EST TRUQUÉ !" EH B'EN SI, C'EST POSSIBLE !.. TOUT SIMPLEMENT ET TOUT BÊTEMENT PARCE QUE LE HÉROS EST EXTRÊMEMENT RAPIDE. TENEZ, REVOYONS CETTE SCÈNE AU RALENTI : EFFECTIVEMENT, AVANT QUE LE HÉROS NE PUISSE FAIRE UN GESTE, LE TRUAND DÉGAINE ET TIRE.
CHICO VA ENFIN VOIR LES YEUX DE COYOTTE DU GRINGO !
PENG
Gotlib
87-2
21.2
J.T.

F'murr (1946–2018, France)
Le Génie des alpages, 1983
Pages 236 A and B

FLAPU
FLAPU
FLAPU
DIGUELINGUELINGUELINGUELINGUELINGUELINGUE
PLAF!
VU?
COMME LA MER...
C'EST MALIN!

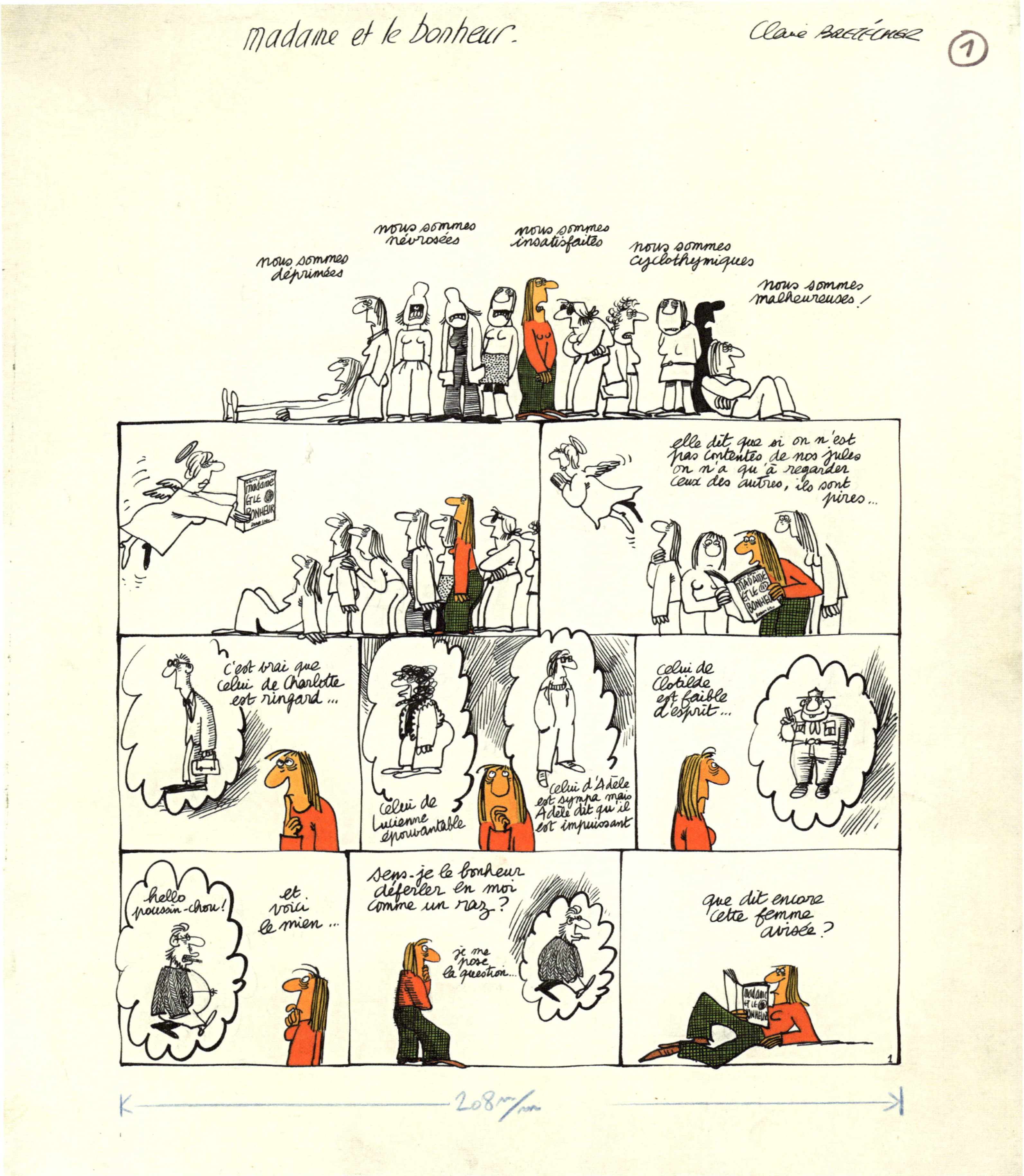

Claire Bretécher (1940–2020, France)
Madame et le bonheur, 1973
Pages 1 & 2

2

" échangeriez-vous votre physique avec une de vos amies ?"
tu veux ma photo ?
Clarisse est belle mais elle couve sûrement un cancer...
donc quand je vois ça je dois ressentir une joie gratinée...
quoi d'autre ?
"le bonheur se fabrique à force d'énergie..."
je vais inviter les Debray à dîner je vais m'avancer dans mon boulot je vais fendre du bois je vais faire du tennis je vais porter des oranges à la vieille d'en-bas...
ça ne va pas non ? je hais cette vieille, en plus je suis crevée...
allô ? je viens te voir...
oui viens ! je suis au bord du suicide...
je t'ai apporté un livre qui va t'achever complètement...
quand tu l'auras parcouru on pourra geindre et dire du mal de tout le monde... oh le bon après-midi
c'est ça le bonheur...
2

208 m/m

Claire Bretécher (1940–2020, France)
Agrippine, vol. 4: *Agrippine et les inclus*, 1993
'Au bagne'

Florence Cestac (born 1949, France)
Harry Mickson, 'Le rock à Mickson', 1979
Page 1

André Franquin (1924, Belgium–1997, France)
Gaston Lagaffe, published on the cover of *Spirou*, no. 1554, 25 January 1968

André Franquin (1924, Belgium–1997, France)
Idées noires, 1978
Gag no. 13 (based on an idea by Yvan Delporte)

Catherine Meurisse (born 1980, France)
Scènes de la vie hormonale, 2015
'Rut de rue' ('Street Mating')

Christophe Blain (born 1970, France), written by Abel Lanzac
Quai d'Orsay. Chroniques diplomatiques (*Weapons of Mass Diplomacy*), vol. 1, 2010
Chapter 5, page 3

Anouk Ricard (born 1970, France)
Animan, 2022
Digital cover art

Anouk Ricard (born 1970, France)
Animan, 2022
'Le modèle', digital artwork

Nicole Claveloux (born 1940, France),
written by Édith Zha
La Main verte (*The Green Hand*), 1976
Page 1 (detail)

COLOUR AND BLACK AND WHITE

Anne Lemonnier

In the years of pop art, colour in comics broke away from the restrictions of naturalism and reached peak saturation, playing a key part in their radical look. By the 1970s, the important work done by colourists – specialists working either at a colouring studio or in partnership with an artist – began to be recognized by the publishing world. In 1971, colourist Évelyne Tran-Lê's name appeared in Pierre Christin and Jean-Claude Mézières's *L'Empire des mille planètes*, and in 1976 Anne Delobel was credited in Jacques Tardi's first Adèle Blanc-Sec adventure. The colouring process started with proofs printed in the correct format for publication, in which the artist's lines were rendered in blueline. These pale outlines, which showed the colourist where to apply the colour, disappeared during the printing process when a reproduction of the original line art was printed over the top in pure black.

But the major revolution in these years was the move away from the blueline technique and towards 'full process colour'. First used by Edmond François Calvo in the 1940s, this practice was resurrected in 1975 when Mœbius's *Arzach* was published in *Métal hurlant*. A fantasy saga with no text, the story took place in desert landscapes populated by strange beasts. In 1976, *Métal hurlant* also published Nicole Claveloux's *The Green Hand*, a fantastical work full of biting wit, featuring a daydreaming young woman and an anxious crow. Colour played a vital role in creating the story's psychedelic feel. From then on, colour was no longer simply a form of decoration to be added later, in flat areas. Instead, it became a vital part of the artwork, and could be applied in a range of media, from inks and watercolours to paint, felt-tips and pastels.

But black and white, the dominant medium for comics since their earliest days, whether in ink or paint, was by no means abandoned. It experienced a resurgence in the *bandes dessinées* of the 1980s, mainly thanks to the monthly *(À suivre)*, which featured comics stories in a literary style, often in darker shades. The high-contrast aesthetic found in the work of Hugo Pratt, Comès, José Muñoz and Jacques Tardi, which explored the depth and subtleties of ink, had a lasting influence on the generations that followed. The vast potential of black and white comics can be seen in the popularity of graphic novels, as well as the exponential growth of manga. Stylistic experiments abounded as illustrators played with chiaroscuro and used light and shade to create atmosphere and depth. Some used ink-wash techniques, while others preferred cross-hatching or, like Swiss artist Thomas Ott, worked with a nib and scratchboard.

In colour comics, creators whose body of work did not conform to commercial stereotypes also began to draw on a broader range of techniques, as well as embracing different aesthetics: the ethereal frozen world of Enki Bilal, in shades of white and cold tones shot through with dark reds, contrasts strongly with the world created by Italian artist Lorenzo Mattotti, which explores the symbolic and emotional aspects of colour – his graphic novel *Fires* (1984) was a major milestone in the exploration of colour in comics art. Nicolas de Crécy's artwork develops the same approach, with a palette characterized by soft harmonies between cloudy blues and reddish ochres, while Brecht Evens's books use transparent layers of colour, bringing a sense of the interplay of light into night-time scenes.

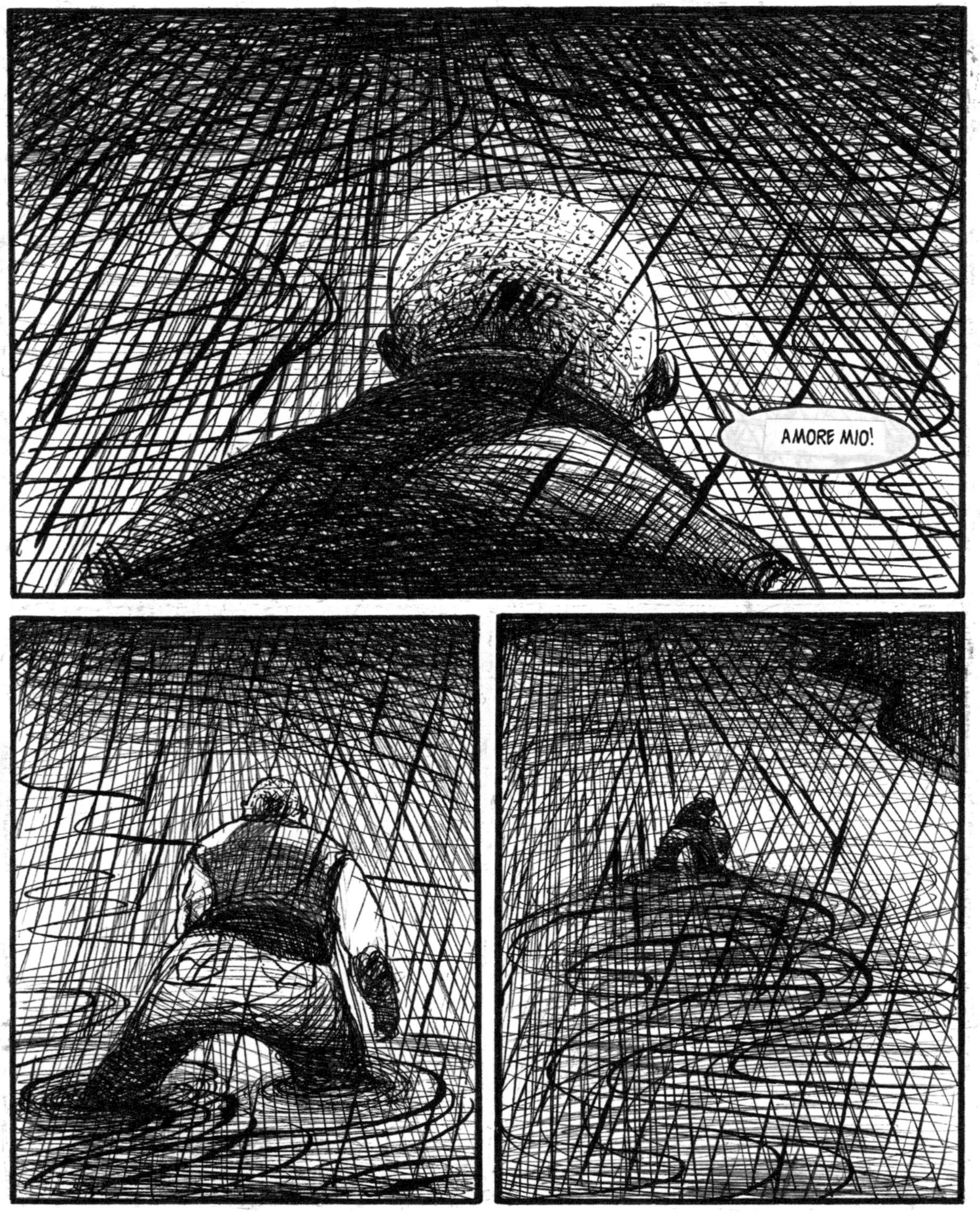

98

Lorenzo Mattotti (born 1954, Italy), written by Claudio Piersanti and Lorenzo Mattotti
Stigmata, 1998
Page 98

Lorenzo Mattotti (born 1954, Italy)
Fuochi (*Fires*), 1986
Page 27

Lorenzo Mattotti (born 1954, Italy)
Bob Dylan Revisited (collective work), 2008
'A Hard Rain's A-Gonna Fall', planche 2

Nicolas de Crécy (born 1966, France)
Le Bibendum céleste (*The Celestial Bibendum*), vol. 2, 1998
Cover art

Mœbius (1938–2012, France)
Ballade, 1977 (inspired by the poem *Fleur* by Arthur Rimbaud)
Page 6

Mœbius (1938–2012, France)
Arzach, 1975
Chapter 1, page 1

Enki Bilal (born 1951, Yugoslavia), written by Pierre Christin
Partie de chasse (*The Hunting Party*), 1982
Page 66

Enki Bilal (born 1951, Yugoslavia)
La Femme piège (*The Woman Trap*), 1986
Page 7

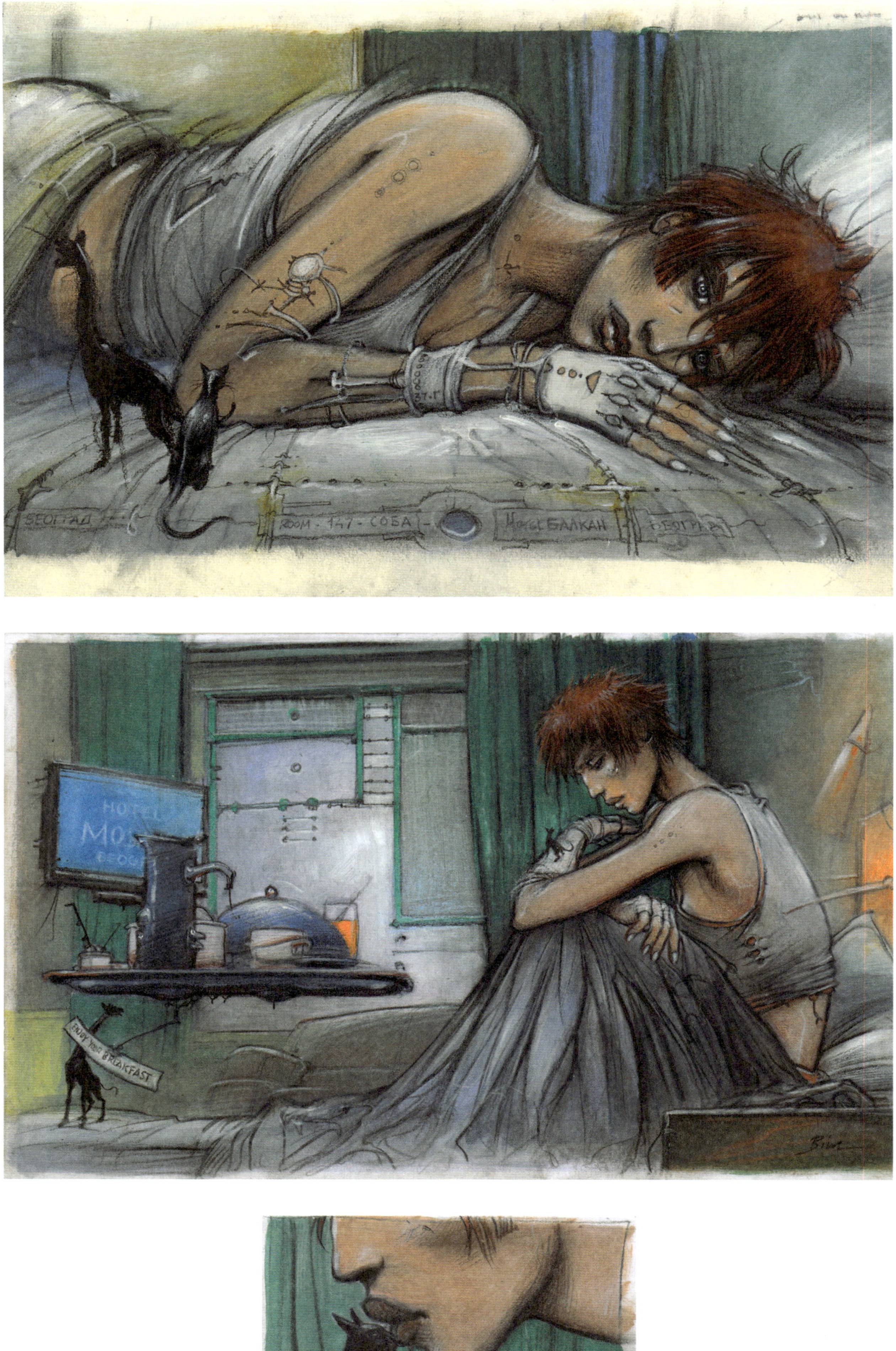

Enki Bilal (born 1951, Yugoslavia)
Le Cycle du monstre (*Monster*), vol. 3: *Rendez-vous à Paris*, 2006
Page 7 in 3 panels

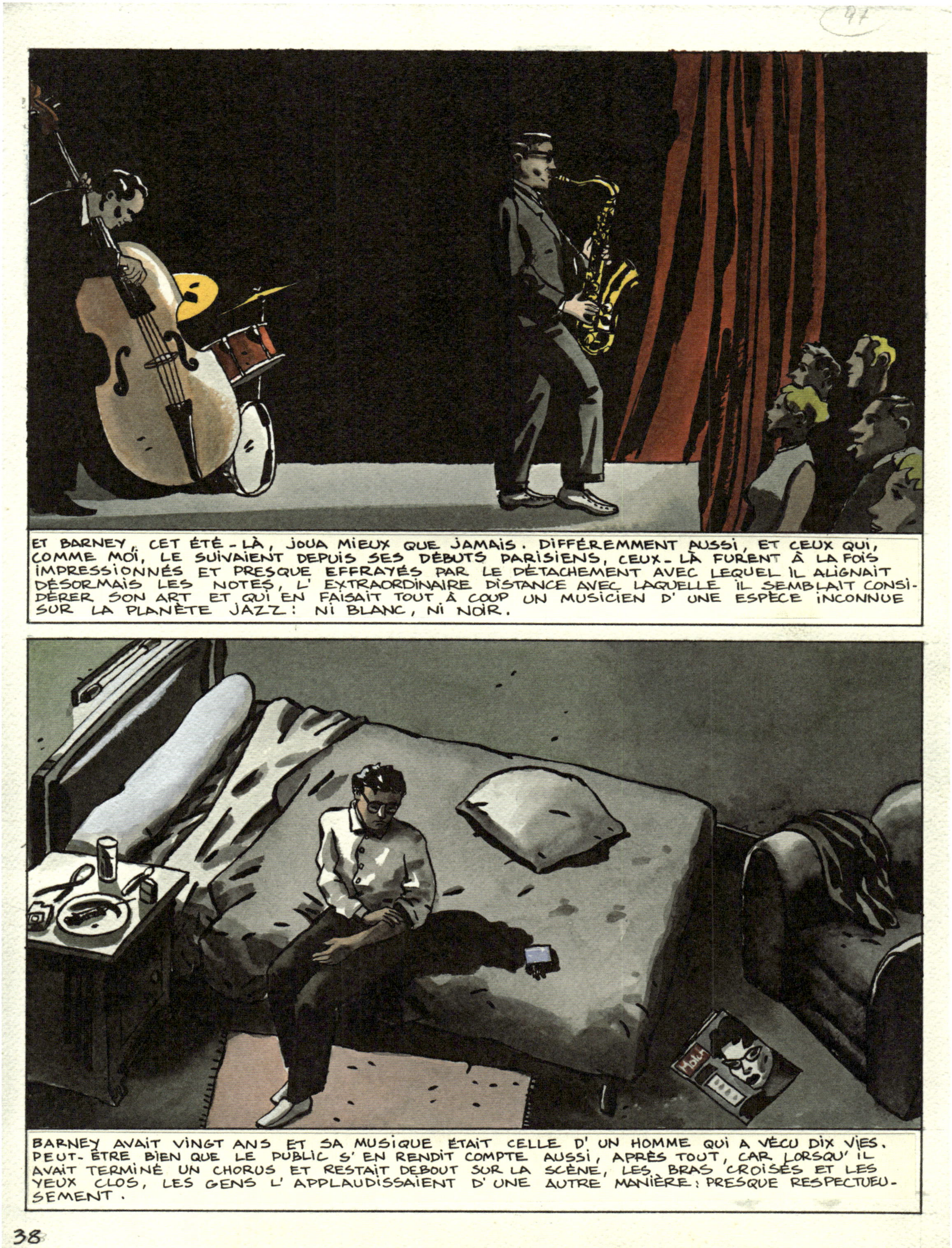

Loustal (born 1956, France), written by Philippe Paringaux
Barney et la note bleue (*Barney and the Blue Note*), 1985
Page 38

Nicole Claveloux (born 1940, France), written by Édith Zha
La Main verte (*The Green Hand*), 1976
Page 1

Brecht Evens (born 1986, Belgium)
Les Amateurs (*The Making Of*), 2011
Cover art

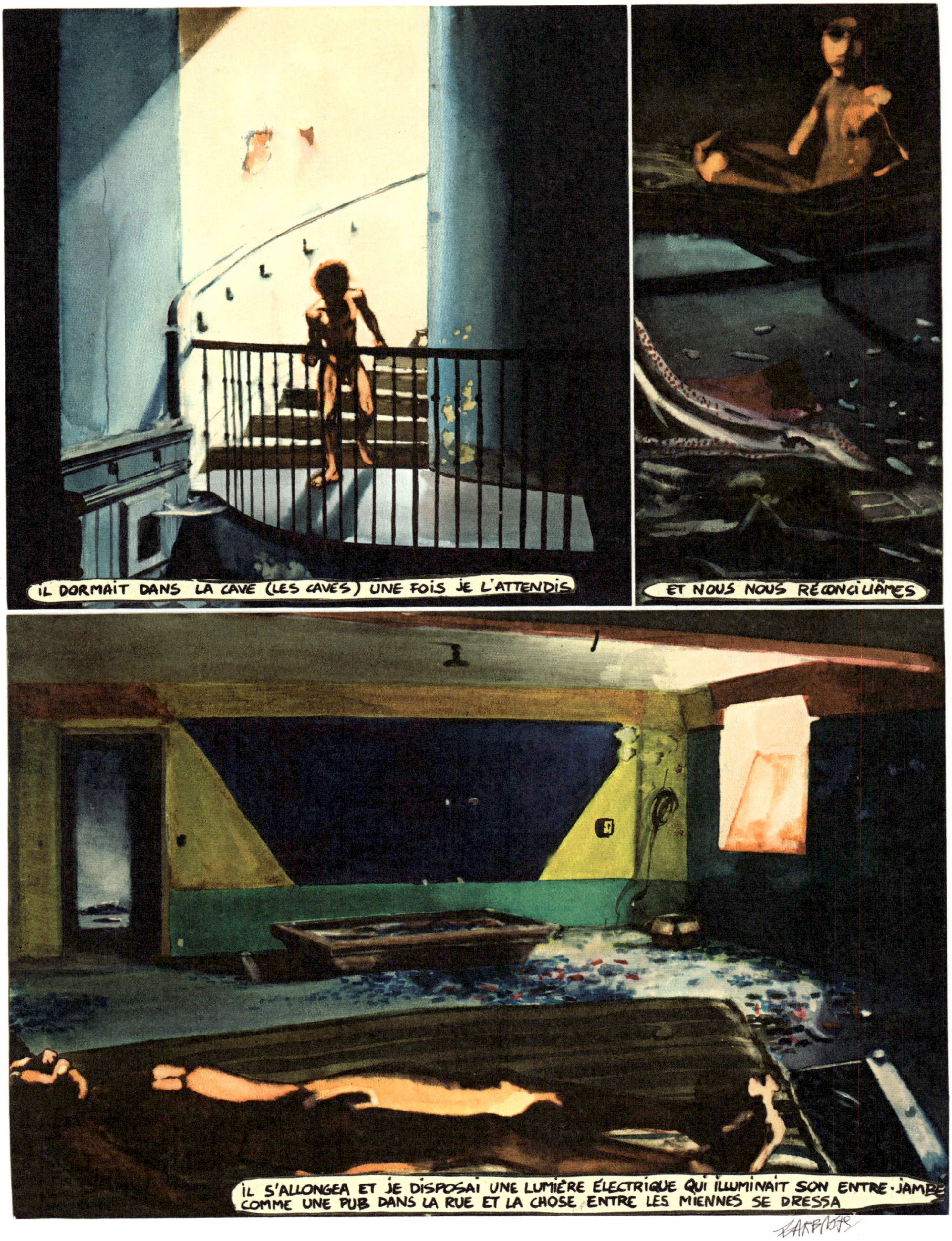

Alex Barbier (1950–2019, France)
Comme un poulet sans tête (*Like a Headless Chicken*), 1994
Page 17

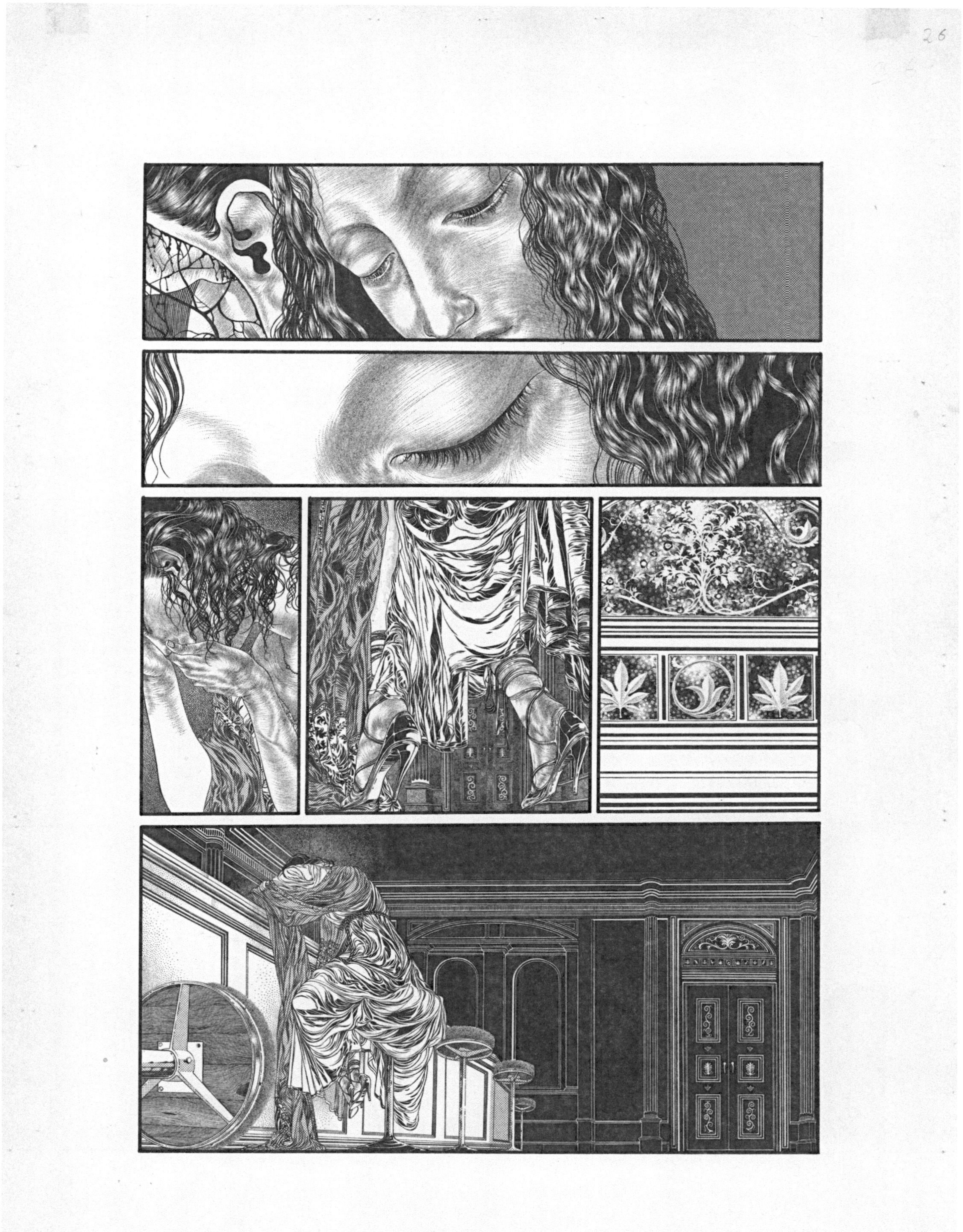

Keizō Miyanishi (born 1956, Japan)
Maila, c. 1970
Page 32

Mike Mignola (born 1960, USA)
Hellboy, vol. 12: *The Storm and the Fury*, 2012
Cover art

Frank Miller (born 1957, USA)
Sin City, vol. 3*: The Big Fat Kill*, 1995
Chapter 3, page 12

Hugo Pratt (1927, Italy–1995, Switzerland)
Corto Maltese: *Les Éthiopiques*
'Et d'autres Roméos et d'autres Juliettes' ('And of Other Romeos and Other Juliets'), 1973
Page 11

Hugo Pratt (1927, Italy–1995, Switzerland)
La Macumba du gringo, 1977
Page 47

José Muñoz (born 1942, Argentina), written by Carlos Sampayo
Alack Sinner, 'Twinkle, Twinkle', 1976
Page 11

Comès (1942–2013, Belgium)
Silence, 1980
Cover art

Thomas Ott (born 1966, Switzerland)
Cinema Panopticum, 2005
'The Prophet', page 14

Nina Bunjevac (born 1973, Canada)
La Réparation, 2022
Page 18

Zeina Abirached (born 1981, Lebanon)
Le Piano oriental, 2015
Pages 90–91, digital artwork

JE TRICOTE DEPUIS MA NAISSANCE UNE LANGUE FAITE DE DEUX FILS FRAGILES ET PRÉCIEUX.

Art Spiegelman (born 1948, Sweden)
Maus #2, 1991
Endpaper illustration (detail)

HISTORY AND MEMORY

Joe Sacco in conversation with Paul Gravett

Paul Gravett: Joe Sacco, you're considered a pioneer of comics journalism, with your work focusing on Palestine, Bosnia, and other parts of the world. Your detailed graphic novels allow you to focus on the local contexts and human experiences of the places you visit, exploring a number of complex questions that other forms of media often neglect. I'd like to talk to you about the way in which you use first-hand research in your work, as well as the roles played by history and memory in your approach.

There are many versions of history – after all, the root of the word is 'story'. So which version do we trust? Equally, memory can be variable, unreliable and highly personal, the same event can be experienced and remembered in multiple ways. Comics have become a medium to speak about sometimes difficult, complex truths, and give an individual's perspective on huge events.

Joe Sacco: Yes, what we're talking here about is the sort of autobiographical or biographical work which places a person, often the author or a family member, into an historical context. People can find themselves dropped into history, within a context of the bigger forces of history, as outside events control your life, for example in *Maus* or *Barefoot Gen*.

P: Were these part of what first interested you in expanding your approach to comics?

J: There's a lot of things that fracture your conventional thinking. EC Comics' *Mad* comic books blew up my ideas about what you can do with comics. And then there was the underground movement. They tried many different things, sometimes not so deeply, but there was an experimental nature to many of them. I think of Spain Rodriguez's historical comics and remember one he did as a reporter for the *East Village Other* about his experiences at the Democratic National Convention in 1968. Robert Crumb did some journalistic work too. They wanted to crack things open and set out flags. What are the boundaries, how far can we go? And I think some put those flags so far out that to today's generation, they seem too far out. They were breaking taboos, and in the broad scope of human experience, the underground pushed how far you can go. However, we judge it – and I judge it quite kindly – if it wasn't for that, I don't think I and a lot of other people would be doing what we're doing now.

P: Your journalistic background means you're comfortable going out there and reporting on what you're seeing and hearing first-hand. But how do you verify memories and deal with researching history?

J: It's a combination. Obviously you have to read up about the people and places before you go. And that can be a security blanket, because when you get there, you find out a lot is going on that you weren't reading about. You learn to not just read books but to go into the archives of newspapers to get a sense. When I was doing *Safe Area Gorazde*,[1] for example, I went to the *Guardian* and the *New York Times* and I got every article that mentioned Gorazde for some years.

P: How do you research deeper history, for example about Palestine?

J: For *Footnotes in Gaza*,[2] I discovered quotes from a United Nations document in a book. So I went to the United Nations Relief and Works Agency archives in New York that deals with refugees around the Middle East, found that document and got copies of it. Reading it all through, I asked for more information. A lot of the stacks are closed, so you have to give the right words to get the right documents back. I even paid a couple of Israeli researchers to look in the archives in Israel for anything they could find in Hebrew. It's not always helpful, but it's doing due diligence, trying to research.

Pictures are super-important too for drawing historic moments. In the photo archive of the United Nations Relief and Works Agency[3] in Gaza City, I found great photographs of two specific places I was mentioning from the 1950s. I said, 'Can I make copies?' And they said, 'No, we've got doubles. Here, you can have these.' So I own these great photographs and from those, I could construct what a refugee camp looked like in those days.

But that was coupled with talking to older people there, who would describe what the streets looked in those days. They would say 'It's not like today, there were cacti on the streets.' Some people would take me to buildings that still had some of the framework or attributes like roof tiles of the houses that were built for them in the 1950s and I took photographs of those locations. It's a way of making me feel that I'm getting it right, or making an effort to get it right.

There's the subjective element in comics that creates a tension between the facts and the quotes. Every medium is subjective on some level. I remember reading about places that I eventually went to and realized I had a completely wrong conception of what the place looked like. My standard is to try to make it so the person from that place will recognize it. In its essential elements, let's say. In some cases, it's possible to recreate the exact, actual building because it still exists.

P: How do you manage when there's no visual evidence, but people have powerful memories that you want to illustrate?

J: The most extreme examples of that are people who have been interrogated and tortured. Everyone's experience might be different. And in some cases people were hooded, so you're trying to recreate something that you haven't seen and that there's no archival document for either. You can research photos of people in hoods being taken to interrogation facilities. There's not much variation between these organizations' methods. It's a great responsibility to try to get it as right as possible.

P: What was your first comic dealing with someone else's memory of history?

J: I did a 22-page story in *Yahoo* #4 (January 1991) about my mother's experiences living in Malta in World War II, when it was under attack by Italian and German air forces. I asked her, 'Ma, can you write to me about living in a shelter?' And she wrote me a letter about what she remembered. And she knows how to draw, she had a good memory in those days. So I asked her what things looked like and she would write me these set pieces, which I put together as her story. And I did *Yahoo* #6 (June 1992), which has never been reprinted, with Susan Catherine, who wrote about her experiences being a stripper in Canada, back in the day. She was living in Berlin when I was there. And I worked with Harvey Pekar on strips for *The Village Voice* (1992–96), mainly about jazz musicians and collectors.

P: So you were building up to something before arriving at *Palestine*[4] in 1993. I'm curious about your decision to portray yourself in this project. Whereas Igort in his *Ukraine Notebooks* and *Russian Notebooks*[5] went there and talked to people, but chose not to put himself into his comics, because he wants these silenced people to have their own voices fully at last.

J: I think that's completely valid. My way isn't necessarily the best way. Frankly, it was accidental, from doing autobiographical comics. When I went to the Palestinian territories, I wasn't thinking in journalistic terms, more of a travelogue about my experiences there. Autobiography and journalism met. I didn't have a theory of why I was putting myself in it, but then I realized it shows that journalism itself is a subjective experience. Journalism is taught in American schools as objective, you are a fly on the wall getting all this information and at a certain point I realized you can't be objective about certain things. I was influenced partly by New Journalism[6] figures, such as Hunter S. Thompson and Michael Herr.

In *Safe Area Gorazde*, I was being invited into people's homes. How are you going to write yourself out of that? Those things can show a lot about a society, they were very happy to see an outsider. And sometimes you become part of a story, for example when the town was still under siege and only journalists, U.N. workers or a few others could come in and out. I became a postman, taking letters from people in Gorazde to their family members, their parents, in Sarajevo. How do you write yourself out of that? It's very poignant. In certain cases, I take a step towards Igort's approach, as with the indigenous people in *Paying the Land*.[7] At times, I contrast my city ways with their ways of thinking and roughing it in the bush. I'm a real advocate for this approach.

P: I know you don't want your personal story to overwhelm the bigger story. But for many readers, you are a point of access into this often complex, unfamiliar context.

J: I remember for some political work, my first inclination was to get human rights reports about what was happening to Palestinians in the West Bank and Gaza. I'd thought, that would hold up in court, but it's so dry. It's supposed to be bloodless to be admitted in court. But I want to meet people, talk with people, interact. When I was there, I realized it was the best possible thing to do, because people are victims, but you don't want to show them as victims with a capital V. That's part of their lives but there's more to their lives. People under extreme conditions are still talking about certain things that matter to them. I want to share the whole person I got to meet and liked and what happened to them. There's a power in that.

P: In many of your stories, there is an underlying injustice. Do you ever want to address how to get justice and how judicial systems are failing?

J: That's an awful big assignment to give yourself. These things matter to me and I want them to matter to other people, but I would like to know how the world works. I don't want to have the wool pulled over my eyes, as I felt in the past, until I researched for myself. When I come back from a research trip and try to relate my experiences to my friends, five minutes into it their eyes cloud over, it's too much. I realize it's better to get these things across on the page where I can filter it into an artistic form.

You've got to put your passion and your anger through a filter and that's what comics are to me. It's where I take that raw material and put it in a way that I can reach and that can reach other people. I have a hard time looking at violent images. What drawing does is filter violence, so people can look at it directly and not turn away.

There are certain questions I have about the psychology of people that can't be answered. After spending time doing all these stories, you begin to think, how could that person lift that hatchet or shoot that gun? This goes way deeper than even the institutional reasons. The journalism gives the geopolitical reasons, which are important, but I'm interested to look into the psychology of humans and why they do what they do.

P: So you want to look into the heart of darkness, and discover what we are all capable of?

J: Exactly. In a lot of my work, I'm trying to figure out the world, because it delights me in many ways and sometimes people are so beautiful. Even under the worst conditions, they can still laugh and search for meaning. That's the beauty of the human spirit, alongside other points that are much darker, which I'd like to explore in other ways. When you've read a lot of history, you begin to wonder about what we are as a species, and in the worst possible sense. I'm not trying to be overly dramatic, but I'm curious and need to find out more. I want to talk to neuroscientists, primatologists, or philosophers.

P: Looking at other approaches to the theme of history and memory, I was struck by Nora Krug's *Belonging*.[8] She comes from a German family, some of whom were Nazis but never spoke about it. While there is plenty of teaching about the Second World War in German schools, I gather people deal less with their own family's role. Krug fearlessly looked into her family's history in archives, tracing their role within the Nazi party. She struck a chord with many other people with skeletons in the closet that they don't speak about or face up to. And she shows how you could do this too.

J: That's enormously brave and very painful. When someone does something like that, they're all also putting out flags. There's so much untrammelled grass. I'd read a number of books about the Holocaust and coming across *Maus*,[9] you might think, how much more do I need to read about this? Yet here's a way of pulling you into the subject, so it feels fresh and offers genuine insights you don't get from other books. That's a real power of comics, because whatever is happening in the foreground, the background is informational too, how people still try to live their lives under these conditions. And readers absorb this, even though it's supposedly secondary. In Bosnia I was fascinated by how people were chopping and stacking wood and this was my chance to draw and record some things that are banal, because they'll never be recorded otherwise. I think cartoonists pick up on those things.

P: I feel one of the powers of comics in our multimedia age is their still images that don't go away. We swipe away so many digital images, but when you close a printed comic, you know that image is still inside to look at again, and it haunts you.

J: Yes, when I'm drawing, I don't need to write descriptions because I can draw it, the graffiti on buildings, the mud in the street, it follows the reader around and sinks into their subconscious.

P: The writer Michel Faber reviewed *The Fixer*[10] in *The Guardian*[11] and commented: 'The cluttered squalor of the flat in which Neven keeps his blind aunt on a sofa hits us like a slap in the face, not gradually as prose would.' With the turn of a page, the reader is suddenly fully present in the new location across a double-page spread. It is all there at once and forever, as long as you want to look.

J: A phrase Edward Saïd wrote in his foreword to *Palestine* always stuck in my head. He said images have 'the power to detain'.

P: Perfect. After your 30-page report on the Dalits or 'untouchables' for the *Virginia Quarterly Review*, you are returning to Uttar Pradesh in northern India for your next graphic novel, *The Once and Future Riot*.

J: It's about how electoral politics and violence between Hindus and Muslims can intertwine and about how narratives are created and shaped to suit people. It's not only about the truth of the situation, or the individual's perception of the truth, but what the community tells itself about what it did and what stories it tells outsiders. A number of people were killed in a village, but the claim was that nothing happened to them, they left, they didn't die there. But journalistically, you can do the research and ascertain that they were, in fact, killed. It's interesting how stories can be created and become your memories. So I speak to the village chief and get his story. But there's a bunch of other men in the room and they're listening to him tell the story and I realize it's probably not the first time they've heard him tell it. But it's the communal story and with the power of suggestion, over time, even people who participated in those events will draw from it and it becomes convenient. I ask a lot of questions in the book about how this is done, the psychological process.

I was interested in this story because of its obscurity, but it helps demonstrate the broader question of why violence happens. That's one of my themes, I realize, so I thought it would be a good way to talk about communal violence in India. Trouble is being stirred up before an election and the tensions are there. People can live with each other, but if you've created this situation where there's a possibility of violence, it's a card that can be played if you push the right buttons. It seems that the authorities decide now is the right time to take some altercation and interpret it as communal violence, and play it up, to the point where you're speaking to your electoral base and some people are energized by that sort of rough talk and others will take it to its logical conclusion.

P: Memories can be rewritten, so that even if you weren't there, or remembered it differently, it becomes an imposed, accepted memory?

J: Yes, and sometimes people create memories because they need to, because otherwise it's too painful. In my book on Gaza, a guy remembers his brother dying, but other people don't remember him being there to see his brother's death. You can't unscramble that. Why would he feel like he needed to have been there? So that it became his memory? And then other memories go down the memory hole, and people like Igort and Nora Krug try to bring them to light.

P: I'm also impressed by Keum Suk Gendry-Kim's work from Korea.[12]

J: I love her work. I was blown away. Her intimate portraits of people are what comics can really do. When you're in their homes, you're seeing them cook and the humanity of these people sinks into your subconscious, but in an oblique way, like a relationship that develops into a story with these deeper layers. I've read something of Korean history, but hers is a whole way of seeing the world, you feel the streets, the atmosphere and it's really affecting.

P: What about Jacques Tardi's work on the Paris Commune and the two World Wars?

J: I consider Tardi a towering figure of comics. I look at his work and shake my head at its pure grit. I don't think something like *It Was the War of the Trenches*[13] can be topped. When I was doing my own book about the first day of the Battle of the Somme, *The Great War*,[14] I took an entirely different approach from the intimacy of his war drawings. I decided to be more clinical and removed, as if a space alien was observing the awful proceedings. I think the two approaches complement each other. I was pleased that my drawing was enlarged as a mural in 2014 in the Montparnasse-Bienvenue metro passageway in Paris. Later I found out that Tardi was their first choice for that, but that he had given up. I was fine being their second choice.

P: Tardi was invited by Comica Festival to London in 2014 on the centenary of the outbreak of World War I to be interviewed by British writer Pat Mills. Tardi admires his *Charley's War* series and wrote a foreword for the French edition.

J: *Charley's War*[15] is great, it's astonishing what Mills and Joe Colquhoun were able to get across about the horrors of war in a boys' comic. Of course Tardi wasn't constrained by such things, as he wasn't targeting the same readership, and didn't pull any punches.

P: In 2019, British cartoonist Ella Baron was sent on a comics commission to South Sudan by Médecins sans Frontières. When she had to introduce herself to the team as a cartoonist, she recalls: 'It came out with a cringe, at worst an apology.' But the person in charge spoke up for her: 'Project visits by cartoonists contribute to the notion of bearing witness. They can illustrate sensitive humanitarian activities, and simultaneously show the vulnerability alongside the resilience and agency of people caught in crisis.'[16] Have you had trouble describing your role?

J: Yes, it was hard to explain myself in Palestine when I first went. I always said I'm doing a journalistic project. When I told people I was doing it in comics, that was a good thing, because immediately people would say, we have this famous cartoonist named Naji al-Ali and he was assassinated.

P: Yes, in London.

J: So they have their own history of cartoonists and there's a relationship. Naji al-Ali was killed in 1987 but he's opened the door for me. I learned about him there and realized he was important. I was in one place where someone had his portrait on the wall. And people wore pendants with the image of his character, the child Handala. Of course, the Palestinian cartoon tradition is alive and well. Someone I admire who's working today is Mohammad Saba'aneh. He's been imprisoned by the Israelis, and so he knows the cost of 'free' expression. His illustrations are a really stark and powerful documentation of life under occupation. Franz Kafka would have really appreciated his work.

One reason I try to interview a number of people who had the same experience is you'll get different stories, different tellings, but sometimes the arc of the story remains similar. My work isn't so much to resolve the problems of memory, as to drop them in the reader's lap and say 'Here are the problems with memory.' I might be doing a disservice to the story by trying to smooth out its rough edges. So I let the reader feel that the question about memory is for them as well.

1. Joe Sacco, *Safe Area Gorazde*, London: Jonathan Cape, 2007.
2. Joe Sacco, *Footnotes in Gaza*, London: Jonathan Cape, 2009.
3. United Nations Relief and Works Agency for Palestine Refugees in the Near East (UNRWA)
4. Joe Sacco, *Palestine*, London: Jonathan Cape, 2003.
5. Igort, *The Ukrainian and Russian Notebooks*, New York: Gallery 13, 2016.
6. A new form of journalistic writing that advocated subjectivity, emerging in the US press in the 1960s, especially in the work of Tom Wolfe.
7. Joe Sacco, *Paying the Land*, London: Jonathan Cape, 2020.
8. Nora Krug, *Belonging*, New York: Scribner, 2023.
9. Art Spiegelman, *Maus*, London: Penguin, 2003.
10. Joe Sacco, *The Fixer*, London: Jonathan Cape, 2004.
11. Michel Faber, 'An Anti-Hero of Our Time', *The Guardian*, 7 August 2004: https://www.theguardian.com/books/2004/aug/07/highereducation.news1
12. See Keum Suk Gendry-Kim, *Grass*, Montreal: Drawn and Quarterly, 2019; and Keum Suk Gendry-Kim, *The Waiting*, Montreal: Drawn and Quarterly, 2021.
13. Jacques Tardi, *It Was the War of the Trenches*, Seattle: Fantagraphics Books, 2010.
14. Joe Sacco, *The Great War*, London: Jonathan Cape, 2013.
15. Pat Mills and Joe Colquhoun, *Charley's War*, Oxford: Rebellion, 2018.
16. Ella Baron, 'She is My Daughter, All of Her is Me', *The Newsletter of The Cartoon Museum*, vol. 2, no. 6, Summer 2023.

Art Spiegelman (born 1948, Sweden)
Maus #2, 1991
Cover flap illustration (1989)

Art Spiegelman (born 1948, Sweden)
Prisoner on the Hell Planet: A Case History, 1972
Page 1

Art Spiegelman (born 1948, Sweden)
The Complete Maus, 1996
Endpaper illustration

Art Spiegelman (born 1948, Sweden)
Maus #2, 1991
Endpaper illustration

Keiji Nakazawa (born 1939–2012, Japan)
Barefoot Gen, 1973–74
Page 252

Jacques Tardi (born 1946, France)
C'était la guerre des tranchées (*It Was the War of the Trenches*), 2014
Illustration from the closing image section

Jacques Tardi (born 1946, France)
C'était la guerre des tranchées (*It Was the War of the Trenches*), 1993
Page 55

Jacques Tardi (born 1946, France)
Moi René Tardi, prisonnier de guerre au Stalag IIB (*I, Rene Tardi, Prisoner of War in Stalag IIB*), vol. 1, 2012
Page 55 (2011)

Jacques Tardi (born 1946, France), written by Dominique Grange
Élise et les nouveaux partisans, 2021
Page 71 (2020)

Joe Sacco (born 1960, USA)
The Underground War in Gaza, 2003
Page 1

Joe Sacco (born 1960, USA)
Gaza Portfolio, 2011

Marjane Satrapi (born 1969, Iran)
Persepolis, vol. 1, 2000
'The Veil', pages 1 & 2

ET AUSSI PARCEQU'UN AN AUPARAVANT, EN 1979 ON ÉTAIT DANS UNE ÉCOLE FRANÇAISE ET LAÏQUE,
OÙ NOUS ÉTIONS GARÇONS ET FILLES ENSEMBLE,
ET SOUDAIN EN 1980....
TOUTES LES ÉCOLES BILINGUES DOIVENT FERMER LEUR PORTE
ELLES SONT LES SYMBOLES DU CAPITALISME MONDIAL
BRAVO!
QUELLE SAGESSE!
DE LA DÉCADENCE
★ CELA S'APPELLE UNE: "RÉVOLUTION CULTURELLE"
NOUS NOUS SOMMES RETROUVÉES VOILÉES ET SÉPARÉES DE NOS COPAINS.
ET VOILÀ!

Fanny Michaëlis (born 1983, France)
Le Lait noir, 2016
Pages 86 & 87

Émile Bravo (born 1964, France)
L'Espoir malgré tout (*Hope Against All Odds*), vol. 2: *Un peu plus loin vers l'horreur* (*A Few Steps Closer to Horror*), 2019
Page 50

Chantal Montellier (born 1947, France)
Tchernobyl mon amour, 2006
Page 8

Emmanuel Guibert (born 1964, France)
Alan's War: The Memories of G.I. Alan Cope, 2009
Cover art for the collected edition

Edmond Baudoin (born 1942, France)
Le Chemin de Saint-Jean, 2002
Page 71 (detail)

PERSONAL STORIES

Autobiographical comics, their forms and themes

Laurent Gerbier

Although there are earlier examples, it was between the late 1980s and the mid-1990s that personal stories emerged as a unique form of narrative in comics, in all three parts of the world that dominate the medium. In Canada, Joe Matt drew the first pages of his autobiographical comic *Peepshow* in 1987; in France, Edmond Baudoin published *Couma acò* with Futuropolis in 1991; in Japan, Yoshihiro Tatsumi started to draw *A Life on the Margins* in 1995. Autobiographical comics can therefore be described as a 'moment' in modern comic production or, more precisely, as one of the stages in the long process, spanning over half a century, by which comics sought to break free from their status as an art form aimed solely at children and to shake off the standard tropes of traditional comics genres. Because they were rooted in the truth of the author's own life, autobiographical comics were a way of embracing greater maturity, as graphic novels had started to do from the 1970s and 1980s onwards; over the course of the 1990s and 2000s, autobiographical comics would also prepare the way for comics to conquer new fields of non-fiction, as comic books based on real life would do in the 2010s and 2020s, adopting such diverse forms as documentary, reportage, travel writing and popular science.

Dividing the history of the genre into distinct periods is an oversimplification, but it is not inaccurate: although it applies most accurately to the French-speaking world, it also describes a phenomenon that was shared by the three major comics territories and allows us to place autobiographical comics in the context of contemporary artistic debates, theories and artforms. It is interesting to note that the emergence of autobiographical comics coincided with the rise of literary autofiction in the late 1980s and mid-1990s; similarly, comics artists began experimenting with illustrated forms of autobiography, which focus on questions about intimate representations of the body, around the same time as social scientists started to explore the problem of 'extimacy'[1] in the era of social media.

However, viewing the history in this way leads us to consider each of these periods as inevitably following on from the one before, bringing it to completion and marking its end. But autobiographical comic books did not spell the end of graphic novels, any more than graphic novels replaced adventure stories or 'the funnies', and nor did autobiographical comics fall out of fashion when non-fiction comics started to appear. Their trajectory did, however, reach a peak that was followed by a drop. In France, a number of classic autobiographical BDs were published in the 1990s (from Fabrice Neaud's *Journal* to David B.'s *Epileptic*), largely by the independent publishers that shaped the early part of that decade, but by the mid-2000s, pioneers of the genre Jean-Christophe Menu and Neaud were arguing that the genre was starting to fossilize.[2] It was a harsh, uncompromising judgment, but it did mean that autobiographical comics avoided being reduced to a trend; instead they once again embraced experimentation, exploring the possibilities of the form.

If we want to understand what is really going on in autobiographical comics, we must begin by looking at these possibilities. While the genre draws on a rich heritage of first-person literature, from the *Confessions* of St Augustine to personal diaries, and from Montaigne's essays to autofiction, comics redefine one of the main characteristics of the form: the complexity of articulating a discourse in which the 'self' is both the speaker and the object. Autobiographical comics give the self a unique physical existence, turning it into a character that is visually distinct from the 'self' that narrates the overall work in the first person. While the former is given material form in the artwork, with direct dialogue reported in speech bubbles, the latter is present not only in the elements that frame the narrative (forewords, afterwords, text boxes), but also more generally throughout all of the text and art that move the story forward. This distinction is not limited to any particular 'era'. On the contrary, it is part of the enduring potential of the medium, rooted in

the very language of comics. It also plays into another difference: the relationship between autobiographical comics and self-portraits.

If we view them within the context of visual representations of the self, autobiographical comics do not seem to belong to the long history of first-person literature as much as to the equally complex history of self-portraiture. Art historians have explored the specific features of this genre in great detail. It first emerged in the late fifteenth century, as part of a revolution in the symbolic and social functions of art, when artists started to include their own portraits in their work. As they grew more commonplace, self-portraits became a way to demonstrate both psychological insight and pictorial skill, approaching the surface of the face as a space that expresses the depths within. However, the crises of the self that dominated the nineteenth century, from romanticism to psychoanalysis, transformed self-portraits into a search for a self that was fractured, and moved away from straightforward representation.

Autobiographical comics are heirs to this impossible task: creating a representation of yourself that does not seem to be looking at itself, trying to glimpse yourself out of the corner of your eye, as if you have been taken by surprise, to capture yourself in the impossible double state of seeing yourself and not being aware of being seen. However, the very nature of comics allows us to reframe this problem, because they do not rely on a single image. In comics, a self-portrait is always made up of a series of images. The figure of the self is repeated, constantly broken down and reconstructed, viewed in different situations, with different poses and gestures, at different scales. The artist is constantly pulling the strings to make this puppet dance: they are not observing themselves so much as creating and recreating themselves over and over again, throughout the series of panels. The reader's experience is therefore built on a clear dissociation between the written self and the self that is writing. But where is the true self? Does it lie in the artist-narrator, shaping the narrative and visual elements that recreate these myriad selves? Or is it in the figures that appear throughout the work, in different poses and emotional states, speaking their own words against the backdrop that the artist has created? When Ulli Lust writes about her punk-inspired trip around Italy in *Zu viel ist nicht genug*, does the authenticity of her story lie in the events experienced by the illustrations of herself that she arranges on the page, or in the reconstructed narrative, in the voice of a narrator who regularly comments on those experiences, and in the passages from her notebooks that she reproduces in the foreword and afterword? The same question arises when we read Neaud's *Journal*, or Dominique Goblet's *Pretending is Lying*: the reader latches onto the gestures, actions and emotions of the self as an illustrated character, while never quite forgetting that, just out of shot, this other self is always present, inviting them to share in their story, almost seeming to lean over their shoulder while they read.

This split is at its most powerful when the illustrations are being used to recount a distressing or traumatic event, such as the rape sequence in Lust's story, or the violent attack that Neaud recounts in the third volume of his *Journal*: in both examples, the reader experiences a dissociation between the self who is writing and the self who is written (and who, in the case of Neaud in particular, is the constant subject of comments in the voice of the author-narrator). Edmond Baudoin's *Les Fleurs de cimetière* offers a different approach: in this remarkable feat of artistic and biographical self-reflection, Baudoin reproduces a number of extracts from his notebooks as well as his published works. The reader's gaze is constantly moving between illustrations from different periods, the author's self-portraits from different eras. But, to complicate his own visual identity, alongside these self-quotations, the author also chooses to reproduce a number of portraits that others have drawn of him. In total, there are more than twenty of these 'alloportraits', which enrich and deepen the gap between the written and visual representations of the self and this 'other self', which arranges, displays and comments on them. In this way, Baudoin's work is the perfect illustration of a comment from Guy-Marc Hinant's afterword to Goblet's *Pretending is Lying*, in which he argues that characters in autobiographical comics are not really self-portraits but more like 'avatars controlled by living people bearing similar names'.[3]

In both Baudoin's work and Goblet's, this deliberate fragmentation alters the status of the author-narrator: they are no longer the omniscient master overseeing the work, the hidden god creating it, but a product of reading every event and noticing every detail. For the reader, the author does not pre-exist the work. The author emerges little by little as a point of view from which all the pieces come together and make sense. Therefore, it is not surprising that many of these personal stories also examine the process of creation itself: Baudoin, Goblet and Tatsumi all reflect on the act of writing about the self. However, this is not simply an abstract way of playing with form: it also touches on the most personal aspect of illustrated narratives, by fundamentally redefining the meaning of intimacy. Because they represent the self in a way that is both physical and emotional, autobiographical comics inevitably have to confront the question of depicting the body at its most banal, everyday and intimate. They also often depict the sexual body, desiring and desired: however, because of the fragmentation mentioned previously, these representations are not necessarily particularly intimate in themselves. When it comes down to it, drawing yourself naked is not as intimate as allowing yourself to be seen by exposing the insecure and vulnerable fragments of your inner self.

If the most intimate self is revealed through the way in which all the components of the narrative come together, then the elements of the landscape, objects, faces and bodies that inhabit the space of the page alongside this self are also part of this visual 'representation of the self': this self is present in every single mark on the page. The details of Kazuichi Hanawa's cell (*Doing Time*) are no less authentic representations of the self than a self-portrait, as are the drawings of trees that appear throughout *Les Fleurs de cimetière*, or the mysterious images in *Pretending is Lying*, where ambiguous, ghostly silhouettes loom out of the darkness. In a first-person comic, every line is in some sense a 'self-portrait' of the person who drew it, a medium for a form of self-representation, so much so that ultimately, it is the precise outlines of this 'self' that vary.

Autobiographical writing is never just about 'the self': it also depicts a time and place, a cultural and political moment, a social and professional realm. It always looks beyond itself and includes its surroundings, captured within the artwork by the hand that also places its self-portrait among them, always part of the same graphic space. The first volume of Tatsumi's *A Drifting Life* combines autobiography with a portrait of post-war Japan; in *The Arab of the Future*, Riad Sattouf tells his own story as well as the stories of Libya and Syria in the 1980s, and that of a high-school student in Brittany in the early 1990s. The deliberately porous boundary between the self and what lies beyond the self is especially striking in Étienne Davodeau's *Le Droit du sol*. This travel book records the artist walking from the painted cave of Pech Merle in the Lot region of France to a site where nuclear waste is buried in Bure in the *département* of Meuse; the journey itself is described, carried out and conceived of as an act of writing, analogous to the act of drawing. The personal story, travel diary and descriptions of the landscape are all part of a broader reflection on the marks that human beings choose to leave upon the surface of the planet where they live: here, the two genres of autobiographical and non-fiction comics are inextricably combined.

While the scope of a person story can expand to include the world, it can also approach the subject in a different way, diving inside the self to analyse the way it is constructed. Family is a popular theme for explorations of the complex borders between the self and the non-self: Sattouf's *The Arab of the Future*, Goblet's *Pretending is Lying* and Baudoin's *Les Fleurs de cimetière* all contain family portraits as well as self-portraits. The self is understood and explained via a sometimes painful exploration of the concept of inheritance and what it means to be part of a lineage, and Baudoin's trees can be seen as a visual extension of this idea, acting as metaphors for an exploration of the family tree. In this way, autobiographical comics can become clinical tools: in *Epileptic*, David B. uses art to create his own diagnosis of the condition that afflicts his brother and affects his entire family, giving the illness and suffering visible form. This touches on one of the most recent forms of autobiographical writing in comics: over the last ten years, autopathography – illustrated accounts of the creator's own illness – has emerged and become the genre known as 'graphic medicine',[4] an unexpected collaboration between the medical world and comics.

1. The term 'extimité' in French, borrowed from Jacques Lacan, is used by Serge Tisseron to describe the tendency to expose our personal lives in public. See Serge Tisseron, *L'Intimité surexposée*, Paris: Ramsay, 2001.
2. Jean-Christophe Menu and Fabrice Neaud, 'Autopsie de l'autobiographie', *L'Éprouvette*, no. 3, L'Association, 2007, pp. 453–472.
3. Guy-Marc Hinant, afterword to Dominique Goblet, *Pretending is Lying*, trans. Sophie Yanow, New York: NYRC, 2017.
4. See Ian Williams, M.K. Czerwiec *et al.*, *Graphic Medicine Manifesto*, University Park, PA: Penn State University Press, 2015.

Aline Kominsky-Crumb (1948, USA–2022, France)
Twisted Sisters, no. 1, 1976
Cover art

7-25

FUN HOME, P.213

Alison Bechdel (born 1960, USA)
Fun Home, 2006
Chapter 7: 'The Antihero's Journey', page 25

Edmond Baudoin (born 1942, France)
Le Chemin de Saint-Jean, 2002
Page 71

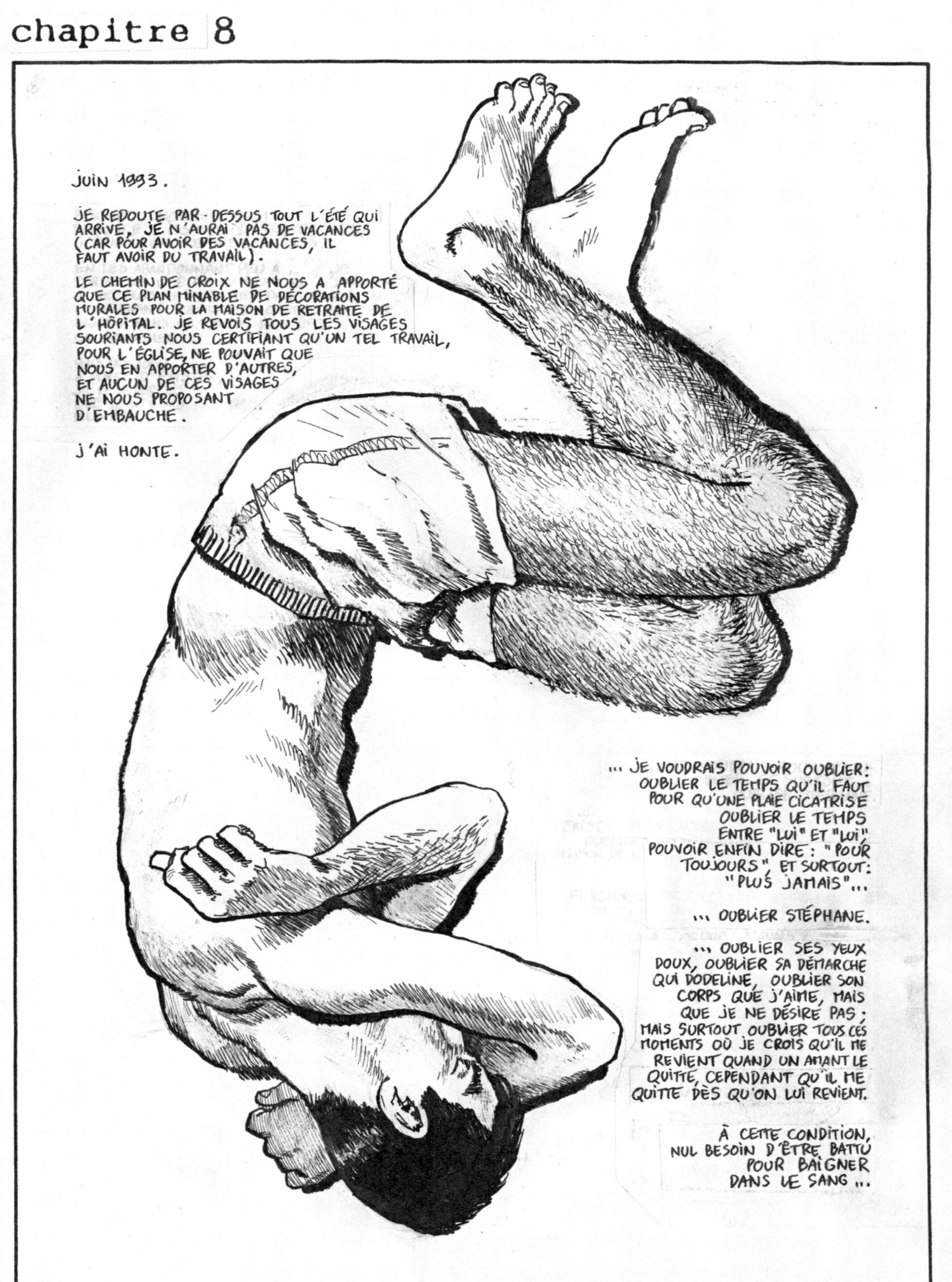

Fabrice Neaud (born 1968, France)
Journal (I), February 1992–September 1993, 1996
Chapter 8, page 1

David B. (born 1959, France)
L'Ascension du Haut Mal (*Epileptic*), vol. 1, 1996
Cover art

David B. (born 1959, France)
L'Ascension du Haut Mal (*Epileptic*), vol. 5, 2000
Cover art

David B. (born 1959, France)
L'Ascension du Haut Mal (*Epileptic*), vol. 6, 2003
Page 1

Dominique Goblet (born 1967, Belgium)
Faire semblant c'est mentir (*Pretending is Lying*), 2007
Chapter 1, pages 12 & 13

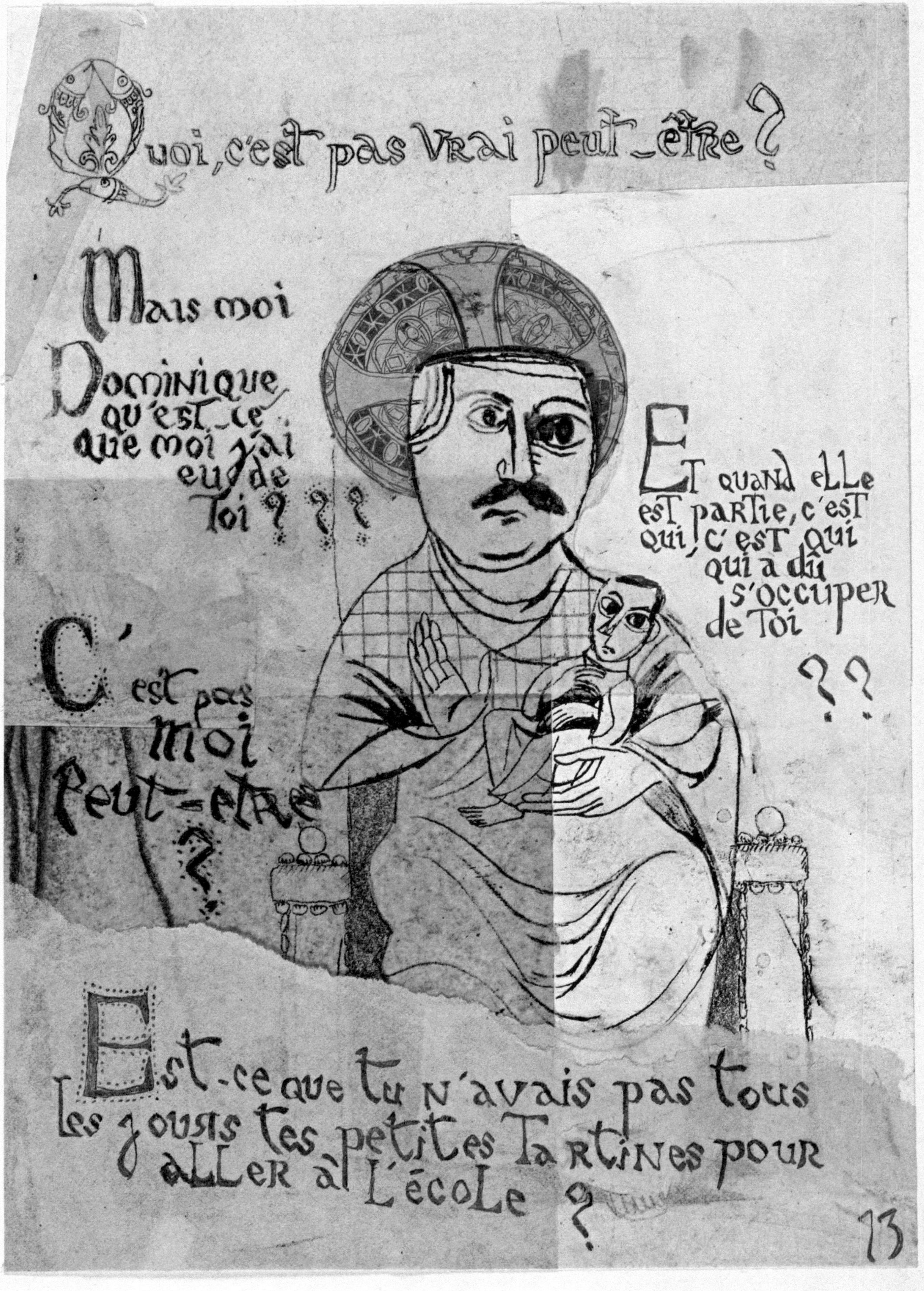
Quoi, c'est pas vrai peut_être ?
Mais moi Dominique qu'est_ce que moi j'ai eu de toi ? ? ?
Et quand elle est partie, c'est qui, c'est qui qui a dû s'occuper de toi ??
C'est pas moi peut_être ?
Est_ce que tu n'avais pas tous les jours tes petites tartines pour aller à l'école ?
13

Étienne Davodeau (born 1965, France)
Le Droit du sol: Journal d'un vertige, 2021
Page 55 (2020)

Ulli Lust (born 1967, Austria)
Heute ist der letzte Tag vom Rest deines Lebens (*Today is the Last Day of the Rest of Your Life*), 2009
Page 229

Lewis Trondheim (born 1964, France)
Approximativement (*Approximate Continuum Comics*), 1995
Page 55

Riad Sattouf (born 1978, France)
L'Arabe du futur (*The Arab of the Future*), vol. 1, 2014
Page 1

Yoshihiro Tatsumi (1935–2015, Japan)
Untitled (detail), c. 1970

EVERYDAY LIFE

Emmanuèle Payen

What does a comic show when nothing is happening? What can a narrative say when it seems like there is no story to tell? Breaking with the tradition of wild adventures featuring heroes and superheroes, and embracing the banality of daily life instead, Hergé was one of the first comics creators to explore the possibilities of a more reflective narrative. Turning away from the action-packed feel that characterized the earlier Tintin adventures, the Belgian writer decided that the twenty-first tale in the series, *The Castafiore Emerald* (1963), would feature a single location (Marlinspike Hall) and a single time period (a month of bed rest for Captain Haddock). The reader is drawn into a world of false pretences and often misleading appearances, of misunderstandings and traps that become the driving force of a relatively minor mystery. But what if there is something vital hidden within the banal, a little something drawn from everyday life, which reveals the humanity and inner lives of the characters?

Not only the repetition of time but also the repetition of space can create boredom: the slow pace at which the days pass is reflected by the characters' meanderings, as they knock against the borders of the comic panels or, in some cases, find gaps through which they can escape.

The setting that best represents everyday life is the home. That is where the dramas play out, where bodies clash, where relationships and fates are woven and broken. In Chris Ware's *Building Stories* (2012), the apartment building is a protagonist in the narrative, which is made up of fourteen separate smaller works that each explore different people's lives. The home can be the backdrop against which intertwined lives play out, as in the dance of physical intimacy in Marion Fayolle's *La Maison nue* (2022), or Anna Sommer's *Damen Dramen* (1996). It is a place inhabited by different people at different times, when the rules of time and space break down: in *Here* (2014), Richard McGuire focuses the reader's gaze on an ordinary living room and makes this shared space the central point from where the stories of its many inhabitants unravel and overlap.

Home is the place where suffering and sadness are expressed, but also the place where children grow up in family tales, sometimes against the odds. As the days go by, friendships are formed, love affairs begin and tender relationships blossom. Life can become a novel, a police procedural, suspense may build slowly or appear out of nowhere, when masks fall away and characters reveal their true selves in the light of an imagined plot (Camille Jourdy's trilogy *Rosalie Blum*, 2007–9). The space expands, the environment grows, wanderings reveal new pathways, and the interior becomes a landscape: the beach, the space explored by David Prudhomme and Pascal Rabaté in *Vive la marée!* (2015), is transformed into a cinema set on which to cast an affectionally mocking eye over bodies in motion, once again offering up a blurred reflection of our own lives.

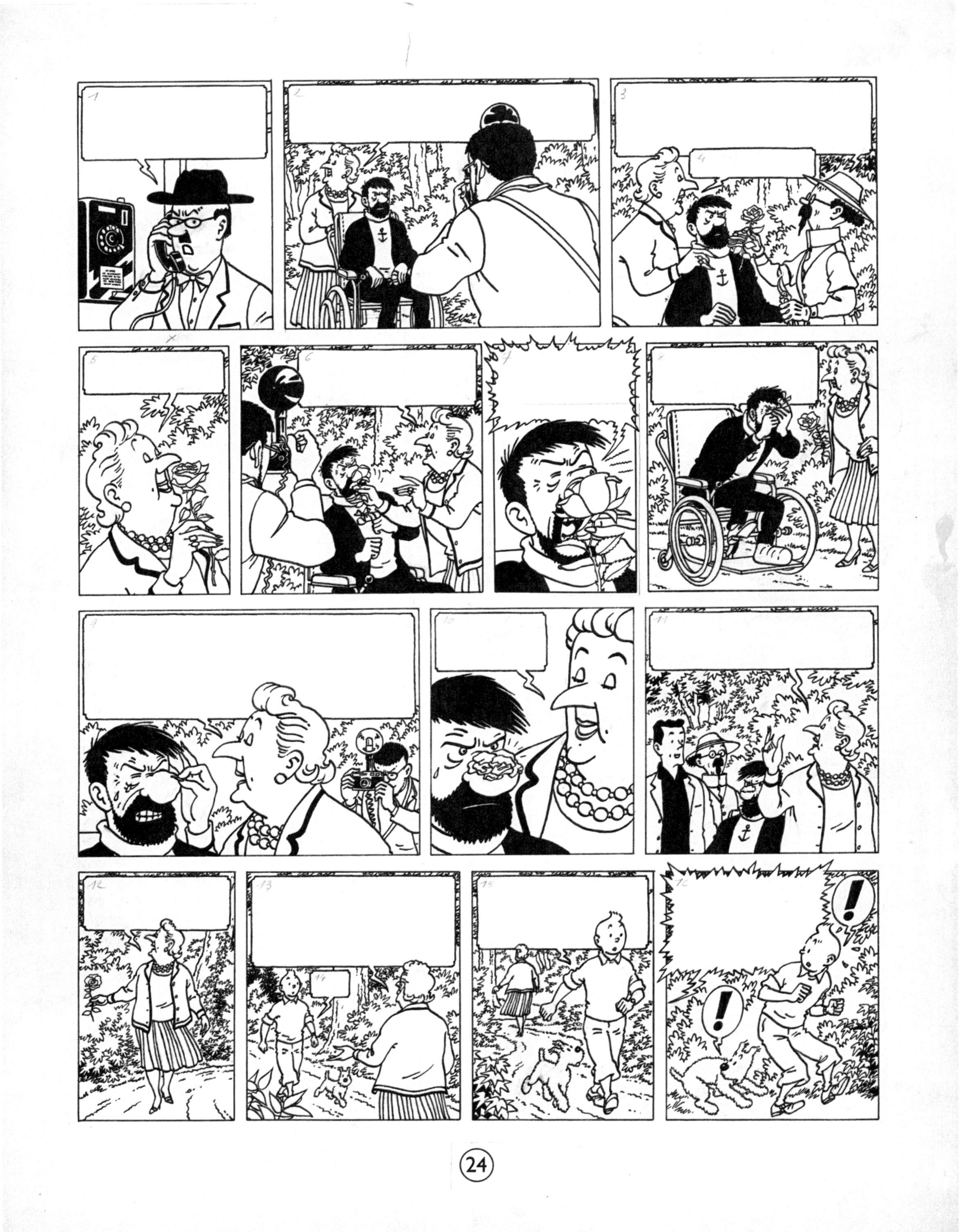

Hergé (1907–83, Belgium)
Les Bijoux de la Castafiore (*The Castafiore Emerald*), 1961–62
Pages 24 & 59

Tintin n° 33 – "Bijoux" p 59

Yoshihiro Tatsumi (1935–2015, Japan)
Untitled, c. 1970

アンローズ
性病
佐藤医院
長編コミック 10/1 7号 折 千色オフ
口絵ウラ

Jirō Taniguchi (1947–2017, Japan)
Aruku Hito (*The Walking Man*), 2003
Chapter 18, page 11

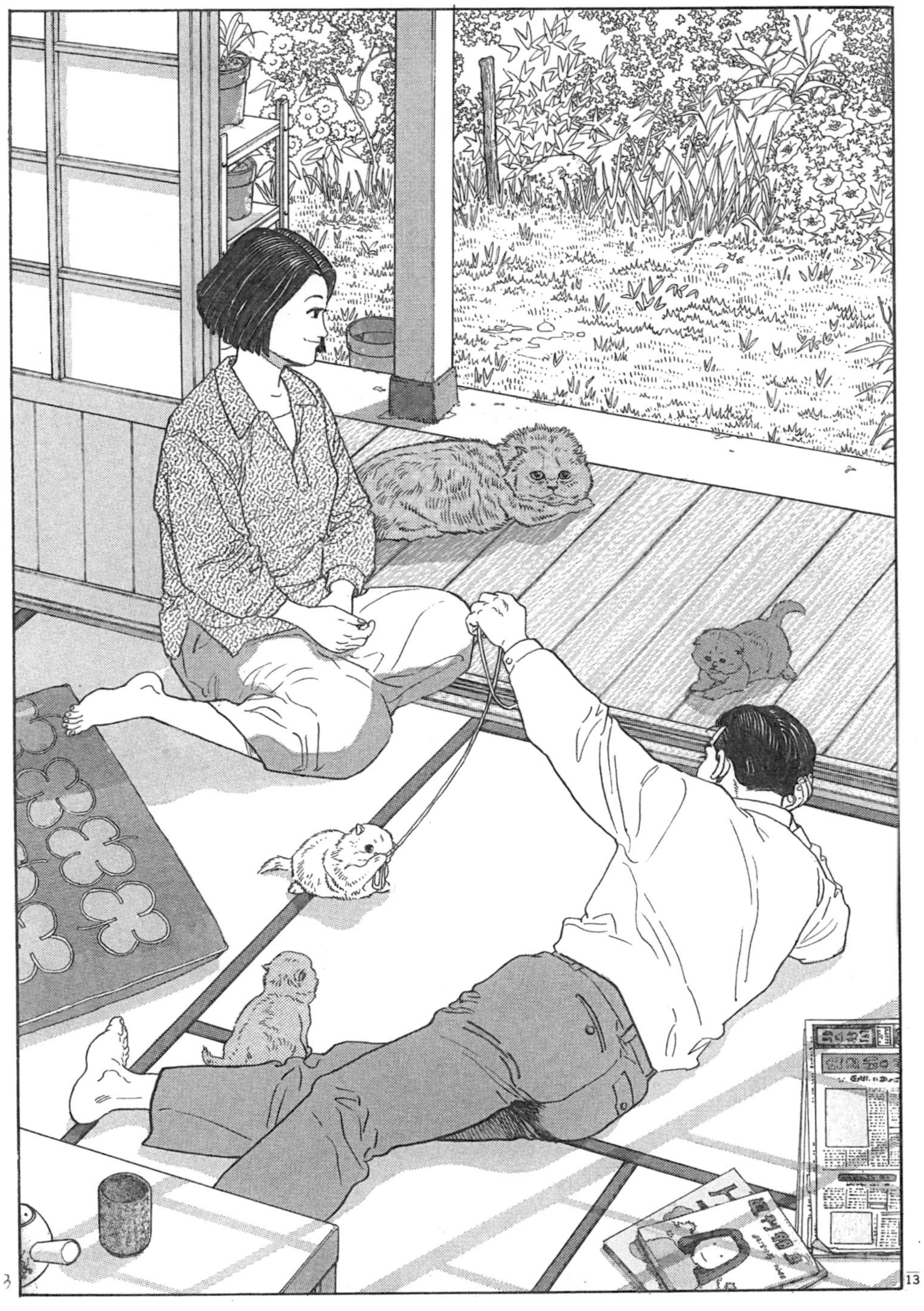

81

Jirō Taniguchi (1947–2017, Japan)
Inu wo Kau (*Land of Dreams*), 1991
'The View of the Garden', page 12

Richard McGuire (born 1957, USA)
Here, 2014
Pages 12–15 (digital comic)

1766
1989
HA
HA
HA
HA
HA
HA
KOF KOF !!
KOF KOF !!
HA
KOF KOF !!

1783
1989
ÇA VA ?
JE VAIS TE CHERCHER UN VERRE D'EAU.
KOF KOF !!
KOF KOF !!!

Chris Ware (born 1967, USA)
Building Stories, 2012
'Actual Size'

GOING BACK
TO SCHOOL WAS ACTUALLY THE HARDEST PART... I'D BEEN GONE FOR SO LONG IT FELT WEIRD, UNFAMILIAR...
AT FIRST, EVERYONE WAS REALLY NICE TO ME, ALMOST OVERLY SO... THE PRETTY GIRLS WHO'D NEVER EVEN GIVEN ME THE TIME OF DAY BEFORE WERE SUDDENLY COMPETING WITH EACH OTHER TO BE MY "FRIEND"... SADLY, I ATE IT ALL UP, THOUGH WHO WOULDN'T?
I'M CARRYING HER BOOKS!
NO, I AM!
HOWEVER, AS TIME WORE ON, THE NOVELTY OF ME WORE THIN, AND AFTER A FEW WEEKS IT WAS CLEAR THAT THE DUST HAD SETTLED AROUND ME... IT WASN'T MEANNESS ON ANYONE'S PART, JUST THE WAY THINGS GO, I GUESS...
ARE YOU OKAY, HONEY?
YES MA'AM, THANK YOU
WHICH IS WHY
WHEN THAT NEW GIRL JOINED OUR CLASS IN THE MIDDLE OF THE YEAR, SHE AND I BECAME FAST FRIENDS...
I WISH I COULD REMEMBER HER NAME, THOUGH... FOR SOME REASON I'VE COMPLETELY FORGOTTEN IT... MEGAN? MELISSA?
IT WASN'T LIKE MY CLASSMATES HAD GIVEN UP ON ME, EITHER, BUT THE AMPUTATION SEEMED TO ONLY AGITATE THE ALREADY CAPRICIOUS CURRENTS OF CHILDHOOD FRIENDSHIP... ONE DAY, I'D FEEL WELCOME, AND THE NEXT I'D BE CAST ASHORE... I SUPPOSE THE NEW GIRL AND I FOUND SOME COMMON GROUND IN OUR MUTUAL UNCERTAINTY...
COME IN, SUZANNE, COME IN!
'SUZANNE,' THAT WAS IT...
YOU GIRLS NEED ANYTHING?
NO MOM WE'RE FINE!
THEN THERE WAS THAT DISASTROUS ATTEMPT AT A SLEEPOVER...
EVERYTHING HAD BEEN GOING FINE AND WE WERE HAVING LOTS OF FUN, ACTUALLY... IT WAS JUST AFTER WE'D GONE TO BED AND A STORM MOVED IN THAT THINGS GOT WEIRD... THE WIND STARTED KNOCKING A TREEBRANCH AGAINST THE WINDOW AND SHE TOTALLY FREAKED OVER IT...
WHAT'S THE PROBLEM?
MOM!
SHE THINKS THERE'S A MONSTER
MOMMA!
SHE WAS SO INCONSOLABLE, IN FACT, THAT HER MOM CAME AND GOT HER...
...SO MUCH FOR OUR SLEEPOVER.
LATER,
IT TURNED OUT THAT SHE HAD SOME PRETTY BAD EMOTIONAL PROBLEMS, AND SHE'D FALLEN IN WITH A DIFFERENT GROUP OF GIRLS, ANYWAY. SO I DIDN'T LET IT BOTHER ME... AT THAT POINT I WAS STARTING TO BECOME ACQUAINTED WITH THE UNFAIRNESS OF LIFE AND WAS LEARNING IT WAS BETTER NOT TO EXPECT ANYTHING RATHER THAN SET YOURSELF UP FOR DISAPPOINTMENT... SOMETIMES I WORRY THAT I GREW UP TOO FAST AS A KID...
NO NO NO
HONEY, IT WAS JUST TH TREE BRANCH, THAT'S ALL... IT WAS JUST TH TREE BRANCH...
DON'T TELL ME I'M PRETTY! I KNOW I'M NOT PRETTY!
THE BAD PART OF THE INCIDENT WAS THAT MY DAD USED IT AS JUSTIFICATION TO FINALLY CUT DOWN MOST OF THE TREES... OR MAYBE I SHOULD SAY HACK DOWN... I'LL NEVER FORGET THE DAY I CAME HOME TO SEE OUR HOUSE SUDDENLY SO EXPOSED, NAKED... IT LOOKED LIKE WHAT IT WAS, TOO... A MEAN LITTLE BOX ON A MOUND...
I DON'T KNOW HOW LONG I STARED AT IT...
ALL OF THE SECRET SPOTS AND HIDEAWAYS THAT UNTIL RIGHT THEN HAD SEEMED AS CERTAIN TO ME AS THE SMALL CONSTELLATION OF BIRTHMARKS ON THE INSIDE OF MY WRIST WERE NOW GONE, AS IF THEY'D NEVER EXISTED... I PASSED THROUGH THE NOW-SMALL FRONT YARD INTO THE STRANGE, BRIGHT HOUSE AND OUT TO THE BACK YARD, WHERE MY FATHER WAS CUTTING UP THE BRANCHES INTO SMALLER PIECES WITH A FEROCITY THAT I FOUND UNCHARACTERISTIC, FRIGHTENING...
AT DINNER THAT NIGHT HE MUST'VE FELT HE NEEDED TO SAY SOMETHING ABOUT IT, BUT IF HE DID, I'VE FORGOTTEN WHAT IT WAS...
SHF
CREAK
MOM
POOR MOM...
AND
GOING DOWNSTAIRS TO APOLOGIZE TO HER, I BREATHE A SIGH OF RELIEF TO FIND HER IN THE KITCHEN, LAUGHING OVER SOMETHING SHE'S READ IN THE NEWSPAPER...
MOM?
MOM ARE YOU OKAY?
snnnfffff
OH MOM DON'T CRY...
DON'T CRY, MOM... I'M HERE... I'M HERE...
snnff
I'M SORRY...
I'M JUST... ...IT'S...
THIS HOUSE CAN GET... PRETTY LONELY, Y'KNOW? snf HA HA.. AND IT'S SO GOOD... TO HAVE YOU HERE... AND...
...AND I JUST WISH HE COULD SEE HOW HAPPY YOU ARE NOW, THAT'S ALL...
HE LOVED YOU SO MUCH
MOM
OH MOM
HE LOVED YOU SO MUCH

Marion Fayolle (born 1988, France)
La Maison nue (*The Naked House*), 2022
Chapter: 'L'effeuilage', pages 2 & 3

·marion·fayolle·

Camille Jourdy (born 1979, France)
Rosalie Blum, vol. 1: *Une impression de déjà-vu*, 2007
Page 41

André Juillard (born 1948, France), written by Pierre Christin
Le Long Voyage de Léna (*Lena's Odyssey*), 2006
Page 13

Anna Sommer (born 1968, Switzerland)
Damen Dramen, 1996
'Die Frau aus der Zoohandlung', page 5

David Prudhomme (born 1969, France) & Pascal Rabaté (born 1961, France)
Vive la marée!, 2015
Cover art

Joanna Hellgren (born 1981, Sweden)
Frances, vol. 3, 2012
Pages 10 & 11

Jacques Tardi (born 1946, France)
Casse-pipe à la Nation (*Death of a Marseilles Man*), published in *(À suivre)*, no. 217, 1996 (based on the novel by Léo Malet, 1957)
Cover art (detail)

LITERATURE

Literature and comics: sister arts

Tristan Garcia

The graphic novel

When *A Contract with God* was published in 1978, the subtitle *A Graphic Novel by Will Eisner* was written on the cover in large letters.[1] To describe this original comic book, which combines childhood memories with observations of daily life to create a loose narrative structure, Eisner borrowed the term 'novel' from the world of literature and added the adjective 'graphic'.[2]

Thierry Groensteen has explained how this borrowing served to elevate comics by integrating them, both in artistic and commercial terms, into a dominant cultural register and allowed them to reach adult readers who were suspicious of what they saw as a trivial medium for children. By claiming the term 'graphic novel', Eisner 'was first and foremost pursuing a tactical goal: his aim was for his book to be placed on the tables in mainstream bookshops, alongside works of literary fiction. (At that time, American bookstores did not have shelves dedicated to comics. Comics were mainly published by the news press – comic strips in newspapers, comic books by specialist publishers – and anthologies of the most popular comic strips [*Peanuts*, *Blondie* and even *Dick Tracy*] were usually found on the "humour" shelf).'[3]

Being classified alongside novels was a symbolic coming of age for comics.[4] Understandably, they gained legitimacy by being assimilated into an older, more recognized art form. However, are comics really a kind of literature? Leaving behind any value judgments about one or the other, let's look at the forms of representation and expression that each medium uses, the logic that governs them, their differences and their similarities.

Words and pictures

It is not easy to answer the question famously posed by Jean-Paul Sartre: 'What is literature?'[5] Defining it etymologically, as an art form that is *written*, means excluding the oral dimension of literature – which was the dominant form for many centuries and still exists today. Literature goes far beyond the written word.[6] Nor should it be confused with the act of storytelling, because it includes poetry, in both verse and prose forms. We might tentatively agree on the vague and simplistic idea that literature is less an object or a field than a certain *way* of dealing with language that is present in all human cultures, and involves playing with it, shaping it, remoulding it and transforming it.

In order for comics to be considered literature, they therefore need to include language. It might be argued that comics generally tell stories through pictures that include words and sentences. Unfortunately, this often means that the medium is viewed as a 'bastardized' art form, because it draws on pictorial and narrative at the same time. Sometimes it is seen as part of a long history that can be traced back to cave art, but often it is viewed as a later product of the printing age, born from a combination of caricatures, illustrated magazines and serialized stories. Caught up in an argument about the legitimacy of popular artforms that have long been viewed as 'minor', the detractors and defenders of comic books both have a tendency to consider them less as an emergent art form than a kind of hybrid.

W.J.T. Mitchell writes that our culture has changed and we are now surrounded by what he calls 'imagetexts',[7] of which comics are only one example. Charles Hatfield writes: 'Both socially and aesthetically, comics are likely to remain an unresolved, unstable, and challenging form. This is what makes them interesting. [...] If comic art is some kind of bastard, to recruit a popular metaphor, then maybe bastardy is just the thing – our culture has it in for aesthetic purity anyway. In our age of new and hybrid media, inter-artistic collaboration is king.'[8]

This interaction within a work, as a form of intermediality, recalls the way in which works can be adapted and thereby cross the boundaries between different artforms. Take for example Virginie Despentes's novel *Vernon Subutex*,[9]

R TIR
SUPER

which was first adapted into a French TV series and then into a comic by Luz. The comic gave the characters and places described by the novelist a visual incarnation, and Luz worked with her to rewrite some of the dialogue. It was not simply the act of integrating text into his artwork that made this a literary work, but the act of shaping it into a narrative, thus creating a new book.

No lexicon, no syntax

No panel in a comic strip is ever 'like a word'. Countless issues arise when we use expressions like 'the language of comics' or 'the syntax of images'. Panels are not comparable to morphemes because they are not symbols with agreed meanings that can be repeated and combined in any number of ways; they are images that represent something in their own right.

Unlike a language, there is no lexicon that is specific to comics, or even to a certain *style* of comics. Although we may recognize familiar elements in *Asterix* or *Tintin*, they cannot be listed in the same way as words in a dialect. At most, we can define a sort of 'illustration style' that is particular to Hergé – although it changes significantly from one comic to the next – or a 'house style' that sets out guidelines for a new artist to follow when they take over an established series. For *Gaston: The Return of Lagaffe* (2023), Delaf scanned thousands of illustrations by original artist Franquin and organized them into a database, with categories including Gaston's eccentric inventions, Gaston's range of poses, Mademoiselle Jeanne's range of poses, the furniture in the offices of *Spirou* magazine, and much more. But this catalogue of *specific* objects cannot be compared to a list of common nouns, verbs or adjectives: Gaston's pet seagull is not potentially 'every seagull', it is only that particular one; an image of Gaston falling is not the verb 'to fall', it is only 'Gaston falling down these stairs'. A lexicon requires a greater degree of generality to allow the speaker to organize objects by category.[10]

What's more, although the 'syntax of comics' is a phrase that's sometimes heard, it's not a correct use of the word. It's possible to identify specific trends in illustration that change according to the time period, aesthetic and medium of publication, and there are established conventions governing the direction of reading (from left to right in the West, from right to left in Japan), but there is no clearly defined system for linking one panel to another that can be applied across all comics. It is not necessarily true that the next panel must represent a later moment in the unfolding of the story, or a close-up or zoomed-out view of the scene depicted in the one before.

When Pénélope Bagieu was adapting Roald Dahl's *The Witches* in 2020, she took a playful approach to the direction in which the reader's gaze moved around the page: while the novel was discursive and linear, she transformed each page into a multidirectional space, through which the witches could come and go.

Isolated images

Let's take a scene from Rébecca Dautremer's 2020 comic adaptation of John Steinbeck's *Of Mice and Men* as an example. Steinbeck provides very little description of the old ranch worker Candy, who is uncomfortable and nervous about going into the barn where George and Lennie are. In Dautremer's comic, we see the door frame isolated on a black background. Candy is standing there, hands clasped together, at first hanging back, then on the threshold, and finally in the shadow of the barn's interior. At the bottom of the page, there are three separate images of him, as if he were three different men; in this way, first we see the multiple poses, then these are pulled together, as if by an invisible thread, to form a single character.

Comics don't simply show us 'a table' or 'a man'; instead, via a series of isolated images, they build up an overall scene in which we can perceive an *outline* of these things. This is completely different from the way in which words work. The isolated image provided by each panel never depicts the table or the man as a complete entity, but only conveys a limited view of them.

A panel in a comic does not necessarily have clearly defined edges. Dautremer makes panels bleed into each other, while, in *A Contract with God*, Eisner did not draw lines around his images or the accompanying blocks of text or dialogue. He knew that he didn't need panels to create visual demarcations. Ludovic Debeurme pushed this logic even further, almost allowing the characters of *Lucille* (2006) to get lost in the white background of the page. With no panel frames, these creators do not isolate individual objects – as if they were words – but entire *scenes*, the fundamental building blocks of comics. Within these scenes, each individual element (the 'nouns') must be isolated by the reader's gaze as they move from one scene to the next.

What comics offer is not primarily commonalities with language, but *differences*. In his grimly inventive adaptation of *Pinocchio* (2008), Winshluss's artwork recalls the morality tales of William Hogarth, depicting the protagonist first as a hero protecting his mother, then as the victim of his father's violence, then as a perpetrator of rape. The way in which our gaze singles out the protagonist each of these very different situations, as he plays conflicting roles, is particular to comics. We see the events, and we read the character's destiny.

A system of visual differences

Here is what distinguishes comics from language and the way it is used in a literary narrative. Literature relies on words, therefore on linguistic commonalities, to try and create a sense of difference. We can see this in the description of Charles Bovary's hat that Gustave Flaubert includes at the start of *Madame Bovary*. However, a similar hat drawn by Posy Simmonds in *Gemma Bovery* (1999), a contemporary reimagining of Flaubert's story, is not as important in itself as the way our gaze moves between different iterations of the hat. We reconstruct it: seen from far away, close up, worn on someone's head, or set down and lost. In a comic, the idea that this hat *at this moment* and this same hat *at a different moment* are simulatanously two separate images and the same object is childishly obvious. This is the same thing we always find in a page from a comic: a system made up of differences, repetitions, variations and alterations; and that is what we learn to decipher.

Comics are never a literary artform, either in the strict sense of the word or in an analogous sense ('like literature'). They have their own distinct mode of being, even when they frequently draw on literature. They borrow from all genres – from autobiographies (*Chīko* by Yoshiharu Tsuge, 1966) to photo stories (Loustal and Paringaux)[11] – and literary styles – long blocks of narration in *Blake and Mortimer* (1950–90) or philosophical musings in *Cerebus* (Dave Sim, 1977–2004). Comics lend themselves well to adaptations of classic works – the short stories of Edgar Allan Poe, H. P. Lovecraft and Ernesto Sabato (Alberto Breccia), kabuki theatre, the plays of William Shakespeare, Anton Chekhov and Samuel Beckett (Osamu Tezuka, *The Rainbow Parakeet*, 1981–83), the prose of Marcel Proust (Stéphane Heuet, 1998–2021) or even Marx's *Das Kapital* in manga form (Variety Artworks, 2008–9). But it is precisely because comics are not a literary form that they can make these genres and styles their own, often in a striking and surprising way, transposing the words we read into a world of visible forms.

Any comic book adaptation is a translation of a system of linguistic commonalities into another system, a system of 'visual differences'.

The third sister

Far from being the late-born bastard child of written and illustrated cultures, comics are the embodiment of a third way of representing the world and expressing the self, by means of a deliberately arranged sequence of images, which can equally be used to tell a story or create a poetic evocation.

In eighteenth-century England, there was an allegory, popularized by the poet John Dryden, which was sometimes used to illustrate the relationship between the arts, especially painting and poetry. Instead of defining one in terms of the other, as in the tradition summed up by Horace's phrase *ut pictura poesis*,[12] it represented them as two sisters, sister arts:[13] one placing a finger on her lips to show that she cannot speak (painting), the other covering her eyes (poetry). This allegory shows the extent to which the expressive potential of each art is born from what it lacks: the inability of one is the ability of the other. Because the two sister disciplines completed one another, there was no hierarchy between them. Comics both see and speak. But they cannot see, or be seen, without speaking or storytelling, and, in a sense, they cannot speak unless they are seen.

Therefore the relationship between comics and literature, like the relationship between comics and painting, is neither one of inclusion (they are not the same), nor of exclusion (they are not entirely different). Instead, comics are the third sister of the sister arts.

1. Will Eisner, *A Contract with God*, New York: Baronet Press, 1978; new ed.: New York: W.W. Norton, 2007.
2. The term 'graphic novel' was first proposed by American critic Richard Kyle in 1964. Although popularized by Will Eisner, it had been already been used before 1978, for example by George Metzger in his *Beyond Time and Again* in 1976.
3. Thierry Groensteen (ed.), 'Roman-graphique', *Le Bouquin de la bande dessinée. Dictionnaire esthétique et thématique*, Paris: Robert Laffont; Angoulême: Cité Internationale de la Bande Dessinée et de l'Image, 2020, p. 689.
4. See Tristan Gaillard, 'Autobiographie et identités', masters thesis, Université Lyon-3, 2022.
5. Jean-Paul Sartre, *What is Literature?*, Abingdon: Routledge Classics, 2001
6. See Jan Vansina, *Oral Tradition as History*, Madison, WI: University of Wisconsin Press, 1985.
7. W.J.T. Mitchell, *What Do Pictures Want? The Lives and Loves of Images*, Chicago: University of Chicago Press, 2006.
8. Charles Hatfield, *Alternative Comics: An Emerging Literature*, Jackson, MS: University Press of Mississippi, 2005, pp. XIII–XIV.
9. TV adaptation produced by Canal+ France, 2019; comic by Luz, Paris: Albin Michel, 2020–22.
10. See Booij Geert, *The Grammar of Words: An Introduction to Linguistic Morphology*, Oxford: Oxford University Press, 2005.
11. Loustal and Philippe Paringaux, *Barney and the Blue Note*, Seattle: Fantagraphics Books, 1988.
12. For more on this subject, see Étienne Souriau, *La Correspondance des arts. Éléments d'esthétique comparée*, Paris: Flammarion, 1947.
13. Jean H. Hagstrum, *The Sister Arts: The Tradition of Literary Pictorialism and English Poetry, from Dryden to Gray*, Chicago: University of Chicago Press, 1958.

Dino Battaglia (1923–83, Italy)
The Fall of the House of Usher, 1969 (based on the story by Edgar Allan Poe, 1839)
Page 1

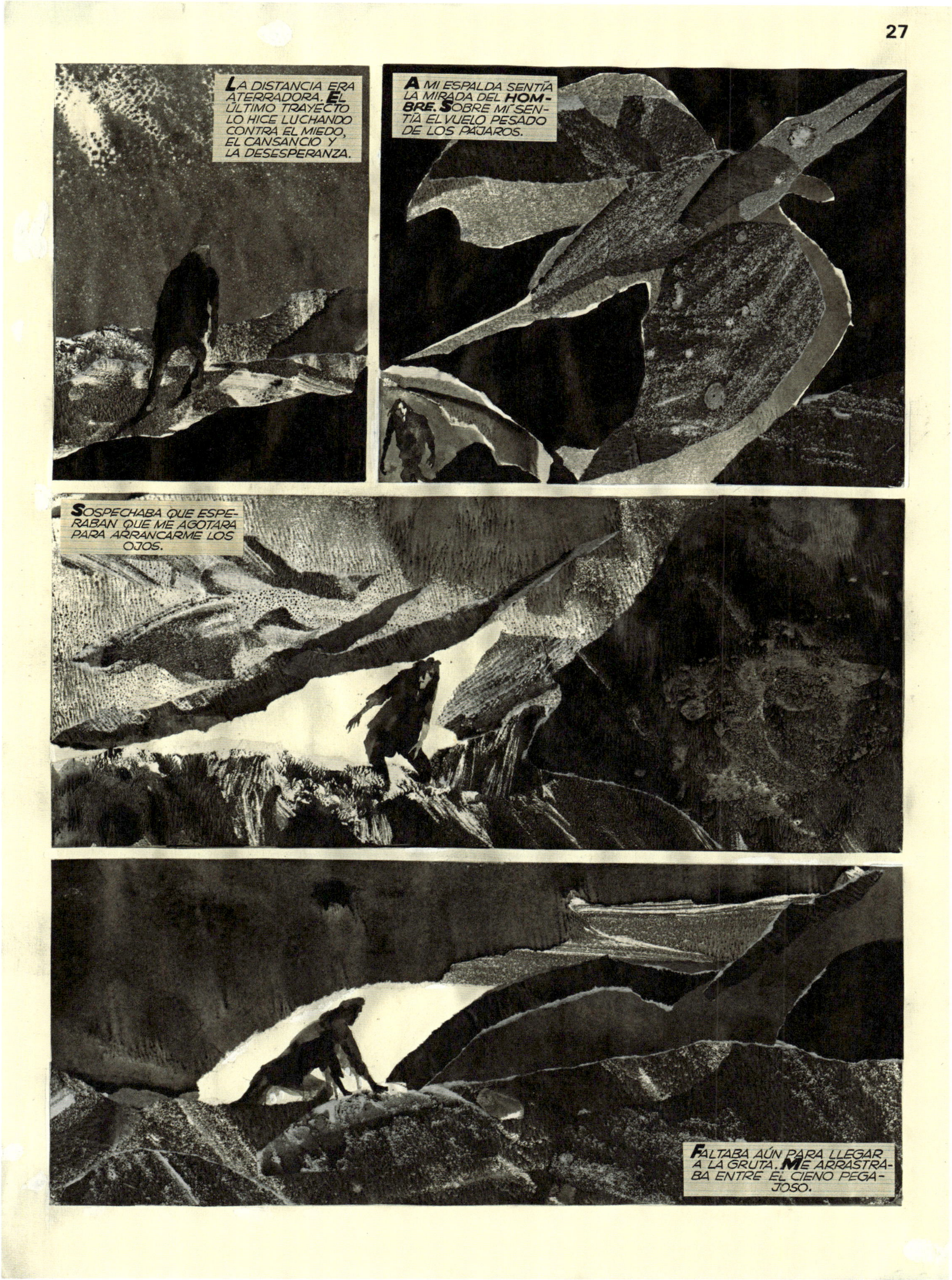

Alberto Breccia (1919, Uruguay–1993, Argentina)
Informe sobre ciegos (*Report on the Blind*), 1993 (based on the novel *On Heroes and Tombs* by Ernesto Sábato, 1961)
Page 27

Alberto Breccia (1919, Uruguay–1993, Argentina)
Caperucita roja (*Little Red Riding Hood*), 1980 (based on the tale by the Brothers Grimm, c. 1857)
Page 3

Alberto Breccia (1919, Uruguay–1993, Argentina)
Dracula, 1993 (freely based on the novel by Bram Stoker, 1897)
Chapter 3: 'A soft and grieving heart', page 5

Jacques Tardi (born 1946, France)
Brouillard au pont de Tolbiac (*Fog over Tolbiac Bridge*), 1981 (based on the novel by Léo Malet, 1956)
Page 60

Jacques Tardi (born 1946, France)
Casse-pipe à la Nation (*Death of a Marseilles Man*), based on the 1957 novel by Léo Malet, published in *(À suivre)*, no. 217, 1996
Cover art

Winshluss (born 1970, France)
Pinocchio, 2008 (freely based on the novel by Carlo Collodi, 1881)
Page 146

Winshluss (born 1970, France)
Pinocchio, 2008 (freely based on the novel by Carlo Collodi, 1881)
Sketch for cover art (unpublished)

Rébecca Dautremer (born 1971, France)
Of Mice and Men, 2020 (based on the novel by John Steinbeck, 1937)
Chapter 4, pages 27–28

..... 3 cours d'Italien avec Emmanuel, l'Invaire Mariette
et la séance photo avec Rona ... 4 jours pour finir ↑ → p 268 - 269 ... bon allons au resto japonais pour se consoler !

Gary Panter (born 1950, USA)
Jimbo in Purgatory, 2004 (based on *The Divine Comedy* by Dante Alighieri, 14th century)
Page 32

Luz (born 1972, France)
Vernon Subutex, vol. 1, 2020 (based on the novel by Virginie Despentes, 2015 & 2017)
Page 250

On that afternoon I, Joubert, was taking my usual circular walk near the chateau.

Posy Simmonds (born 1945, UK)
Gemma Bovery, 1997 (freely based on *Madame Bovary* by Gustave Flaubert, 1857)
'Normandy', page 64

Pénélope Bagieu (born 1982, France)
The Witches, 2020 (based on the book by Roald Dahl, 1983)
Pages 146 to 149 (digital publication)

Mœbius (1938–2012, France)
Upon a Star, 1987
Cover art (detail)

SCIENCE FICTION

Lucas Hureau

The 1950s saw a major change in adventure comics. Narratives taking place in 'exotic lands' no longer held the same appeal in a world that had been explored and mapped out. So comics creators turned to the stars and started to embrace the conquest of space.

Space opera – a subgenre of science fiction that deals with voyages through space and descriptions of intergalactic civilizations – first made a major impact in France in the early 1960s. Following in the footsteps of *Barbarella* (Jean-Claude Forest) and *Lost in Time* (Paul Gillon and Jean-Claude Forest), Philippe Druillet created the series *Lone Sloane*, which was later followed by *Vuzz* and *Yragaël*. The frenzied energy of his illustration style intensified the chaotic feel of the cosmos. The narrative and panels are explosive, embracing excess throughout. The original artwork, often designed in the Grand Aigle format (75 × 106 cm), is some of the largest in the history of comics.

Working alongside Druillet on the magazine *Métal hurlant*, Mœbius embraced a more metaphysical form of science fiction that drew on a number of different influences, such as mysticism, environmentalism, parapsychology and pantheism. In 1976, he published the first instalment of the serial *The Airtight Garage* in *Métal hurlant*, without having the story planned out in advance. This was followed by *The Incal* (1980–88), which he created in collaboration with Alejandro Jodorowsky, and then *The World of Edena* (1983–2001), his third major science-fiction series.

In Japan, manga had been speculating about developments in robotics and human enhancement since the 1950s, notably in the series *Astro Boy* by Osamu Tezuka, *Cyborg 009* and *Kamen Rider* by Shōtarō Ishinomori, and later *Mazinger Z*, *UFO Robo Grendizer* and *Great Mazinger* by Gō Nagai.

In the wake of the atomic bombs dropped on Hiroshima and Nagasaki and the impact of natural disasters, post-apocalyptic stories also started to spring up in Japan. The most prevalent themes in this genre are survival, violence, being pushed to the limit, hostile environments and the hope of a new world. Two especially iconic works emerged in the 1980s: Hayao Miyazaki's *Nausicaä of the Valley of the Wind* (1982–1994), a story that embraces environmentalism and pacifism and focuses heavily on nature, and Katsuhiro Ōtomo's *Akira* (1982–1990), which features more political and social commentary and plays out in the purely urban environment of Neo Tokyo. Both were adapted by their authors into feature-length animated films.

In the US, the 1960s brought the 'Silver Age' of comics and the emergence of new superheroes. Over the course of less than ten years, Marvel Comics built up its pantheon, creating the Fantastic Four, Hulk, Spider-Man, Thor, Iron Man, Dr. Strange, the Avengers, the X-Men, Daredevil, Nick Fury, the Silver Surfer and Black Panther. A parallel trend saw heroes from the earlier Golden Age being revived, after almost fifteen years of absence: the Human Torch, Namor the Sub-Mariner and Captain America. A new mythology was born.

In the 1980s, superheroes began to suffer from doubts, madness, depression and old age, marking a profound change in the comics that appeared over the following decades. Frank Miller's *The Dark Knight Returns* and Alan Moore and Dave Gibbons's *Watchmen* were the main drivers of this change, inviting us to see these characters in a new light, their surprising fragility resonating with our contemporary age.

Philippe Druillet (born 1944, France)
Lone Sloane, vol. 4: *Gail*, 1978
Pages 8–9

Philippe Druillet (born 1944, France)
Lone Sloane, vol. 4: *Gail*, 1978
Pages 10–11

Mœbius (1938–2012, France)
Le Monde d'Edena (*The World of Edena*), vol. 3: *La Déesse* (*The Goddess*), 1990
Page 35

Mœbius (1938–2012, France)
Upon a Star, 1987
Cover art

Mœbius (1938–2012, France)
Starwatcher, 1986

Frederik Peeters (born 1974, Switzerland)
Aâma, vol. 4: *Tu seras merveilleuse, ma fille* (*You Will Be Glorious, My Daughter*), 2014
Page 4

Jack Kirby (1917–94, USA), inked by Joe Sinnott
Fantastic Four, no. 95, Marvel Comics, February 1970
Cover art

Jack Kirby (1917–94, USA), inked by Joe Sinnott
Thor, no. 257, Marvel Comics, March 1977
Cover art

Marie Severin (1929–2018, USA), inked by Joe Sinnott
Captain America, no. 124, Marvel Comics, April 1971
Cover art

Gene Colan (1926–2011, USA), inked by Jim Steranko
Daredevil, no. 44, Marvel Comics, September 1968
Cover art

Neal Adams (1941–2022, USA), inked by Mike Esposito
Superman, no. 204, February 1968
Cover art © & ™ DC

Frank Miller (born 1957, USA)
The Dark Knight Returns, 1997

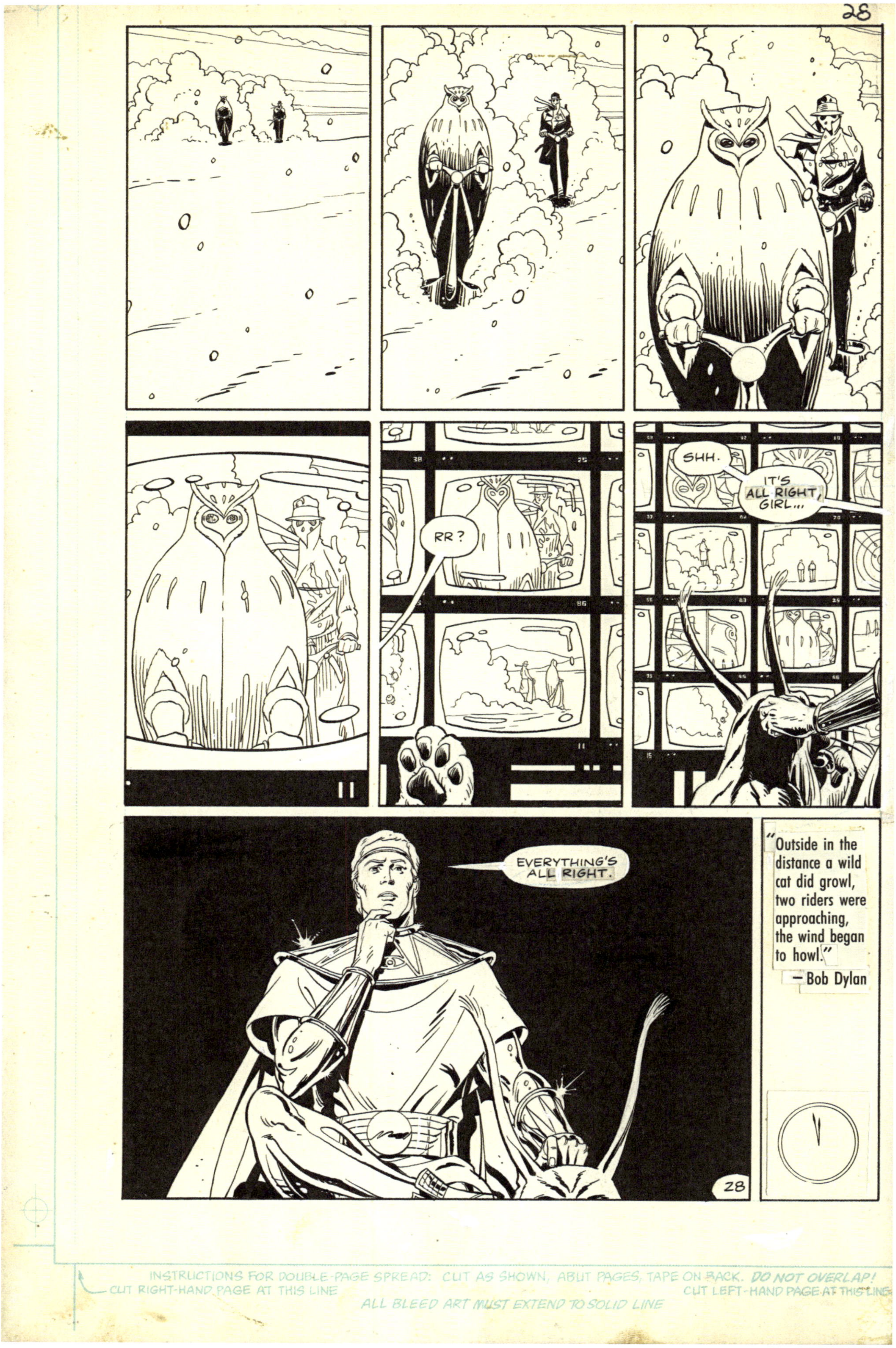

Dave Gibbons (born 1949, UK), written by Alan Moore
Watchmen, 1986
Chapter 7, page 28 © & ™ DC

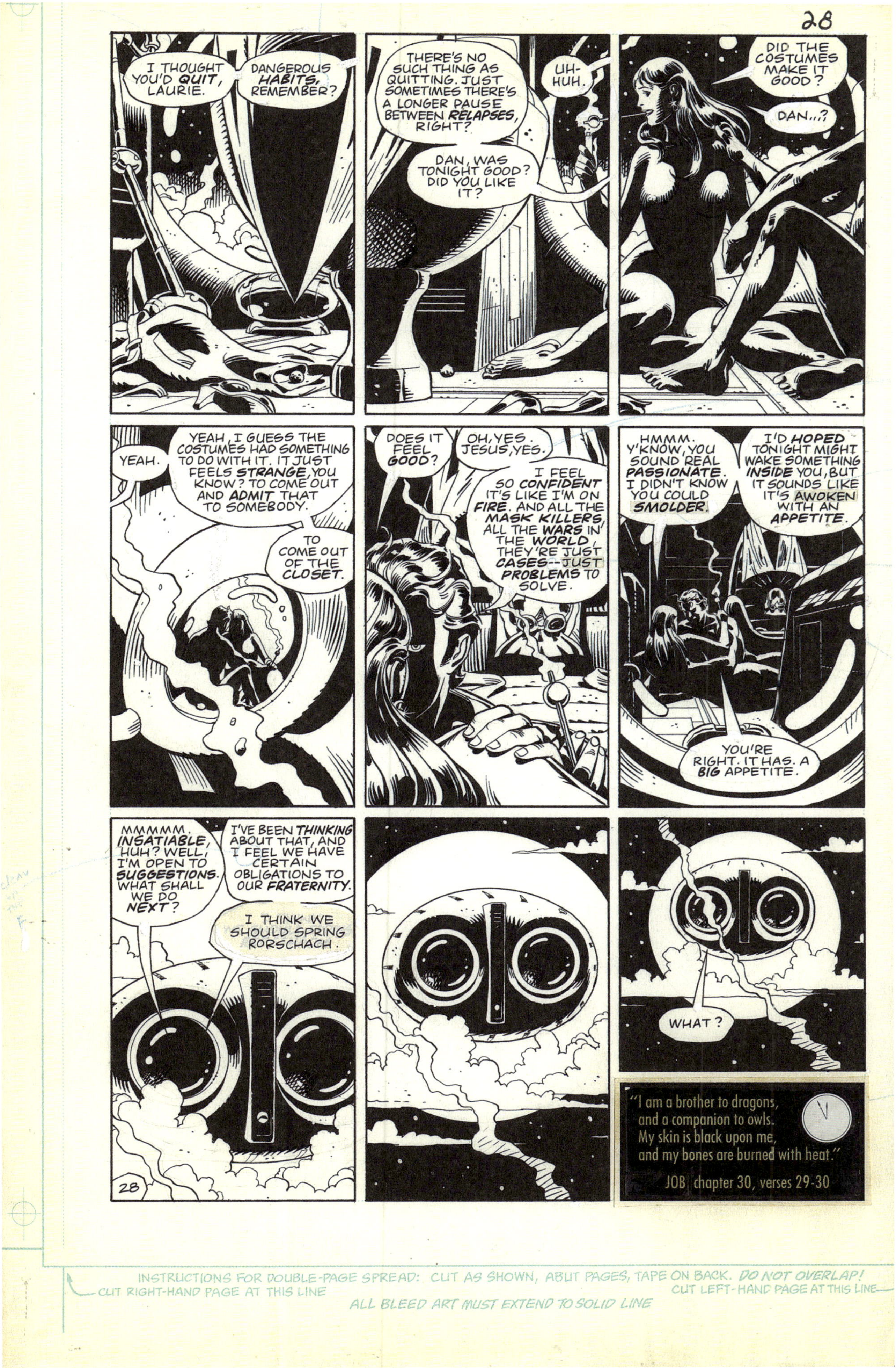

Dave Gibbons (born 1949, UK), written by Alan Moore
Watchmen, 1986
Chapter 10, page 28 © & ™ DC

Osamu Tezuka (1928–89, Japan)
Astro Boy, 1956
Title page artwork

Osamu Tezuka (1928–89, Japan)
Astro Boy, 'Robio & Robiette', 1965
Title page artwork

Nicolas de Crécy (born 1966, France)
The Cathedral, version 2 (detail), 2023
Unpublished art created for this exhibition

CITIES

Emmanuèle Payen

In comics, the rectangle of the page and the outline of each panel very quickly came to be seen as structural spaces in which to depict the urban environment, drawing pathways for the protagonists to walk down, with the aim of exploring the many potential interactions between the characters in the story and their constantly changing surroundings.

In the early twentieth century, Winsor McCay used these structural spaces as a framework for the dreamlike wanderings of *Little Nemo* (1905); the young hero climbed the buildings and tower blocks of an imagined city, like a toy construction set that has been distorted by the change of scale. The myth of the sprawling city, a space that is built to be conquered and mastered, was born. From the 1930s onwards, American megacities became the playgrounds of comic book superheroes, from Superman to *Watchmen*. A new toponymy was born, with imaginary urban spaces such as Metropolis, Gotham City or Sin City. They became the backdrop against which violent, sometimes deadly struggles between good and evil played out, the outlines of the buildings casting their threatening shadow over lives that are hanging on by a thread. American creator Will Eisner drew on this aesthetic but sought to make the presence of humans more evident, first in the adventures of *The Spirit* (1940), then in his later works set in New York City, which feature some of his most beautiful art (*New York: The Big City*, 1986; *The Building*, 1987).

Drawing on his interest in geometry and architecture, Chris Ware placed a building at the heart of his graphic novel (*Building Stories*, 2012); Seth's *Clyde Fans* (2000-03), a saga that follows two brothers, also features a wonderfully inventive urban setting. In Japan, the city of New Tokyo that appears in *Akira* (1984–93), created by Katsuhiro Ōtomo, was born from the ashes of the former Japanese capital, which has been destroyed by the Third World War.

In French and Belgian comics, a number of heroes also explored cities: Tintin, Blake and Mortimer, Spirou, and Gaston. Street furniture, road signs, cityscapes and traffic all come together to create a sense of reality as well as conveying the beauty of the city itself. Paris becomes the dark setting for the characters of Jacques Tardi, from Adèle Blanc-Sec to Nestor Burma, and for the events of *Le Cri du peuple* (2001–4), a magnificent historical tale tracing the history of the Paris Commune.

But the city is first and foremost a place in which the artist's imagination can be given free rein: in *The Celestial Bibendum* (1994–2002), Nicolas de Crécy creates a fantasy vision of 'New York on the Loire', populated by anthropomorphic creatures. This city provides the setting for a number of comic books, illustrations and paintings. For more than thirty years, François Schuiten and Benoît Peeters have created the magnificent series *Obscure Cities* (1983–2023), set in a parallel universe of such richness and complexity that it invites us to reconsider our own political and social structures.

The urban environment is also a space in which worlds can be upended and reversed, as can be seen in Marc-Antoine Mathieu's series *Julius Corentin Acquefacques* (1990–2020), especially in the story *L'Épaisseur du miroir*, a conceptual narrative that can be read both forwards and backwards, transforming the city into the palindromic setting for a never-ending story full of reflections and inversions of space and time.

Imagined cities, real cities, cities of the future: the urban world is undergoing a constant metamorphosis.

Will Eisner (1917–2005, USA)
A Contract with God, 1985
Back cover art

Will Eisner (1917–2005, USA)
City People Notebook, 1989
'Empty Street', unpublished illustration

François Schuiten (born 1956, Belgium), written by Benoît Peeters
Revoir Paris, vol. 2: *La Nuit des constellations*, 2016
Page 99

François Schuiten (born 1956, Belgium), with Benoît Peeters
Les Cités obscures (*The Obscure Cities*), vol. 3: *La Tour*, 1987
Page 2

François Schuiten (born 1956, Belgium), with Benoît Peeters
Les Cités obscures (*The Obscure Cities*), vol. 4: *La Route d'Armilia*, 1988
Page 29

Nicolas de Crécy (born 1966, France)
Le Bibendum céleste (*The Celestial Bibendum*), vol. 3, 2001
Page 35

Nicolas de Crécy (born 1966, France)
The Cathedral, version 2, 2023
Unpublished art created for this exhibition

Seth (born 1962, Canada)
Clyde Fans, 2017
Part 5: '1957', pages 29 & 32

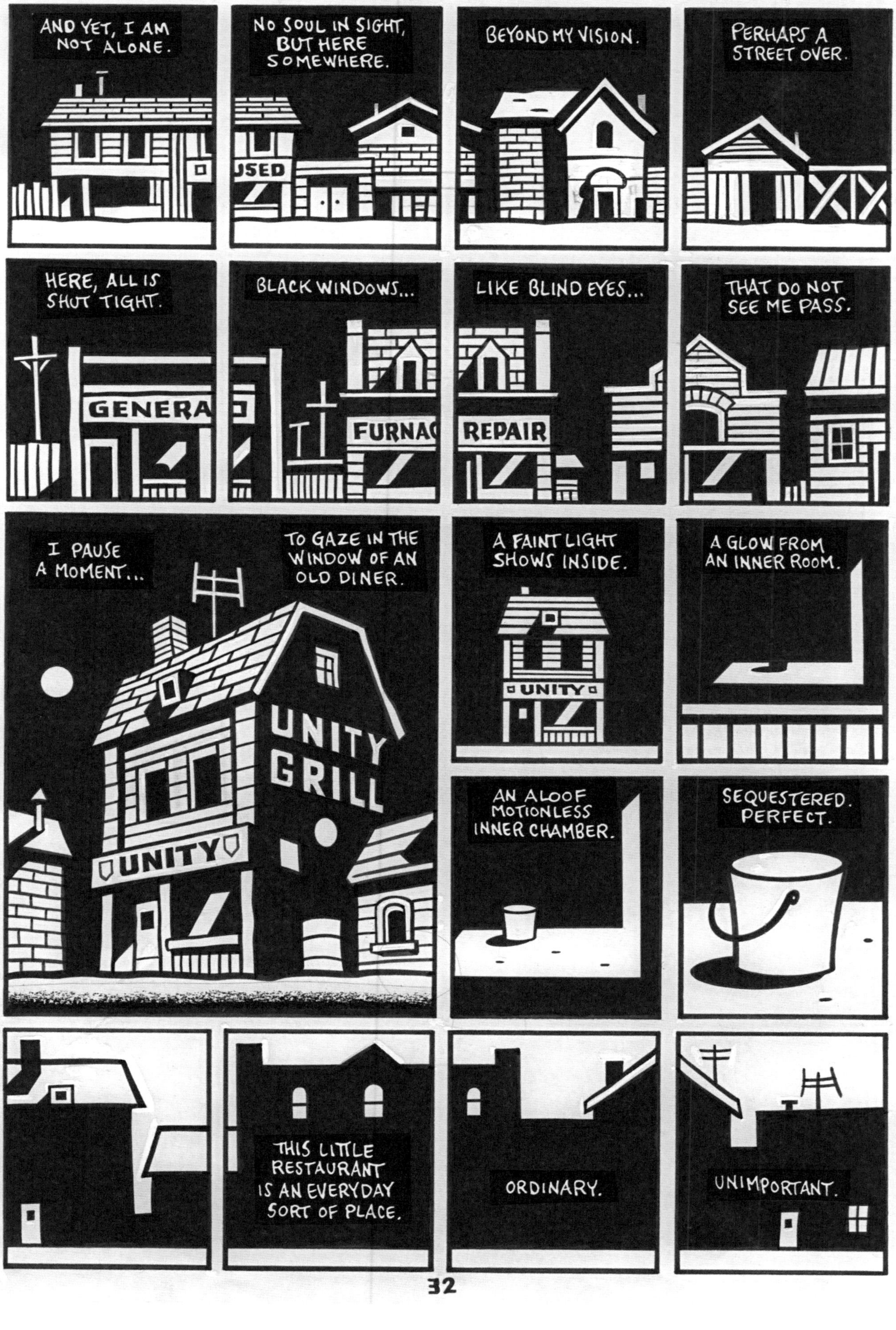
AND YET, I AM NOT ALONE.
NO SOUL IN SIGHT, BUT HERE SOMEWHERE.
USED
BEYOND MY VISION.
PERHAPS A STREET OVER.
HERE, ALL IS SHUT TIGHT.
GENERA
BLACK WINDOWS...
FURNAC
LIKE BLIND EYES...
REPAIR
THAT DO NOT SEE ME PASS.
I PAUSE A MOMENT...
TO GAZE IN THE WINDOW OF AN OLD DINER.
UNITY GRILL
UNITY
A FAINT LIGHT SHOWS INSIDE.
UNITY
A GLOW FROM AN INNER ROOM.
AN ALOOF MOTIONLESS INNER CHAMBER.
SEQUESTERED. PERFECT.
THIS LITTLE RESTAURANT IS AN EVERYDAY SORT OF PLACE.
ORDINARY.
UNIMPORTANT.

Marc-Antoine Mathieu (born 1959, France)
Julius Corentin Acquefacques, vol. 4: *L'Épaisseur du miroir*, 1995
'2. La fin du début', page 18

Marc-Antoine Mathieu (born 1959, France)
Julius Corentin Acquefacques, vol. 4: *L'Épaisseur du miroir*, 1995
'1. Le début de la fin', page 22

Chris Ware (born 1967, USA)
Poster art for the 49th Angoulême International
Comics Festival (detail), 2022

GEOMETRY

Bringing infinity within reach

Marguerite Demoëte

From fantasy architecture in the form of imagined cities to the most inventive visual experiments, comics have always had an instinctive and formal relationship with the space of the page. Although it is a codified, regulated space, it is also a landscape that offers an infinite number of narrative possibilities. Drawing up a (non-exhaustive) list of the connections between comics and geometry does not lead us to the portrait of a cold, abstract art form, but to an examination of a constantly shifting and emotional relationship with the page, in which the author and reader are in constant collaboration to come up with new approaches.

As a sequential art form governed by the principle of 'iconic solidarity',[1] the term coined by Thierry Groensteen, a comic might be defined as follows: a network made up of multiple images, connected by relationships of various kinds – sequential, coexisting and/or interdependent. From this perspective, any study of comics must be combined with a study of how comics creators construct pages, using an approach 'like geometricians',[2] following specific principles or axioms to determine how to organize the space of the page. Dividing the narrative into separate fragments of space and time, cutting out and rearranging, changing the format and scale, allowing images to overlap – all these techniques invite us to see things from the point of view of the creator, the person controlling the architecture of the page.

By listing and examining the different strategies by which comics creators can play with geometry, invent new forms, take the page to pieces and remake it, we can imagine different points of origin and pinpoint the geographies of these creative spaces within the history of comics.

Strips, panels and experiments in geometry

Winsor McCay (1869–1934), one of the pioneers of these experiments in geometry, abandoned traditional grids and embraced less regulated ways of organizing a narrative, changing the size of panels to suit the needs of the story and thereby creating surprising, dreamlike spaces. In *Little Nemo in Slumberland* (1905), as Benoît Peeters writes, 'The page is not simply a vector pointing towards its end (the reader knows that Nemo will wake up in the final panel). It becomes a place in which every element plays a part, a genuine box of tricks that we can wander through in many different ways. Over the weeks, McCay adopts a number of different organizational principles for his pages: little by little, he builds up an overall picture, creates a sense of moving through a series of settings, setting up illusions and reflections.'[3]

As we move through the pages of *Little Nemo*, we can trace the evolution of a narrative that always tends towards profusion and diffraction, characteristics of the ethereal realm in which the young hero finds himself as his dreams plunge him into ever more fantastical worlds. We move progressively from regular rectangular panels, labelled with numbers and captions that give a sense of order to the action, to compositions in which speech bubbles and numbers form part of the image itself.

George Herriman (1880–1944) was one of the other leading lights in these experiments in geometry, rearranging the centre and margins of the page to transform it into a space that was constantly shifting. By playing with different kinds of grid, large panoramic or circular frames, and panels arranged in symmetrical or asymmetric designs, the creator of *Krazy Kat* – and other comic strips that are less famous but just as experimental – invented his own style: he allowed the relationships between his characters to evolve, their ambiguities being presented to a reader via a narrative that was sometimes sustained and sometimes disrupted by these shifts of geometry. What is the strange relationship between Krazy, the ambiguous, androgynous cat, and Ignatz the mouse? Their connection is made concrete in the form of bricks thrown by the mouse, recalling the Freudian game of '*Fort/Da*', in which the contradictory drives of attachment

and separation are misinterpreted by the cat as signs of affection. The scattergun arrangement of panels allows the reader to grasp, both at first glance and as their gaze moves back and forth around the page, the ambiguous nature of the relationship between these two characters.

Building and unbuilding

For both the pioneers of abstraction and the contemporary artists who experiment in this way, playing with geometry is never gratuitous. Splitting a panel into pieces emphasizes the sense that there are multiple narratives, whether in a filmic, architectural or organic way. George Herriman's approach to using panels, strips and vignettes is reminiscent of a cinema screen (or TV); they overlap in a way that resembles cross-cutting, with different phases in a story isolated and reordered in a way that makes them easier to read, in strips of different lengths that form one or more possible epilogues. Chris Ware adopts an architectural model, culminating in his *Building Stories* (2012), which means that the reader can both immediately perceive and then later decode the many spaces in which his characters find themselves, which correspond to different layers of time but also to their different perspectives on intimacy and solitude, whether they are isolated in tiny boxes or lost within huge vertical panels. In this way, experiments in geometry and narrative dynamics create an infinite number of different perceptions of the intimate worlds of these characters, each hidden inside the other like Russian dolls. In some of Guido Crepax's page designs, the female body is broken down into pieces to convey the complexity of desire, split into panels that have a photographic feel. In an approach that is sometimes fetishizing, sometimes objectifying, Crepax depicts the body in fragmented form, in a series of strips or panels of unequal sizes, in order to recreate the intensity of pleasure or the ambivalence of the gaze. Who is looking? Who is being looked at? Hands, feet, backsides and backgrounds are all dislocated, and the reader becomes a voyeur or even a photographer, like the character of Valentina, through whose eyes we are invited to see. These geometric variations establish a new hierarchy of meaning created by our reading, which is not only about finding the 'right' meaning but about taking different paths, recognizing the importance of details, changing perspective and embracing different points of view.

The skeleton of the page

Paradoxically, it is by dismantling the skeleton of the page grid that comics reach the pinnacle of their graphic potential, building a narrative structure with its own rules, organization and grammar. Jochen Gerner's research, in which he isolates and analyses visual elements of comic strips, has revealed a number of recurring motifs and figures in the narrative space of the *Tintin* comics.[4] Through a series of formal experiments designed to explore Hergé's original structure, as both a system and a narrative, Gerner created a new work that borders on abstraction. Earlier, in a work bearing the apt title *Abstraction (1941–1968)* (2011), Gerner used the technique of *blacking out* elements, but here he uses a process of *extraction* to draw up an inventory of forms in black and white, classifying them according to both their geometry and their meaning. By listing the elements associated with different colours, he uses the Tintin books as the basis for a classification system that shows how colours are associated with different symbolic meanings (blue with the night sky in *The Blue Lotus*, gold with power in *King Ottokar's Sceptre*, etc.).

The construction of meaning, which is both deliberate and obscured, is accomplished by revealing the unconscious structure of the work. Drawing on the phenomenon of synthesis in dreams, this process of extraction emphasizes relationships of scale, of detail and in framing, which exist in Hergé's illustrations in a way that we might describe as unconscious or latent. In this manner, Gerner was able to spot, in one panel in *The Castafiore Emerald*, a visual relationship between the flowers in a speech bubble and the notes from a piece of contemporary music. Isolating the narrative structure through this kind of reading is an act of deciphering, like interpreting a dream or solving a puzzle, translated into terms that are both geometric and poetic. The collected repertoire of forms creates a kind of enduring dynamic, bringing the tiny details of the work back to life. From an inventory of motifs to the reader rearranging the syntax of comics, different levels of engagement with geometry can be perceived. Together these form a single dynamic, moving from abstraction to a perceptible, almost synaesthetic kind of connection between forms and narrative.

Some creators build their entire work around the task of revealing this underlying geometric structure and of stripping comics of the constituent elements from which they are made. In his hybrid projects, which lie somewhere between comics, installations, painting and manga, the artist Yuichi Yokoyama invites us to see 'the comic strip at work'. Like an architect placing the maquette and the finished building on the same level, he draws the dislocated faces and bodies of his characters, in hidden or nested spaces. In *Public Works*[5] (2004), for example, he depicts the movements of workers, the way they use their bodies, their relationship with materials and constructions at different stages, without the reader ever being able to see the whole picture, the end result or the finished product. What are the 'works' being carried out? What tools are being used, and for what purpose? We are told almost nothing, apart from what we see in the mysterious faces and bodies of the workers, cogs in a machine that look like ancient colossi, enormous stones to be carved, raw material offered up to the reader, like a kind of metonymy, representing Yokoyama's own creation. A work that shows the mechanics of its own construction, created in his workshop with the aid of rulers and templates, grey outlines that are cut and pasted together, taken apart and reassembled once again.

Deconstructing comics

Dots, curves, lines, circles, figures, outlines: the surface of the page or the screen, criss-crossed by parallel lines that could form strips or panels, seems in itself to require a clear geometric division of space in order to make it easier to read. After all, this, first and foremost, is what defines comics, as a medium that not only has its own history – as an art form, an industry and a publishing format – but also has a pact of readability with the reader, who is tasked with deciphering a series of images that make up a narrative, as the space of the page suggests. With this in mind, the entire history of comics could be reinterpreted in light of what the various marks and lines say about its relationship with the page, a pure geometric space that is both cohesive and fragmented at the same time. A tension can be seen between two geometric traditions: on one hand, the development of a narrative tradition that prioritizes readability above all else and insists on 'the clarity of the line'[6] beyond all other stylistic considerations; on the other hand, the variations and visual experiments that seek to push the limits of abstraction ever further.

However, this would mean losing sight of the fact that comics are always designed to be seen, or read. They make a unique pact with the reader, in which the mechanics of the medium are constantly deconstructed both for and by the reader, who is an active player in this geometric game of shapes and lines. This framework for reading means that an infinite number of variations are possible. Today, comics creators such as Léa Murawiec,[7] Martin Panchaud,[8] and Martin Nadé[9] are embracing new ways of exploring the relationships between comics and geometry, reinventing the principles of perspective, narrative and figuration. As in the work of Chris Ware, the undisputed master of narrative tricks and twists, they say to the reader: 'Turn the book every which way, break it down, remake it... You will see an infinite number of possible worlds appear.'

1. A concept developed by Thierry Groensteen, mainly in *Système de la bande dessinée*, Paris: PUF, 'Formes sémiotiques' series, 1999.
2. To use the words of Spinoza in *Ethics*, when the philosopher invites the reader to adopt the principles of geometry, approaching the task of examining human passions 'in the way of geometricians' (*more geometrico*).
3. Benoît Peeters, *La Bande dessinée entre la presse et le livre*, Paris: Bibliothèque Nationale de France, 2019, p. 21.
4. *RG: Renseignements généraux. Lecture chromatique des aventures de Tintin (1929–1976), Hergé*, text by Emmanuel Rabu, illustrations by Jochen Gerner, Paris: L'Association, 2016.
5. English-language adaptation published in Yūichi Yokoyama, *New Engineering*, New York: PictureBox, 2007.
6. *Töpffer. L'invention de la bande dessinée*, eds. B. Peeters and T. Groensteen, Paris: Hermann, 1994, p. 43. Quoted by T. Groensteen in 'Ligne claire', *Le Bouquin de la bande dessinée. Dictionnaire esthétique et thématique*, Angoulême: Cité Internationale de la Bande Dessinée et de l'Image; Paris: Robert Laffont, 2020, p. 433.
7. Léa Murawiec, *Le Grand Vide*, Strasbourg: Éditions 2024, 2021.
8. Martin Panchaud, *La Couleur des choses*, Bussy-Saint-Georges: Çà et Là, 2022.
9. Martin Nadé, *Quelques miettes à géométrie variable*, Montreuil: Éditions Matière, 2017.

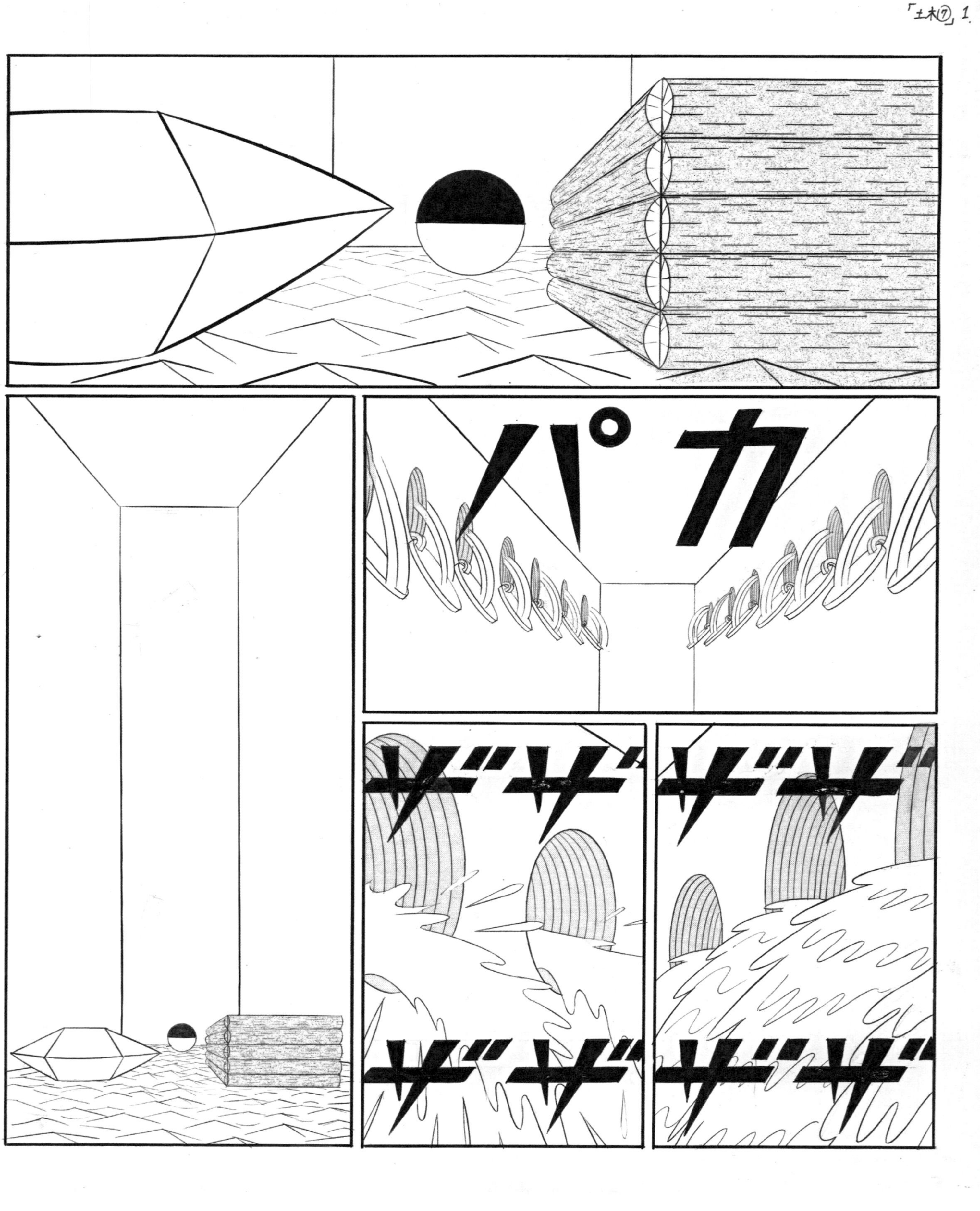

Yūichi Yokoyama (born 1967, Japan)
Public Works, c. 2005
Pages 1 & 2

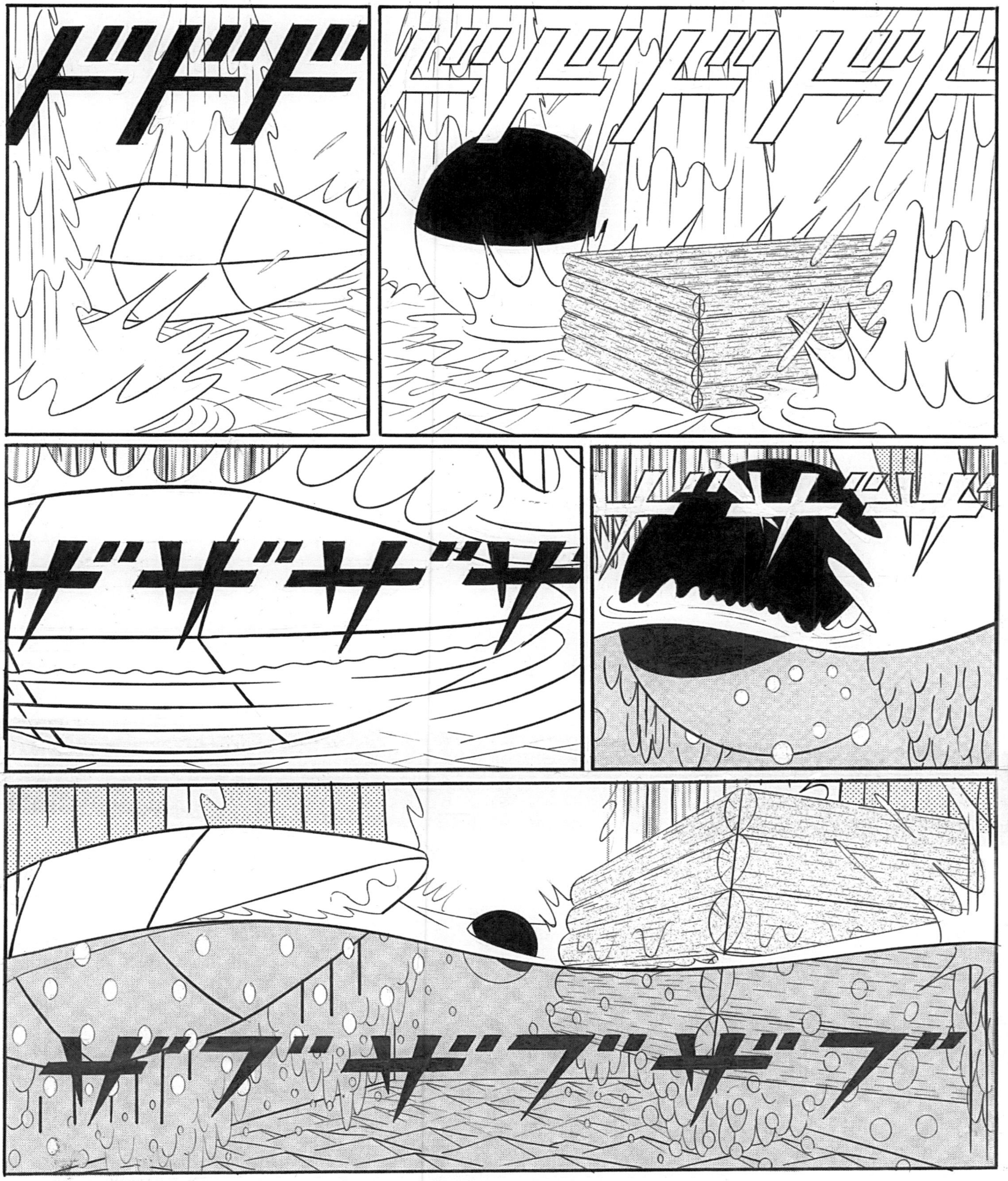
ドドドドド
ドドド
ザザザ
ザザザザ
ザブザブザブ

Guido Crepax (1933–2003, Italy)
Bianca: La casa matta, 1969
Page 28

Guido Crepax (1933–2003, Italy)
Valentina, 'Anthropology', 1977–78
Page 51

Jochen Gerner (born 1970, France)
RG, 2013–15
'Ectoplasm' (detail)

Jochen Gerner (born 1970, France)
RG, 2013–15
'Megacycle', page 12

Martin Panchaud (born 1982, Switzerland)
Die Farbe der Dinge (*The Colour of Things*), 2022
Pages 20 & 21 (digital artwork)

Tu vois,
on pourrait
croire que
Moonlight Cloud
est le favori,
mais j'ai plus
confiance en
Restiadargent.
C'est curieux,
comme nom de
cheval...

Chris Ware (born 1967, USA)
Poster art for the 49th Angoulême International Comics Festival, 2022

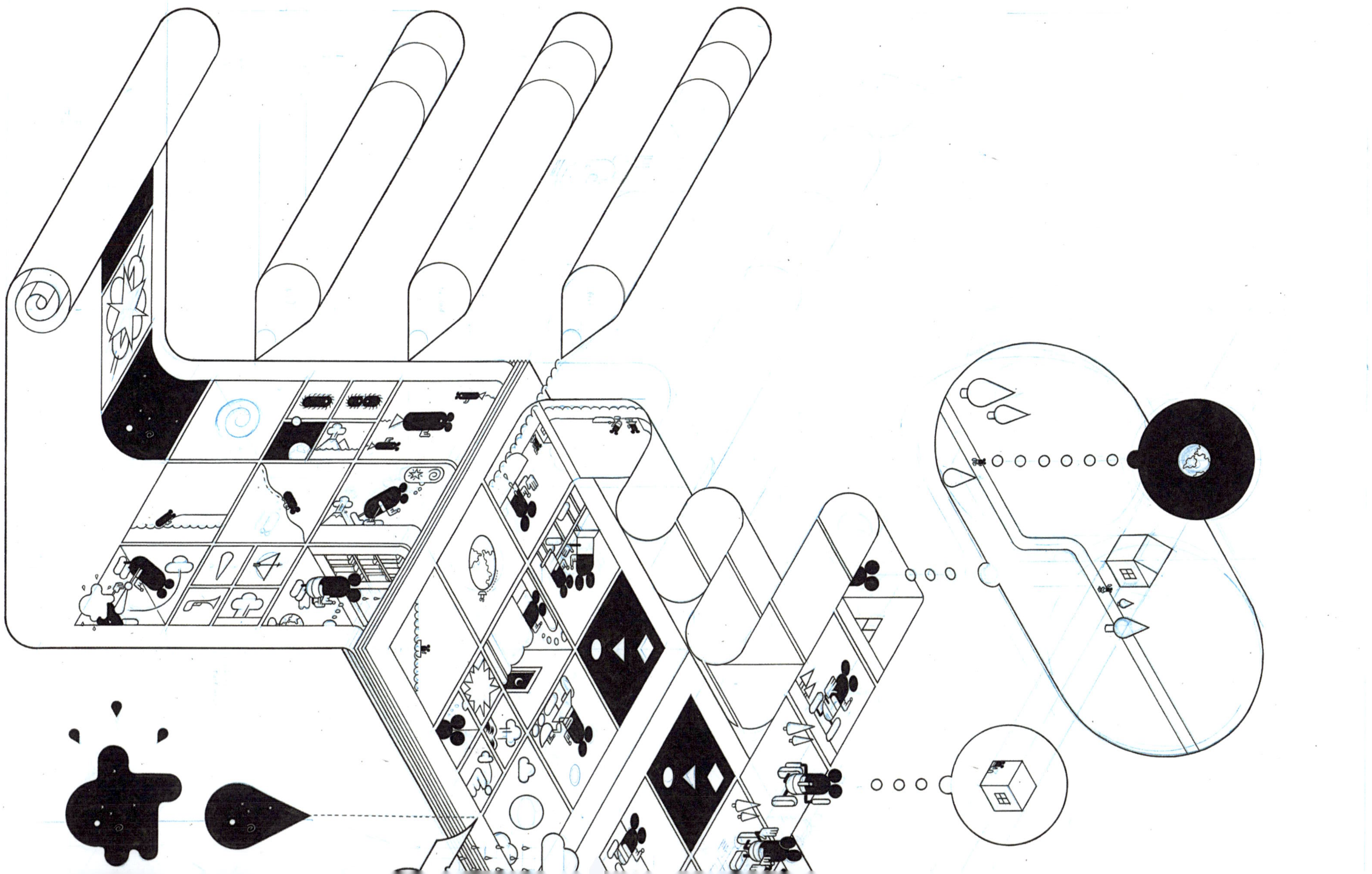

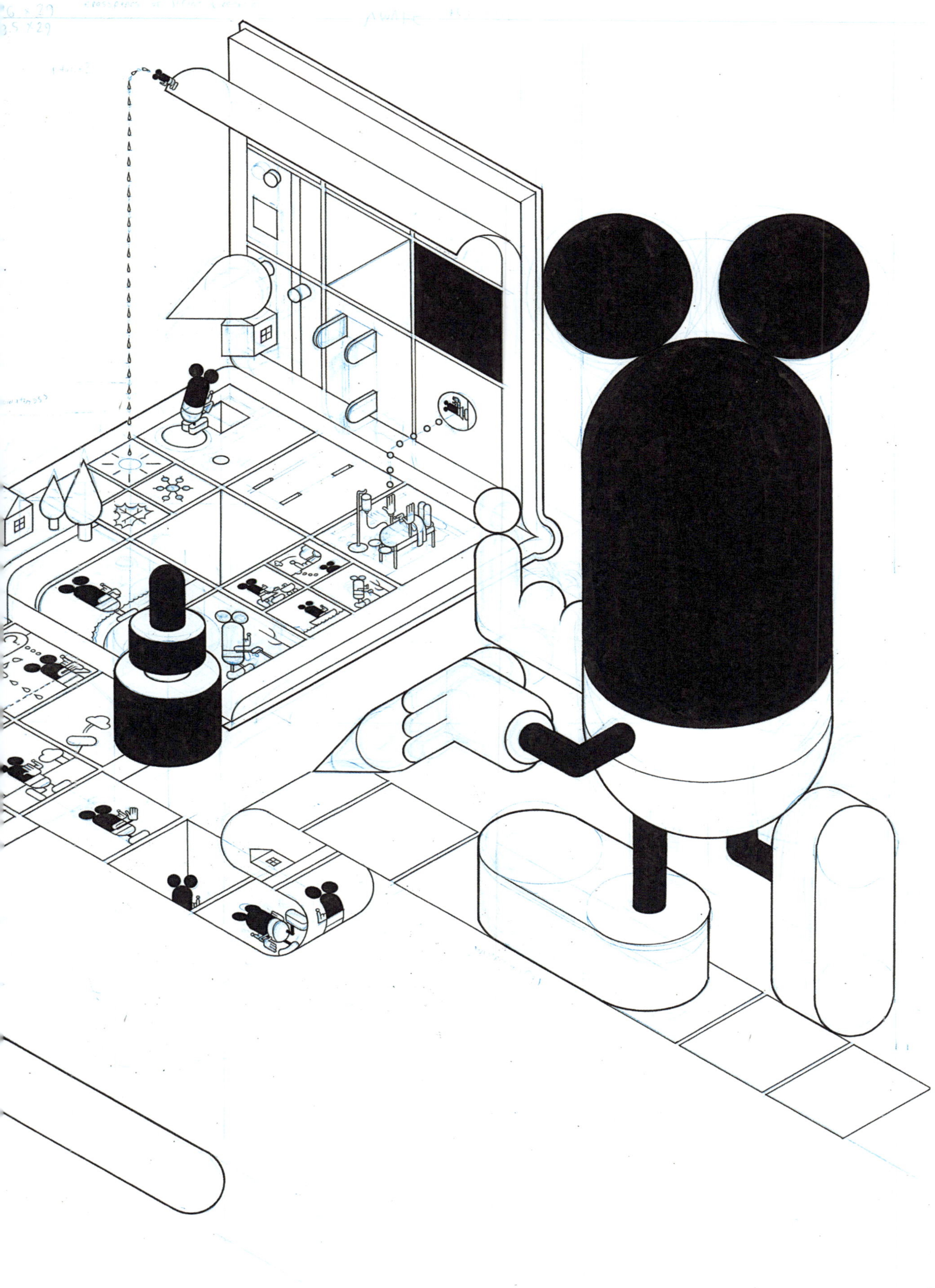

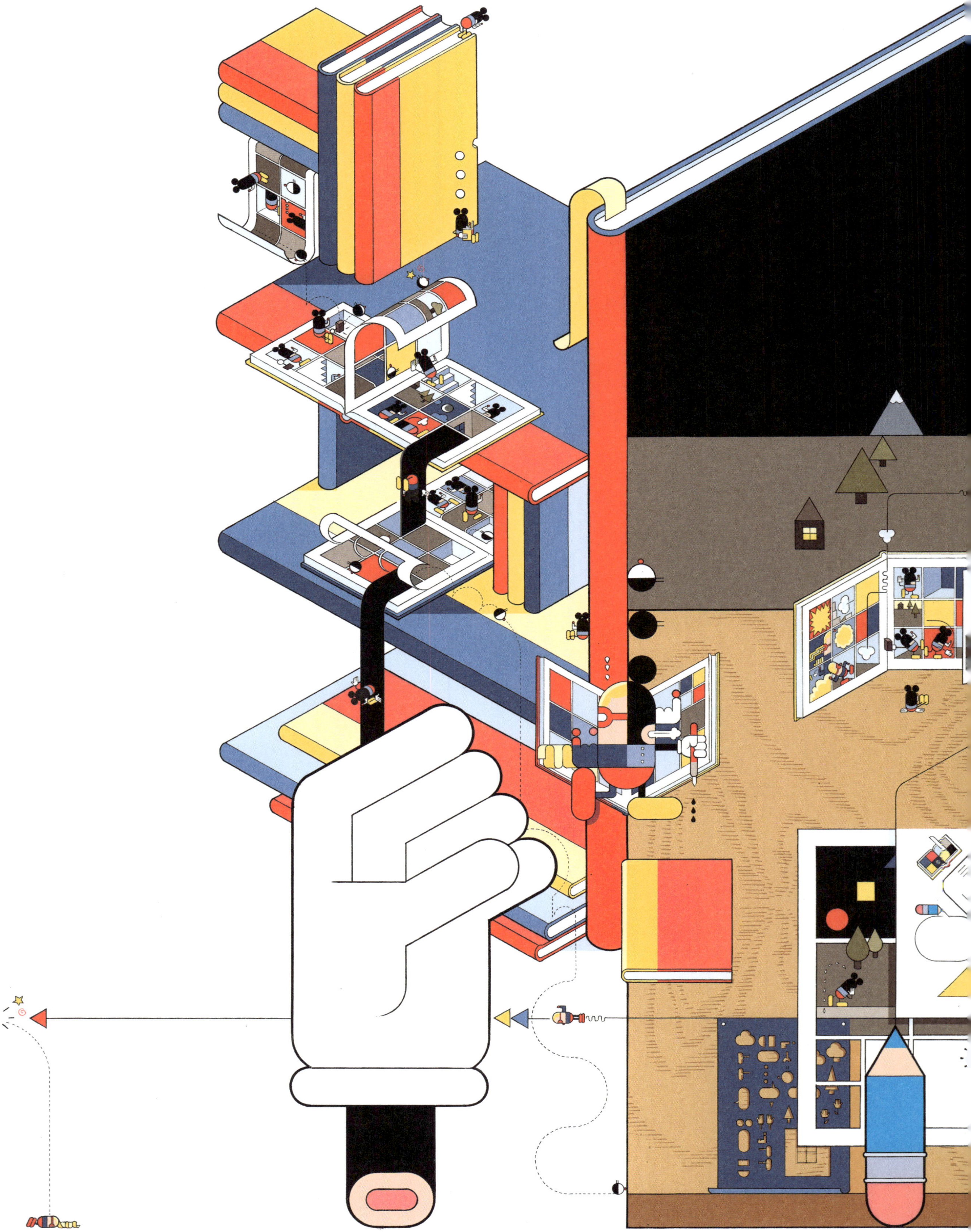

Previous pages

Chris Ware (born 1967, USA)
Drawing Table, 2024
Wall art created for this exhibition

LIST OF EXHIBITED WORKS

Note:

At the time of going to press, technical information for some works was not available. Apologies to the artists, rights holders and lenders for any unintentional omissions.

Dates given refer to the creation of the original art (where known), or to the date of first publication.

COUNTERCULTURE

I. PRINTED WORKS

Hara-Kiri
Éditions du Square, Paris
No. 1, September 1960
No. 2, October 1960
No. 5, February 1961 [repr. p. 42]
No. 6, March 1961
No. 9, June 1961
No. 11, September 1961
No. 12, November 1961
No. 13, December 1961
No. 15, March 1962
No. 16, April 1962 [repr. p. 42]
No. 17, May 1962
No. 19, July–August 1962
No. 20, September 1962
No. 22, November 1962
No. 24, January 1963
No. 26, March 1963
No. 28, May 1963
No. 31, September 1963
Covers by Fred
Bibliothèque Patrimoniale de la Cité Internationale de la Bande Dessinée et de l'Image, Angoulême

Garo
Seirindō, Tokyo
No. 1, September 1964
Cover by Sanpei Shirato
No. 9, May 1965
Cover by Sanpei Shirato
No. 10, June 1965
Cover by Sanpei Shirato
No. 17, January 1966
Cover by Sanpei Shirato
No. 45, May 1968
Cover by Shigeru Mizuki
No. 58, April 1969
Cover by Sanpei Shirato
No. 59, April 1969
Cover by Yū Takita
No. 64, August 1969
Cover by Sanpei Shirato
No. 70, January 1970
Cover by Yū Takita
No. 72, February 1970
Cover by Seiichi Hayashi
No. 76, May 1970
Cover by Ryōichi Ikegami
No. 85, December 1970
Cover by Kuniko Tsurita [repr. p. 30]
No. 96, August 1971
Cover by Seiichi Hayashi
No. 100, December 1971
Cover by Seiichi Hayashi
No. 103, March 1972
Cover by Susumu Katsumata
No. 119, July 1973
Cover by Genpei Akasegawa
No. 126, February 1974
Cover by Seiichi Hayashi
No. 128, April 1974
Cover by Seiichi Hayashi
Claude Leblanc Collection

Yoshiharu Tsuge
Garo
Seirindō, Tokyo
No. 19, March 1966; contains the story 'Chīko'
No. 38, October 1967; contains the story 'Red Flowers'
No. 47, June 1968: special issue: Yoshiharu Tsuge
No. 91, April 1971, dedicated entirely to this artist
Claude Leblanc Collection

Jean-Claude Forest
Barbarella
1964
Le Terrain Vague
Bibliothèque Patrimoniale de la Cité Internationale de la Bande Dessinée et de l'Image, Angoulême
[repr. p. 36]

Philippe Druillet
Lone Sloane: Le Mystère des abîmes
1966
Éd. Éric Losfeld
Bibliothèque Patrimoniale de la Cité Internationale de la Bande Dessinée et de l'Image, Angoulême

Nicolas Devil (Nicolas Deville)
Saga de Xam
Written by Jean Rollin
1967
Éd. Éric Losfeld
Bibliothèque Patrimoniale de la Cité Internationale de la Bande Dessinée et de l'Image, Angoulême
[repr. p. 36]

Robert Gigi
Scarlett Dream
Written by Claude Moliterni
1967
Éd. Éric Losfeld
Bibliothèque Patrimoniale de la Cité Internationale de la Bande Dessinée et de l'Image, Angoulême
[repr. p. 36]

Guido Crepax
Valentina
1969
Éd. Éric Losfeld
Bibliothèque Patrimoniale de la Cité Internationale de la Bande Dessinée et de l'Image, Angoulême
[repr. p. 40]

Caza (Philippe Cazaumayou)
Kris Kool
1970
Éd. Éric Losfeld
Bibliothèque Patrimoniale de la Cité Internationale de la Bande Dessinée et de l'Image, Angoulême
[repr. p. 40]

Georges Pichard
Lolly-Strip
Written by Danie Dubos
1972
Éd. Éric Losfeld
Bibliothèque Patrimoniale de la Cité Internationale de la Bande Dessinée et de l'Image, Angoulême

Zap Comix
Apex Novelties / The Print Mint Inc., San Francisco
No. 1, 1967
Cover by Robert Crumb
No. 2, August 1968
Cover by Robert Crumb
No. 3, 1968
Cover by Rick Griffin
No. 4, August 1969
Cover by Victor Moscoso
No. 5, May 1970
Cover by Robert Williams
No. 6, March 1973
Cover by Gilbert Shelton
[repr. p. 51]
No. 7, March 1974
Cover by Spain Rodriguez
The Print Mint Inc., San Francisco
No. 8, August 1975
Cover by Robert Crumb
Bibliothèque Patrimoniale de la Cité Internationale de la Bande Dessinée et de l'Image, Angoulême
[repr. p. 51]

Yellow Dog
The Print Mint Inc. Berkeley
No. 6, 1968
Vol. 2, nos. 9 & 10, 1969
[repr. p. 50]
Vol. 2, no. 13, July 1969
Covers by Robert Crumb
Bibliothèque Patrimoniale de la Cité Internationale de la Bande Dessinée et de l'Image, Angoulême

Motor City Comics
No. 1, April 1969
Rip Off Press, San Francisco
Cover by Robert Crumb
Bibliothèque Patrimoniale de la Cité Internationale de la Bande Dessinée et de l'Image, Angoulême

Big Ass Comics
Rip Off Press, San Francisco
No. 1, June 1969
No. 2, August 1971
Covers by Robert Crumb
Bibliothèque Patrimoniale de la Cité Internationale de la Bande Dessinée et de l'Image, Angoulême

Bijou Funnies
No. 8, November 1973
Kitchen Sink
Cover by Harvey Kurtzman
Bibliothèque Patrimoniale de la Cité Internationale de la Bande Dessinée et de l'Image, Angoulême

Arcade
The Print Mint Inc., San Francisco
No. 1, Spring 1975
No. 2, Summer 1975
No. 6, Summer 1976
Covers by Robert Crumb
Bibliothèque Patrimoniale de la Cité Internationale de la Bande Dessinée et de l'Image, Angoulême

Bazooka (collective)
Un regard moderne
Published by the newspaper *Libération*
No. 1, March 1978
Cover by Loulou Picasso
No. 3, May 1978
Cover by Olivia Clavel
No. 5, July 1978
Cover by Lulu Larsen
Private collection, Courtesy MEL Publisher

II. ORIGINAL ARTWORK

Shin'ichi Abe
born 1950, Japan

That Miyoko Asagaya Feeling
Title page and pages 12 to 14
Published in *Garo*, no. 88, March 1971
Indian ink and white gouache
34.5 × 24.5 cm each
Private collection, Courtesy MEL Publisher
[repr. p. 34-35]

Bazooka (collective)

Olivia Clavel
born 1955, France

Les Aventures de Télévision
'Télé voyage', part 2
Page 1
Published in *Charlie Mensuel*, no. 140, 1980
Indian ink and coloured felt-tips
50 × 32 cm
Private collection, Courtesy MEL Publisher
[repr. p. 59]

Kiki Picasso
(Christian Chapiron)
born 1956, France
Loulou Picasso
(Jean-Louis Dupré)
born 1954, France

My Grandpa's Name is Modern Art, But I Can Do Better Than Him
Published in *Un regard moderne*, no. 1, March 1978
Back cover illustration
Indian ink, felt-tip, gouache, wash and collage
54.9 × 38.5 cm
Private collection, Courtesy MEL Publisher
[repr. p. 58]

Kiki Picasso
(Christian Chapiron)

L'Atelier de l'artiste
Published in *Un regard moderne*, no. 2, April 1978
Indian ink, felt-tip, screentones and collage
34 × 25 cm
Private collection, Courtesy MEL Publisher

Bernard Vidal
born 1954, Algeria

Rééduquons / Let's Rehabilitate
Published in *Bulletin périodique*, no. 7, 1978
Indian ink, collage and gouache
32.7 × 50.2 cm
Private collection, Courtesy MEL Publisher

Guido Crepax
1933–2003, Italy

Valentina, 'I sotterranei'
Page 12
1968
Published in the magazine *Linusfabri*
Milano Libri, Milan, 1968
Indian ink
51 × 36.5 cm
Private collection, Courtesy MEL Publisher
[repr. p. 41]

Robert Crumb
born 1943, USA

Fritz the Cat, 'Secret Agent for the C.I.A.'
Page 16
1965
Originally drawn for *Help!*
First published: *R. Crumb's Fritz the Cat*, 1969
Indian ink
28 × 21.4 cm
Private collection, Courtesy MEL Publisher
[repr. p. 55]

Eggs Ackley in Eggs Escape
Page 3
Published in *Big Ass Comics*, no. 2, Rip Off Press, August 1971
Indian ink
31 × 21 cm
Philippe Simay Collection

Arcade: The Comics Revue
'Those Cute Little Bearzy-Wearzies'
No. 6, Summer 1976
Cover art
Indian ink, pasted title
36 × 29 cm
9e Art Références Collection, Paris

Nicolas Devil
(Nicolas Deville)
born 1943, France

Saga de Xam
Written by Jean Rollin
Page 80
Éd. Éric Losfeld, 1967
Indian ink and black gouache
104.7 × 74.8 cm
Private collection, Courtesy MEL Publisher
[repr. p. 39]

Jean-Claude Forest
1930–98, France

Barbarella
First published in *V-Magazine*
Le Terrain Vague, 1964
Page 45
Indian ink and blue ink wash
51.3 × 37 cm
Private collection, Courtesy MEL Publisher
[repr. p. 37]

Barbarella
First published in *V-Magazine*, no. 572/8, Autumn 1963
Page 54
Le Terrain Vague, 1964
Indian ink and blue ink wash
50 × 34.5 cm
Private collection, Courtesy MEL Publisher

Barbarella
First published in *V-Magazine*, no. 572/8, Autumn 1963
Page 55
Le Terrain Vague, 1964
Indian ink, white gouache, blue ink wash, Letraset and applied paper
51 × 35.6 cm
Private collection, Switzerland

Fred
(Frédéric Othon Théodore Aristidès)
1931–2013, France

Le Petit Cirque
Pages 1 & 2
Published in *Hara-Kiri*, no. 44, October 1964
Éd. Dargaud, 1973
Indian ink and wash
44.5 × 35.5 cm
Private collection
[repr. pp. 44–45]

Gébé
(Georges Blondeaux)
1929–2004, France

On ne se dit pas tout entre époux
Published in *Hara-Kiri*, no. 29, March 1961
2 pages
Indian ink, white gouache and collage on cardboard
50 × 32.5 cm each
Courtesy of Galerie Anne Barrault

Berck essaie des chapeaux
Published in *Hara-Kiri*, no. 48, February 1965
Indian ink and collage on cardboard
44 × 65 cm
Courtesy of Galerie Anne Barrault
[repr. pp. 46–47]

Susumu Katsumata
1943–2007, Japan

Ghost of Spring
Cover art
Published in *Garo*, no. 103, March 1972
Indian ink, gouache and watercolour
47 × 38 cm
Private collection, Courtesy MEL Publisher
[repr. p. 33]

Ghost of Spring
Pages 12 to 15
Published in *Garo*, no. 103, March 1972
Indian ink, white gouache and pasted speech bubbles
34.5 × 25 cm each
Private collection, Courtesy MEL Publisher
[repr. p. 32]

Aline Kominsky-Crumb
1948, USA–2022, France
Robert Crumb
born 1943, USA

Aline and Bob's Dirty Laundry Comics
Cover art
1974
Indian ink
35.6 × 28 cm
Erwin and Alfred Bergdoll Collection of Underground Comics and Original Art
The Ohio State University Billy Ireland Cartoon Library & Museum
[repr. p. 54]

Jay Lynch
1945–2017, USA

Nard n' Pat
Published in *Nard n' Pat*, no. 1, 1974
The Cartoonists Co-op Press, 1974
Indian ink and graphite pencil
40.8 × 30.4 cm
Jay Lynch Papers and Collection of Original Art
The Ohio State University Billy Ireland Cartoon Library & Museum
[repr. p. 57]

Featuring Richard Corben, Robert Crumb, Kim Deitch, Evert Geradts, Justin Green, Bill Griffith, Denis Kitchen, Harvey Kurtzman, Willy Murphy, Pepe Poplaski, Trina Robbins, Gilbert Shelton, Spain Rodriguez, Art Spiegelman, Robert Williams, Skip Williamson and S. Clay Wilson
Nard n' Pat
2 pages
Published in *Nard n' Pat*, no. 1, 1974
The Cartoonists Co-op Press, 1974
Indian ink, graphite pencil, blue pencil, screentone and collage
46.8 × 33.9 cm each
Jay Lynch Papers and Collection of Original Art
The Ohio State University Billy Ireland Cartoon Library & Museum

Georges Pichard
1920–2003, France

Lolly-Strip
Written by Danie Dubos
1967
First published in *Le Rire*, no. 187
Page 20
Éd. Éric Losfeld, 1972
Indian ink on cardboard
49.7 × 30.2 cm
Private collection, Switzerland
[repr. p. 38]

Jean-Marc Reiser
1941–83, France

Untitled
c. 1965
Indian ink
31.8 × 19.8 cm
Private collection, Courtesy MEL Publisher

Untitled
Published in *Hara-Kiri*, no. 69, May 1967
Indian ink
32.6 × 25 cm
Private collection, Courtesy MEL Publisher

Unpublished illustration for *Hara-Kiri*, no. 79, April 1968

Indian ink and collage
32 × 25 cm
Marina Vlady Collection
[repr. p. 43]

Gilbert Shelton
born 1940, USA

The Fabulous Furry Freak Brothers
1969
T-shirt design
Indian ink
31 × 25 cm
Galerie de la Bande Dessinée
[repr. p. 52]

Fat Freddy's Cat
1974
Published in *Les Fabuleux Freak Brothers. Intégrale*, vol. 4
Artefact, 1983
Indian ink
58.1 × 37 cm
Private collection,
Courtesy MEL Publisher

Art Spiegelman
born 1948, Sweden

Short Order Comix, no. 1
Cover art
Head Press, 1973
Indian ink and opaque white
45.7 × 29.8 cm
Art Spiegelman Collection

Don't Get Around Much Anymore
1973
Published in *Short Order Comix*, no. 2, 1974
Reprinted in *Breakdowns*, Belier Press, New York, 1977
Indian ink, opaque white and collage
36.8 × 25.4 cm
Art Spiegelman Collection

Comics as a Medium for Self-Expression
1981
Cover art for *PRINT Magazine*, May–June 1981
Reprinted in *Read Yourself Raw*, 1987
Indian ink, opaque white and watercolour
41.3 × 29.8 cm
Art Spiegelman Collection
[repr. p. 56]

Kuniko Tsurita
1947–85, Japan

My Wife is an Acrobat
Pages 1 to 5
Published in *Garo*, no. 128, April 1974
Indian ink and white gouache
36.3 × 24.5 cm each
Private collection
[repr. p. 31]

Willem (Bernhard Willem Holtrop)
born 1941, Netherlands

Il y a déjà longtemps...
Pages 1 & 2
Published in *Hara-Kiri*, no. 84, September 1968
Indian ink
30 × 24 cm each
Bibliothèque Nationale de France, Département des Estampes et de la Photographie

Quelques fois par an...
Pages 1 & 2
Published in *Hara-Kiri*, no. 86, November 1968
Indian ink
30 × 24 cm
Bibliothèque Nationale de France, Département des Estampes et de la Photographie
[repr. p. 48–49]

S. Clay Wilson (Steve Clay Wilson)
1941–2021, USA

Shorts in The Bowls
1969
Indian ink and graphite pencil
29.2 × 41.5 cm
Erwin and Alfred Bergdoll Collection of Underground Comics and Original Art
The Ohio State University Billy Ireland Cartoon Library & Museum

The Nocturnal Bad Biter
Page 1
1970
Indian ink and graphite pencil
23.9 × 30.4 cm
Erwin and Alfred Bergdoll Collection of Underground Comics and Original Art
The Ohio State University Billy Ireland Cartoon Library & Museum
[repr. p. 53]

Georges Wolinski
1934–2015, Tunisia

Unused cover design for *Hara-Kiri*
Published in *Hara-Kiri*, no. 69, May 1967
Gouache, watercolour and Indian ink
16.5 × 12.5 cm
Bibliothèque Nationale de France, Département des Estampes et de la Photographie
[repr. p. 42]

Unused cover design for *Hara-Kiri*
Published in *Hara-Kiri*, no. 69, May 1967
Gouache, watercolour and Indian ink
17 × 12.5 cm
Bibliothèque Nationale de France, Département des Estampes et de la Photographie

Unused cover design for *Hara-Kiri*
Published in *Hara-Kiri*, no. 69, May 1967
Gouache, watercolour and Indian ink
14.3 × 12.5 cm
Bibliothèque Nationale de France, Département des Estampes et de la Photographie

Unused cover design for *Hara-Kiri*
Published in *Hara-Kiri*, no. 69, May 1967
Gouache, watercolour and Indian ink
17 × 12.1 cm
Bibliothèque Nationale de France, Département des Estampes et de la Photographie

FEAR

Charlie Adlard
born 1966, UK

The Walking Dead, no. 153
Image Comics, Portland, OR, 2016
Cover art
Indian ink and black felt-tip
43.2 × 28.2 cm
Private collection,
Courtesy MEL Publisher
[repr. p. 68]

Stéphane Blanquet
born 1973, France

Silence hypnotique
2011
Published as the cover of *La Tranchée Racine*, no. 2 bis
Indian ink
41.1 × 32 cm
Private collection,
Courtesy MEL Publisher

La Pythie face aux signes
2015
Tapestry designed by the artist, woven by TextielLab
Indian ink
75 × 110 cm
Private collection,
Courtesy MEL Publisher
[repr. pp. 76–77]

Charles Burns
born 1955, USA

El Borbah
1988
Back cover art for *Hard-Boiled Defective*
Penguin Books Ltd, March 1990
Indian ink
29.7 × 21 cm
Private collection,
Courtesy MEL Publisher

Black Hole
No. 4: *Bag Action*
Kitchen Sink Press, Princeton, NJ, 1997
Endpapers
Indian ink
38 × 30.5 cm each
Private collection,
Courtesy MEL Publisher

Black Hole
c. 1997
Unpublished illustration
Indian ink
38 × 49 cm
Private collection,
Courtesy MEL Publisher

X'ed Out
Page 22
Pantheon Books, New York, 2010
Indian ink
45.8 × 35 cm
Private collection,
Courtesy MEL Publisher

Daniel Clowes
born 1961, USA

Like a Velvet Glove Cast in Iron
Chapter 10, page 12
Fantagraphics Books, Seattle, 1993
Ink, graphite and Letraset collage on cardboard
48 × 31 cm
Daniel Clowes, Galerie Martel

Like a Velvet Glove Cast in Iron
Fantagraphics Books, Seattle, 2017
Sketch for cover art
Coloured pencil, graphite and ink
61 × 45.5 cm
Daniel Clowes, Galerie Martel
[repr. p. 71]

Gene Colan
1926–2011, USA

Tomb of Dracula, no. 22: '...In Death Do We Join! Gorna... Lord of the Living Lightning!'
Written by Marv Wolfman
Inked by Tom Palmer
Pages 14–15
Marvel Comics Group, New York, July 1974
Indian ink and blue pencil
29.5 × 44.4 cm
Private collection,
Courtesy MEL Publisher
[repr. p. 70]

Ludovic Debeurme
born 1971, France

Le Grand Autre
Cover art and pages 78 & 81
Éd. Cornélius, 2007
Indian ink
38.5 × 30 cm approx. each
Ludovic Debeurme Collection
[repr. p. 78]

Emil Ferris
born 1962, USA

Ghastly
2018
Ballpoint pen
35 × 28 cm
Galerie Martel
[repr. p. 75]

Anke Feuchtenberger
born 1963, Germany

Die Hure H wirft den Handschuh (W the Whore)
Written by Katrin de Vries
Reprodukt, Berlin, 2007
Illustrations from pages 151 (below), 152, 153, 154, 155 (above), 156 (below) & 159 (above)
Charcoal
29.7 × 42 cm each
Anke Feuchtenberger Collection
[repr. p. 79]

Ada
2013
Illustration from a series of 5, not yet published
Graphite pencil, gouache and acrylic
49.3 × 49.3 cm
Private collection, Courtesy MEL Publisher

Hideshi Hino
born 1946, China

Kyofu Jigoku Shojo (*Hell Baby*)
Tairiku Shobou, 1982
Cover art
Inks and Indian ink
25.5 × 19 cm
Private collection, Courtesy MEL Publisher
[repr. p. 64]

Kyofu Jigoku Shojo (*Hell Baby*)
Pages 6–7 to 114–115
Tairiku Shobou, 1982
Indian ink and white gouache
27.1 × 39.3 cm each
Private collection, Courtesy MEL Publisher
[repr. pp. 62–63]

Suehiro Maruo
born 1956, Japan

The Scream
Illustration for Edogawa Ranpo's short story *The Human Chair*, 1988
Published in *Maruo Graph DX I*, Éditions Treville, 1996
Reprinted in *Ranpo Panorama*, Le Lézard noir, 2013
Gouache on cardboard
25.5 × 36.2 cm
Private collection, Courtesy MEL Publisher
[repr. p. 66]

Vampyre
2001
Published in *Maruo Graph DX II*, Éditions Treville, 2005
Gouache
40.7 × 29.7 cm
Private collection, Courtesy MEL Publisher

Shigeru Mizuki
1922–2015, Japan

GeGeGe no Kitaro
'The Great Yokai War'
Published in *Weekly Shonen Jump*, April 1966
Reprinted on the cover of *Gegege no Kitaro*, vol. 3, Sun Comics
Indian ink, coloured ink and white gouache
39 × 54 cm
Private collection, Courtesy MEL Publisher. With the kind permission of Mizuki Pro

GeGeGe no Kitaro
'The Great Tanuki War'
Published in *Weekly Shonen Magazine*, no. 34, Kōdansha, August 1967
Title page
Indian ink and white gouache
38 × 27 cm
Private collection, Courtesy MEL Publisher. With the kind permission of Mizuki Pro

GeGeGe no Kitaro
'Bake-Neko'
Published in *Weekly Shonen Magazine*, Kōdansha, 1968
Reprinted in *Shigeru Mizuki Manga Complete Works, Gegege no Kitaro 8*
Indian ink and graphite pencil
39 × 54 cm
Private collection, Courtesy MEL Publisher. With the kind permission of Mizuki Pro

Kappa no Sanpei
1962
Cover art
Asahi Sonorama, 1970
Indian ink and coloured ink
22.3 × 15.7 cm
Private collection, Courtesy MEL Publisher.With the kind permission of Mizuki Pro

Joann Sfar
born 1971, France

Grand Vampire, vol. 4: *Quai des brunes*
Cover art
Éd. Delcourt, 2003
Indian ink
42 × 29.7 cm
Private collection, Courtesy MEL Publisher

Grand Vampire, vol. 5: *La Communauté des magiciens*
Title page artwork
Éd. Delcourt, 2004
Indian ink
42 × 29.5 cm
Private collection, Courtesy MEL Publisher
[repr. p. 74]

Gō Tanabe
born 1975, Japan

The Shadow over Innsmouth, vol. 2
Based on the novella by H. P. Lovecraft (1936)
Chapter 9: 'Nightmare', pages 26–27, 32 to 39
Enterbrain, 2020
Indian ink
42 × 29.7 cm each
Private collection
[repr. p. 67]

Kazuo Umezz
born 1936, Japan

God's Left Hand, Devil's Right Hand, vol. 6
Cover art
Published in *Big Comic Spirits*
Shogakukan, 1988
Ink and watercolour
36.1 × 25.5 cm
Kazuo Umezz Collection

God's Left Hand, Devil's Right Hand
Chapter 37: 'The Tongue of the Spider Queen', page 4
Published in *Big Comic Spirits*
Shogakukan, 1987
Indian ink
33.9 × 23.7 cm
Kazuo Umezz Collection
[repr. p. 65]

God's Left Hand, Devil's Right Hand
Chapter 54: 'Shadow of the Departed', page 14
Published in *Big Comic Spirits*
Shogakukan, 1988
Indian ink
33.9 × 23.7 cm
Kazuo Umezz Collection

Bernie Wrightson
(Bernard Albert Wrightson)
born 1948, USA

Frankenstein, or The Modern Prometheus
based on the novel by Mary Shelley (1818)
Page 17
Tyrannosaurus Press, 1977
Indian ink on cardboard
50.7 × 38 cm
Private collection, Courtesy MEL Publisher
[repr. p. 69]

DREAMS

David B.
(Pierre-François Beauchard)
born 1959, France

Les Complots nocturnes (*Nocturnal Conspiracies*)
Dream no. 17: 'The Heads'
7 pages
Futuropolis, 2005
Indian ink
32 × 24 cm each
Courtesy of the artist and Galerie Anne Barrault
[repr. pp. 88–89]

Blutch
(Christian Hincker)
born 1967, France

La Volupté
Pages 43 to 46
Futuropolis, 2006
Graphite pencil and coloured pencils
29.7 × 21 cm
Private collection, Courtesy MEL Publisher
[repr. pp. 86–87]

Collective

Peur(s) du noir / Fear(s) of the Dark
2007
4 of 6 segments:
Blutch, 'L'aristocrate aux chiens', 1:57 mins.
Charles Burns, 'L'insecte', 2:37 mins.
Lorenzo Mattotti, 'La bête', 2:10 mins.
Richard McGuire, 'La maison dans la neige', 2:10 mins.
2D animation
Prima Linea Productions, La Parti Production, Def2shoot, Denis Friedman Productions

Julie Doucet
born 1965, Canada

Là là, chu tanney là!!! ou le rêve récidiviste (*My Most Secret Desire*)
27 panels
Mille Putois, Montreal, 1995
Reprinted in *Ciboire de Criss!*, L'Association, 1996
Indian ink, white gouache and screentones
12.6 × 9.6 cm each
Private collection, Courtesy MEL Publisher
[repr. pp. 92–93]

Jean-Claude Forest
1930–98, France

Barbarella, vol. 3: *Le Semble-Lune* (*The Moon Child*)

Pages 25 (3 strips) and 26
(1st and 2nd strips)
Éd. Pierre Horay, 1977
Indian ink, graphite pencil,
black felt-tip and white gouache
36.7 × 94.8 cm each
Private collection,
Courtesy MEL Publisher
[repr. p. 84]

Barbarella, vol. 3: *Le Semble-Lune*
(*The Moon Child*)
Page 26 (3rd strip)
Éd. Pierre Horay, Paris, 1977
Indian ink, graphite pencil,
black felt-tip and white gouache
36.6 × 97.2 cm
Private collection, Switzerland

Fred
(Frédéric Othon Théodore Aristidès)
1931–2013, France

Philémon, vol. 5: *Simbabbad de Batbad*
Page 8
First published in *Pilote*, no. 564, 1970
Éd. Dargaud, 1974
Indian ink
41.5 × 32.5 cm
Private collection,
Courtesy MEL Publisher

Philémon, vol. 14: *L'Enfer des épouvantails*
Page 11
First published in *Pilote mensuel*, no. 108, May 1983
Éd. Dargaud, 1983
Indian ink
44 × 35.1 cm
Private collection,
Courtesy MEL Publisher
[repr. p. 13]

Philémon, vol. 14: *L'Enfer des épouvantails*
Page 25
First published in *Pilote mensuel*, no. 110, July 1983
Éd. Dargaud, 1983
Indian ink
44 × 35 cm
Private collection,
Courtesy MEL Publisher
[repr. p. 85]

Killoffer
(Patrice Killoffer)
born 1966, France

Billet SVP
'Chabadabada…', 2 pages
L'Association, 1995
Indian ink, graphite pencil
and coloured gouache
41 × 30 cm
Private collection,
Courtesy MEL Publisher

Les Cauchemars de l'amateur
2016
Panels 1 to 32 (of 64)
Unpublished
Indian ink and white gouache
29 × 42 cm each
Private collection,
Courtesy MEL Publisher
[repr. pp. 90–91]

HUMOUR

Fujio Akatsuka
1935, China–2008, Japan

Osomatsu-kun
1966
Fujio Productions
Indian ink and watercolour
35.3 × 26.2 cm
Fujio Productions Ltd.

The Genius Bakabon
1967
Fujio Productions
Indian ink and watercolour
33.7 × 27.9 cm
Fujio Productions Ltd.

The End of Unagi-Inu (*Eel-Dog*)
1973
4 pages
Fujio Productions
Indian ink
Title page: 31 × 24.9 cm
Following pages: 31 × 22.2 cm
Fujio Productions Ltd.
[repr. p. 102]

Christophe Blain
born 1970, France

Quai d'Orsay. Chroniques diplomatiques, vol. 1
Written by Abel Lanzac
Chapter 5, page 3
Éd. Dargaud, 2010
Indian ink
40.3 × 29.6 cm
Private collection,
Courtesy MEL Publisher
[repr. p. 121]

Quai d'Orsay. Chroniques diplomatiques, vol. 2
Written by Abel Lanzac
Chapter 7, page 1
Éd. Dargaud, 2011
Indian ink
40.3 × 29.6 cm
Private collection,
Courtesy MEL Publisher

Claire Bretécher
1940–2020, France

Agrippine, vol. 3: *Les Combats d'Agrippine*
'Un cri'
Self-published, 1993
Indian ink
25.5 × 19.3 cm
Private collection

Agrippine
'Au bagne'
First published in *Le Nouvel Observateur*
Reprinted in vol. 4: *Agrippine et les inclus*, self-published, 1993
Coloured inks
31.7 × 24.9 cm
Private collection
[repr. p. 116]

Les Frustrés (*Frustration*)
'Nos amies les bêtes'
First published in *Le Nouvel Observateur*
Reprinted in *Les Frustrés*, vol. 2, self-published, 1976
Indian ink
39 × 28.6 cm
Private collection

Les Frustrés (*Frustration*)
'La frisée aux lardons'
First published in *Le Nouvel Observateur*
Reprinted in *Les Frustrés*, vol. 3, self-published, 1978
Indian ink
39 × 26.3 cm
Private collection

Les Frustrés (*Frustration*)
'La femme du pionnier'
First published in *Le Nouvel Observateur*
Reprinted in *Les Frustrés*, vol. 4, self-published, 1979
Indian ink
41 × 28.5 cm
Private collection

Madame et le bonheur
Pages 1 & 2
Published in *Pilote*, no. 689, 18 January 1973
Indian ink and coloured inks
41 × 32.2 cm each
Private collection,
Courtesy MEL Publisher
[repr. pp. 114–115]

Florence Cestac
born 1949, France

Harry Mickson
'Le rock à Mickson'
1979
2 pages
Published in *Métal hurlant*, no. 39 bis, 1979
Black felt-tip and Indian ink
42.6 × 32.6 cm each
Private collection,
Courtesy MEL Publisher
[repr. p. 117]

F'murr (Richard Peyzaret)
1946–2018, France

Le Génie des alpages
Pages 236 A & B
First published in *Pilote mensuel*, no. 109, 1983
Reprinted in *Cheptel maudit*, Éd. Dargaud, 2004
Indian ink
44.7 × 33.9 cm each
Private collection,
Courtesy MEL Publisher
[repr. pp. 112–113]

André Franquin
1924, Belgium–1997, France

Gaston Lagaffe
Gag no. 472
First published in *Spirou*, no. 1531, 17 August 1967
Reprinted in *Un Gaffeur sachant gaffer*, Éd. Dupuis, 1969
Indian ink
45.4 × 36.2 cm
Private collection,
Courtesy MEL Publisher

Gaston Lagaffe
Published on the cover of *Spirou*, no. 1554, 25 January 1968
Reprinted in *Un Gaffeur sachant gaffer*, Éd. Dupuis, 1969
Indian ink
25.9 × 25.5 cm
Private collection,
Courtesy MEL Publisher
[repr. p. 118]

Gaston Lagaffe
Gag no. 625
First published in *Spirou*, no. 1684, 23 July 1970
Reprinted in *Le Cas Lagaffe*, Éd. Dupuis, 1971
Indian ink
45 × 33 cm
Bernadette Bienfait Collection

Gaston Lagaffe
Gag no. 776
First published in *Spirou*, no. 1845, 3 August 1973
Reprinted in *Le Gang des gaffeurs*, Éd. Dupuis, 1974
Indian ink
44.7 × 35.2 cm
Private collection,
Courtesy MEL Publisher

Idées noires
Gag no. 13 (based on an idea by Yvan Delporte)
First published in *Fluide glacial*, no. 20, 1978
Éd. Audie, 1981
Indian ink
Two parts; 25.8 × 36.5 cm each
Donated in 1979 - Salon International de la Bande Dessinée, loan from the Musée de la Bande Dessinée, CIBDI, Angoulême
[repr. p. 119]

Fujiko F. Fujio (Hiroshi Fujimoto)
1933–96, Japan

Doraemon
'Fishing Indoors', 6 pages
Published in *Shogaku Ichinensei*, April 1982
Series created in 1969
Indian ink and watercolour
Approx. 38.1 × 27.2 cm each
Fujiko F. Fujio Pro Co., Ltd.
[repr. p. 103]

Gotlib (Marcel Gottlieb)
1934–2016, France

Rubrique-à-brac
'Spaghetti-western', 4 pages
Published in *Pilote*, *no.* 528, 1969
Reprinted in *Rubrique-à-brac*, vol. 2
Éd. Dargaud, 1971
Indian ink
45 × 36.8 cm each
Michel Lieuré Collection
[repr. pp. 110–111]

Rubrique-à-brac, vol. 5
Cover art
Éd. Dargaud, 1974
Indian ink
37.5 × 29 cm
Bernadette Bienfait Collection
[repr. p. 109]

Benito Jacovitti
1923–97, Italy

Ridete, prego (*Laugh, Please*)
1964
Published in *Il Giorno*
Indian ink and coloured inks on verso
47.5 × 65.6 cm
Private collection, Courtesy MEL Publisher
[repr. pp. 104–105]

Harvey Kurtzman
1924–93, USA

Hey Look!
Published in *Georgie Comics*, no. 14, January 1948
Indian ink
51.3 × 38.7 cm
Ulrich Schröder Collection
[repr. p. 97]

Jungle Book
'Decadence Degenerated', pages 128 and 129
Ballantine Books, New York, 1959; repr. Kitchen Sink, 1986
Indian ink, wash and white gouache
31.5 × 19 cm each
Private collection, Courtesy MEL Publisher
[repr. p. 96]

Catherine Meurisse
1980, France

Scènes de la vie hormonale
'Rut de rue' ('Street Mating')
2015
First published in *Charlie Hebdo*
Éd. Dargaud, 2016
Page 25
Indian ink
33 × 24 cm
Catherine Meurisse Collection
[repr. p. 120]

Humaine, trop humaine
'Langue vivante', 2 pages
First published in *Philosophie Magazine*
Éd. Dargaud, 2022
Indian ink
35 × 25 cm each
Private collection, Courtesy MEL Publisher

Morris (Maurice De Bevere)
1923–2001, Belgium

Lucky Luke, vol. 19: *Les Rivaux de Painful Gulch* (*The Rivals of Painful Gulch*)
Written by René Goscinny
Pages 1 to 4
First published in *Spirou*, no. 1186, 1961
Éd. Dupuis, 1962
Indian ink
52.8 × 36.5 cm (pp. 1 & 2), 53.9 × 36.5 cm (p. 3), 52.1 × 36.5 cm (p. 4)
Morris Family
[repr. pp. 106–107]

Anouk Ricard
born 1970, France

Animan
Éd. Exemplaire, 2022
Cover art
Page 14: 'The Model'
Page 52: 'Good Hair'
Page 53: 'Secrets'
Digital artwork
[repr. pp. 122–123]

Charles M. Schulz
(Charles Monroe Schulz)
1922–2000, USA

Peanuts
Strip for 26 April 1964
Distributed by United Feature Syndicate
Indian ink
43.2 × 60 cm
Private collection, Courtesy MEL Publisher
[repr. pp. 98–99]

Peanuts
Strip for 7 November 1995
Distributed by United Feature Syndicate
Indian ink
43 × 60 cm
9ᵉ Art Références Collection, Paris

Albert Uderzo
1927–2020, France

Astérix chez les Belges (*Asterix in Belgium*)
Written by René Goscinny
Pages 10 to 13
First published in *VSD*, no. 68, 21 December 1978
Éd. Dargaud, 1979
Indian ink
56.5 × 43.6 cm approx. each
Bibliothèque Nationale de France, Rare Books Archive
[repr. p. 108]

Bill Watterson
(William Boyd Watterson II)
born 1958, USA

Calvin and Hobbes
Strip for 2 May 1993
Distributed by Universal Press Syndicate
Reprinted in *Homicidal Psycho Jungle Cat*, 1994
Indian ink
27.7 × 35.4 cm
Bill Watterson Deposit Collection
The Ohio State University Billy Ireland Cartoon Library & Museum

Calvin and Hobbes
Strip for December 1993
Distributed by Universal Press Syndicate
Reprinted in *There's Treasure Everywhere*, 1996
Indian ink
27.7 × 35.4 cm
Bill Watterson Deposit Collection
The Ohio State University Billy Ireland Cartoon Library & Museum
[repr. p. 16]

Zep (Philippe Chappuis)
born 1967, Switzerland

Titeuf, vol. 4: *C'est pô juste...*
'C'est pô grave'
Éd. Glénat, 1995
Indian ink
42 × 29.7 cm
Private collection, Courtesy MEL Publisher
[repr. p. 101]

COLOUR AND BLACK AND WHITE

Zeina Abirached
born 1981, Lebanon

Le Piano oriental
Pages 90–91
Casterman, 2015
Digital recreation from the published original
[repr. pp. 148–149]

Alex Barbier
1950–2019, France

Lycaons
First published in *Charlie Mensuel*, no. 109, 1978
Éditions du Square, 1979
Coloured inks
50 × 40 cm
Galerie Martel
Comme un poulet sans tête (*Like a Headless Chicken*)
Page 17
Éd. Delcourt, 1994
Coloured inks
50 × 40 cm
Galerie Martel
[repr. p. 138]

Lettres au maire de V. (*Letters to the Mayor of V*), vol. 2: *Autoportrait du vampire d'en face* (*Self-Portrait of the Vampire Across the Street*)
Éd. Fréon / FRMK, 2000
Coloured inks
48 × 34 cm
Galerie Martel

Edmond Baudoin
born 1942, France

Arleri
Notebooks 1 to 3
Original manuscripts of the published version, Éd. Gallimard, 2008
Indian ink, gouache and collage
27 × 42 cm
Private collection, Courtesy MEL Publisher

Enki Bilal (Enes Bilal)
born 1951, Yugoslavia

Partie de chasse (*The Hunting Party*)
Written by Pierre Christin
Page 66
First published in *Pilote*, no. 99, August 1982
Éd. Dargaud, 1983
Indian ink, gouache and graphite pencil
48 × 35.5 cm
Private collection, Courtesy MEL Publisher
[repr. p. 132]

La Femme piège (*The Woman Trap*)
Page 7
Les Humanoïdes Associés, 1986
Indian ink, gouache, graphite pencil and wax pencil
44.6 × 33 cm
Private collection, Courtesy MEL Publisher
[repr. p. 133]

Le Cycle du monstre (*Monster*), vol. 3: *Rendez-vous à Paris* (*Rendez-vous in Paris*)
Casterman, 2006
Pencil, gouache and acrylic on card board
Page 7 in 3 panels
Varying dimensions: 29.3 × 41.7 cm – 26.2 × 41 cm – 8.5 × 17.5 cm
Private collection, Courtesy MEL Publisher
[repr. p. 134]

Nina Bunjevac
born 1973, Canada

La Réparation
Pages 18 to 21
Éd. Martin de Halleux, Paris, 2022
Indian ink
35.5 × 28 cm each
Nina Bunjevac Collection
[repr. p. 147]

Nicole Claveloux
born 1940, France

La Main verte (*The Green Hand*)
Written by Édith Zha
Pages 1 & 2
First published in *Métal hurlant*, no. 9, 1976
Les Humanoïdes Associés, 1978; repr. Éd. Cornélius, 2019
Indian ink, gouache and airbrush on cardboard
26 × 20 cm
Private collection, Courtesy MEL Publisher
[repr. p. 136]

Comès
(Dieter Herman Comes)
1942–2013, Belgium

Silence
Chapter 2: 'La nuit de la sorcière', page 9
First published in *(À suivre)*, no. 14, 1979
Casterman, 1980
Indian ink
51 × 36.5 cm
Private collection, Courtesy MEL Publisher

Silence
Cover art
Casterman, 1980
Indian ink
39.5 × 31 cm
Bernadette Bienfait Collection
[repr. p. 145]

Nicolas de Crécy
born 1966, France

Foligatto
Page 59
Les Humanoïdes Associés, 1991
Indian ink, gouache and acrylic
37 × 28.6 cm
Private collection, Courtesy MEL Publisher

Le Bibendum céleste (*The Celestial Bibendum*), vol. 2
Cover art
Les Humanoïdes Associés, 1998
Pastels, gouache, acrylic
39 × 29.8 cm
Private collection, Courtesy MEL Publisher
[repr. p. 129]

Brecht Evens
born 1986, Belgium

Les Amateurs (*The Making Of*)
Cover art
Actes Sud, 2011
Indian ink, gouache and ink
65 × 59.2 cm
Private collection, Courtesy MEL Publisher
[repr. p. 137]

Panthère (*Panther*)
Cover art
Actes Sud, 2014
Gouache
41 × 50 cm
Private collection, Courtesy MEL Publisher

Panthère (*Panther*)
Endpapers
Actes Sud, 2014
Gouache
46 × 150 cm
Private collection, Courtesy MEL Publisher

Loustal (Jacques de Loustal)
born 1956, France

Barney et la note bleue (*Barney and the Blue Note*)
Written by Philippe Paringaux
Page 38
First published in the magazine *(À suivre)*, 1985
Casterman, 1987
Indian ink and watercolour
38.5 × 28.5 cm
Private collection, Courtesy MEL Publisher
[repr. p. 135]

Lorenzo Mattotti
born 1954, Italy

Fuochi (*Fires*)
Cover art
First published in *Alter alter*, 1984
Pastels and wax pencil
45.6 × 33 cm
Private collection, Courtesy MEL Publisher

Fuochi (*Fires*)
Pages 26 & 27
First published in *Alter alter*, 1984
Pastels and pencil
48 × 34 cm each
Lorenzo Mattotti Archives
[repr. p. 127]

Stigmata
Pages 98, 99 & 100
Written by Claudio Piersanti and Lorenzo Mattotti
Éd. Seuil, 1998
Indian ink
33 × 24 cm each
Lorenzo Mattotti Archives
[repr. p. 126]
Quaderno indiano (*Indian Notebook*) no. 2
2000
Watercolour and Indian ink on Lokta paper
22 × 15 cm closed
Lorenzo Mattotti Archives

Quaderno indiano (*Indian Notebook*) no. 3
2000
Watercolour and Indian ink on Lokta paper
22 × 15 cm closed
Lorenzo Mattotti Archives

Stanze (*Rooms*)
Notebook
2003
Indian ink and coloured inks on Lokta paper
19 × 18,5 cm closed
Lorenzo Mattotti Archives

Angkor
Notebook
2004
Watercolour and Indian ink on Lokta paper
19 × 18,5 cm closed
Lorenzo Mattotti Archives

Nell' Acqua
Notebook
2006
Watercolour and Indian ink on Lokta paper
22 × 15 cm closed
Lorenzo Mattotti Archives

Bob Dylan Revisited (collective)
'A Hard Rain's A-Gonna Fall'
Pages 1 to 10
Éd. Delcourt, Paris, 2008
Pastels and pencil
50 × 35 cm each
Private collection, Courtesy MEL Publisher
[repr. p. 128]

Mike Mignola
born 1960, USA

Hellboy, vol. 1: *Seeds of Destruction*
Written by John Byrne
Cover art
Dark Horse Comics, 1994
Indian ink
40.5 × 29.3 cm
Private collection

Hellboy, vol. 12: *The Storm and the Fury*
Cover art
Dark Horse Comics, 2012
Indian ink
48 × 30 cm
Private collection, Courtesy MEL Publisher
[repr. p. 140]

Frank Miller
born 1957, USA

Sin City, vol. 3: *The Big Fat Kill*
Chapter 3, page 12
Dark Horse, 1994
Indian ink
48 × 30 cm
Private collection, Courtesy MEL Publisher
[repr. p. 141]

Sin City, vol. 3: *The Big Fat Kill*
Chapter 5, pages 8 & 26
Dark Horse, 1994
Indian ink
48 × 30 cm each
Private collection, Courtesy MEL Publisher

Keizō Miyanishi
born 1956, Japan

Maila
c. 1970
Pages 32 & 33
Peyotl Studio, 1999
With accompanying CD by the band Onna
Indian ink, black felt-tip, white gouache and screentone
36.3 × 23.3 cm each
Private collection, Courtesy MEL Publisher
[repr. p. 139]

Mœbius (Jean Giraud)
1938–2012, France

Arzach
Chapter 1, page 1
Published in *Métal hurlant*, no. 1, January 1975
Les Humanoïdes Associés, 1976
Indian ink and coloured inks on cardboard
33 × 26 cm
Bernadette Bienfait Collection
[repr. p. 131]

Arzach
Chapter 1, page 6
Published in *Métal hurlant*, no. 1, January 1975
Les Humanoïdes Associés, 1976
Indian ink and coloured inks

31.7 × 25 cm
Private collection,
Courtesy MEL Publisher

Arzach
Chapter 2, page 6
Published in *Métal hurlant*, no. 2, April 1975
Les Humanoïdes Associés, 1976
Indian ink and coloured inks
28.5 × 22 cm
Deposited by Thierry Smolderen at the Musée de la Bande Dessinée, CIBDI, Angoulême

Ballade
Page 6
Inspired by the poem *Fleur* by Arthur Rimbaud
Published in *L'Homme est-il bon?*, Les Humanoïdes Associés, 1977
Indian ink and coloured inks
35.5 × 27.8 cm
Private collection,
Courtesy MEL Publisher
[repr. p. 130]

José Muñoz
born 1942, Argentina

Alack Sinner
Written by Carlos Sampayo
'Twinkle, Twinkle', page 11
First published in *Charlie Mensuel*, no. 94, November 1976
Alack Sinner, Éditions du Square, 1977; repr.: *Viet Blues*, Casterman, 1986
Indian ink
42.7 × 32.7 cm
Private collection,
Courtesy MEL Publisher
[repr. p. 144]

Alack Sinner
Written by Carlos Sampayo
'Città oscura', page 16
Reprinted in *Flic ou privé*, Casterman, 1983
Indian ink
43 × 31.7 cm
Private collection,
Courtesy MEL Publisher

Thomas Ott
born 1966, Switzerland

Cinema Panopticum
'The Prophet', 16 pages
L'Association, 2005
Scraperboard
18 × 13.5 cm each
Private collection,
Courtesy MEL Publisher
[repr. p. 146]

Hugo Pratt (Ugo Eugenio Pratt)
1927, Italy–1995, Switzerland

Corto Maltese
'L'ange à la fenêtre d'Orient', page 10
First published in *Pif Gadget*, no. 135, 1971
Reprinted in *Les Celtiques*, Casterman, 1980
Indian ink
46.5 × 36 cm
Private collection,
Courtesy MEL Publisher

Corto Maltese: Les Éthiopiques
'Et d'autres Roméos et d'autres Juliettes' ('And of Other Romeos and Other Juliets'), page 11
First published in *Pif Gadget*, no. 204, 1973
Casterman, 1978
Indian ink
In two parts
24.6 × 36 cm each
Private collection
[repr. p. 142]

Corto Maltese, vol. 8: *La Maison dorée de Samarkand*
Bottom of page 68 and top of page 69
First published in *(À suivre)*, 1980, and in *Corto*, 1985–86
Casterman, 1986
Indian ink
67 × 48 cm, in 4 strips
Private collection

La Macumba du gringo
Page 47
First published in *Pilote*, 1977
Éd. Dargaud, 1978
Indian ink
43.5 × 33 cm
Private collection,
Courtesy MEL Publisher
[repr. p. 143]

Joann Sfar
born 1971, France

Klezmer
Books 1 & 2 of vol. 1: *Conquête de l'Est* (*Tales of the Wild East*)
Books 1 & 2 of vol. 2: *Bon anniversaire Scylla* (*Happy Birthday Scylla*)
Manuscript originals of the published editions, Éd. Gallimard, 2005 & 2006
Indian ink and watercolour
24 × 32.5 cm each (open)
Joann Sfar Collection

HISTORY AND MEMORY

Émile Bravo
born 1964, France

L'Espoir malgré tout (*Hope Against All Odds*), vol. 2: *Un peu plus loin vers l'horreur* (*A Few Steps Closer to Horror*)
Pages 47 to 50
Éd. Dupuis, 2019
Indian ink
50 × 32.5 cm each
Émile Bravo Collection
[repr. p. 170]

Emmanuel Guibert
born 1964, France

La Guerre d'Alan (*Alan's War: The Memories of G.I. Alan Cope*), vol. 2
L'Association, 2002
Pages 42 to 45
Indian ink
42 × 30 cm each
Emmanuel Guibert Collection
La Guerre d'Alan (*Alan's War: The Memories of G.I. Alan Cope*), vol. 2
L'Association, 2002
Pages 46 & 47
Indian ink
42 × 29.7 cm each
Emmanuel Guibert Collection

La Guerre d'Alan (*Alan's War: The Memories of G.I. Alan Cope*), vol. 3
2007
L'Association, 2008
Page 114
Indian ink and coloured inks
42 × 30 cm
Emmanuel Guibert Collection

La Guerre d'Alan (*Alan's War: The Memories of G.I. Alan Cope*)
Cover art of the collected edition
L'Association, 2012
Indian ink
42 × 60 cm
Emmanuel Guibert Collection
[repr. pp. 172-173]

Fanny Michaëlis
born 1983, France

Le Lait noir
Pages 77, 78, 86, 87 & 88
Éd. Cornélius, 2016
Graphite pencil
29 × 21 cm
Fanny Michaëlis Collection
[repr. pp. 168–169]

Chantal Montellier
born 1947, France

Tchernobyl mon amour
Page 8
Actes Sud, 2006
Indian ink, graphite pencil, white gouache and collage
42 × 29.7 cm
Private collection,
Courtesy MEL Publisher
[repr. p. 171]

Tchernobyl mon amour
Page 12
Actes Sud, 2006
Digital print, collage, white gouache and graphite pencil
42 × 29.7 cm
Private collection,
Courtesy MEL Publisher

Keiji Nakazawa
1939–2012, Japan

Barefoot Gen
Pages 249 to 255, 271
Published in *Weekly Shonen Jump*, 1973–74
Shueisha, 1975
Indian ink, white gouache, screentone and pasted speech bubbles
Approx. 36.1 × 26 cm each
Hiroshima Peace Memorial Museum
[repr. p. 159]

Joe Sacco
born 1960, Malta

The Underground War in Gaza
4 pages
Published in *The New York Times Magazine*, 2003
Reprinted in *Reportages*, Futuropolis, 2011
Indian ink
40 × 30 cm each
Private collection,
Courtesy MEL Publisher
[repr. p. 164]

Gaza Portfolio
5 pages
Illustrations to accompany a report by Chris Hedges
Published in *Reportages*, Futuropolis, 2011
Indian ink
42.5 × 30 cm each (4 pages), 22.5 × 17.5 cm (1 page)
Private collection,
Courtesy MEL Publisher
[repr. p. 165]

Marjane Satrapi
born 1969, Iran

Persepolis, vol. 1
'The Veil', pages 1 & 3
L'Association, 2000
Indian ink
40.5 × 29.7 cm each
Private collection,
Courtesy MEL Publisher
[repr. p. XX]

Persepolis, vol. 1
'The Veil', pages 2 & 4
L'Association, 2000
Indian ink
40.5 × 29.7 cm each
Private collection – Fondation Boon

Art Spiegelman
born 1948, Sweden

Prisoner on the Hell Planet: A Case History
1972
4 pages
Published in *Short Order Comix*, no. 1, Head Press, 1973

Reprinted in *Breakdowns*,
Nostalgia Press, 1978
Maus, vol. 1, chapter 5: 'Mouse Holes'
Indian ink, collage and opaque white on scraperboard
58.1 × 47 cm each
Art Spiegelman Collection
[repr. p. 157]

Maus
1980–91
17 sketches and preparatory drawings for the eleven chapter openers
Mixed media
Varying dimensions
Art Spiegelman Collection

Maus
Printed inserts of the first seven chapters, packaged with *RAW* magazine nos. 2 to 8 (1980–86)
Art Spiegelman Collection

RAW
Volume 2, nos. 1 to 3
Penguin Books, 1989–91
Including chapters 8, 9 & 10 of *Maus*
Art Spiegelman Collection

Maus #2
Endpaper illustration
Pantheon Books, New York, 1991
Scraperboard
29.8 × 38.1 cm
Art Spiegelman Collection
[repr. p. 158]

Maus #2
1989
Cover flap illustration (1989)
Pantheon Books, New York, 1991
Indian ink and opaque white
41.9 × 33 cm
Art Spiegelman Collection
[repr. p. 156]

Maus #2
Flammarion, 1992
Opening of the eleventh and final chapter (previously unpublished)
Private collection

Maus, collected edition, 1996
Endpaper illustration
Scraperboard
29.8 × 38.1 cm
Art Spiegelman Collection
[repr. p. 158]

Jacques Tardi
born 1946, France

C'était la guerre des tranchées (It Was the War of the Trenches)
Pages 52 to 55
1992–93
First published in *(À suivre)*, no. 181, February 1993
Casterman, 1993
Screentones and Indian ink
44 × 32.5 cm each
Jacques Tardi Collection
[repr. p. 161]

C'était la guerre des tranchées (It Was the War of the Trenches)
Cover art for the monthly magazine *(À suivre)*, no. 185, March 1993
Indian ink and coloured ink
37.2 × 28.7 cm each
Jacques Tardi Collection
C'était la guerre des tranchées (It Was the War of the Trenches)
Illustration from the closing image section in the 2014 edition
Coloured ink on print
40 × 29.7 cm
Jacques Tardi Collection
[repr. p. 160]

Moi René Tardi, prisonnier de guerre au Stalag II B (I, Rene Tardi, Prisoner of War in Stalag II B), vol. 1
Pages 55 to 58
2011
Casterman, 2012
Indian ink
44.2 × 32.5 cm
Jacques Tardi Collection
[repr. p. 162]

Cover art, *Le Monde*, special issue, no. 39: *14–18. Les leçons d'une guerre*, February 2014
Indian ink and coloured ink
44 × 32.5 cm
Jacques Tardi Collection

Élise et les nouveaux partisans
Written by Dominique Grange
Pages 69 to 72
2020
Éd. Delcourt, 2021
Indian ink
43.8 × 32.5 cm each
Jacques Tardi Collection
[repr. p. 163]

PERSONAL STORIES

David B.
(Pierre-François Beauchard)
born 1959, France

L'Ascension du Haut Mal (Epileptic)
Cover art for volumes 1 to 6
L'Association, 1996–2003
Indian ink
Varying dimensions: from 31.8 to 34 × 47.5 to 64.5 cm
Private collection, Courtesy MEL Publisher
[repr. p. 182]

L'Ascension du Haut Mal (Epileptic), vol. 6
Page 1
L'Association, 2003
Indian ink
50 × 32.5 cm
Thierry Mallet Collection
[repr. p. 183]

L'Ascension du Haut Mal (Epileptic), vol. 6
Pages 81 to 86
L'Association, 2003
Indian ink
47.2 × 32.5 cm each
Private collection, Courtesy MEL Publisher

Edmond Baudoin
born 1942, France

Le Chemin de Saint-Jean
Page 71
L'Association, 2002
Indian ink, white gouache, print and collage
41 × 27 cm
Donation of Edmond Baudoin, loaned from the Musée de la Bande Dessinée, CIBDI, Angoulême
[repr. p. 180]

Les Fleurs de cimetière
Pages 113, 114 & 116
L'Association, 2021
Indian ink, watercolour, white gouache, print and collage
29.9 × 21 cm each
Donation of Edmond Baudoin, loaned from the Musée de la Bande Dessinée, CIBDI, Angoulême

Alison Bechdel
born 1960, USA

Fun Home
Chapter 4: 'In the Shadow of Young Girls in Flower', pages 2 & 3
Chapter 7: 'The Antihero's Journey', page 25
Houghton Mifflin Company, Boston, 2006
Indian ink, pencil, colours on transparent film
37.5 × 28 cm each
Private collection, Courtesy MEL Publisher
[repr. p. 179]

Étienne Davodeau
born 1965, France

Le Droit du sol. Journal d'un vertige
Pages 51, 53, 54 & 55
2020
Futuropolis, 2021
Indian ink and wash
42 × 29.7 cm each
Étienne Davodeau Collection
[repr. p. 186]

Dominique Goblet
born 1967, Belgium

Faire semblant c'est mentir (Pretending is Lying)
Cover art & chapter 1, pages 8 to 13
L'Association, 2007
Graphite pencil, wax pencil and oil
29.7 × 21 cm each
Dominique Goblet Collection
[repr. pp. 184–185]

Aline Kominsky-Crumb
1948, USA–2022, France

The Bunch Has A Friend
1975
2 pages
Published in *The Bunch's Power Pak Comics*
Kitchen Sink Press, 1979
Indian ink
35.5 × 28 cm each
Erwin and Alfred Bergdoll Collection of Underground Comics and Original Art
The Ohio State University Billy Ireland Cartoon Library & Museum

Twisted Sisters, no. 1
Cover art
Last Gasp, San Francisco, June 1976
Indian ink
35.5 × 23 cm
Erwin and Alfred Bergdoll Collection of Underground Comics and Original Art
The Ohio State University Billy Ireland Cartoon Library & Museum
[repr. p. 178]

Ulli Lust (Ulli Schneider)
born 1967, Austria

Heute ist der letzte Tag vom Rest deines Lebens (Today is the Last Day of the Rest of Your Life)
Avant Verlag, Berlin, 2009
Pages 226, 228, 229 & 230
Graphite pencil
42 × 29.7 cm each
Ulli Lust Collection
[repr. p. 187]

Fabrice Neaud
born 1968, France

Journal (I), February 1992–September 1993
Chapter 15, pages 18 & 19; chapter 8, page 1
Ego comme X, 1996
Indian ink
42 × 29.7 cm each
Private collection, Courtesy MEL Publisher
[repr. p. 181]

Journal (I), September 1993–December 1993
Chapter 3, page 7
Ego comme X, 1996
Indian ink
42 × 29.7 cm each
Private collection, Courtesy MEL Publisher

Notebook with notes and sketches for *Le Dernier Sergent*, vol. 1
9 October 1999–28 March 2000
108 pages
Mixed media: Pilot-G-Tec-C, felt-tip, black ballpoint, collage
21.5 × 15 cm (closed)
[repr. p. XX]

Spiral-bound notebook
Summer 2006–5 March 2007
50 pages
Original handdrawn pages, G-Tec-C, pen and Indian ink
42 × 29.7 cm
Fabrice Neaud Collection

Notebook
24 May 2013–November 2013
Preprinted panels, Pilot G-Tec-C, pen and Indian ink
29.7 × 21 cm (closed)
Fabrice Neaud Collection

Spiral-bound notebook
Undated, c. 2015–2020
8 pages
Illustrations, G-Tec-C, pen and Indian ink, graphite
42 × 29.7 cm
Fabrice Neaud Collection

Riad Sattouf
born 1978, France

L'Arabe du futur (*The Arab of the Future*), vol. 1: *Une jeunesse au Moyen-Orient (1978–1984)* (*A Childhood in the Middle East, 1978–1984*)
2013
Complete storyboard
Graphite pencil
29.7 × 21 cm
Riad Sattouf Collection

L'Arabe du futur (*The Arab of the Future*), vol. 1: *Une jeunesse au Moyen-Orient (1978–1984)* (*A Childhood in the Middle East, 1978–1984*)
Pages 1 to 4
Allary Éditions, 2014
Indian ink
30 × 21 cm each
Riad Sattouf Collection
[repr. p. 189]

Yoshihiro Tatsumi
1935–2015, Japan

A Drifting Life
Seirinkogeisha, 2008, 2 vols.
Heading illustrations for chapters 20, 31 & 45, created between 1999 and 2006
Indian ink, white gouache, screentones and collage
36 × 26 cm each
Private collection

Lewis Trondheim
(Laurent Chabosy)
born 1964, France

Approximativement (*Approximate Continuum Comics*)
Pages 53 to 57
Éd. Cornélius, 1995
Indian ink
29.5 × 21 cm each
Artist's collection
[repr. p. 188]

EVERYDAY LIFE

Marion Fayolle
born 1988, France

La Maison nue (*The Naked House*)
'L'effeuillage', pages 1 to 8
Éd. Magnani, 2022
Rhodoid sheets and Indian ink
Pages 1 to 7: 31 × 22.7 cm each, page 8: 29.4 × 44.7 cm
Private collection, Courtesy MEL Publisher
[repr. pp. 202–203]

Joanna Hellgren
born 1981, Sweden

Frances, vol. 3
Ordfront Galago, 2012
Pages 8 to 11
Graphite pencil
29.7 × 21 cm each
Joanna Hellgren Collection
[repr. pp. 208–209]

Hergé (Georges Remi)
1907–83, Belgium)

Les Bijoux de la Castafiore (*The Castafiore Emerald*)
Pages 22 to 24
First published in *Tintin*, 1961–62
Casterman, 1963
Indian ink and gouache
47.9 × 35.6 cm approx.
Fondation Hergé
[repr. p. 192]

Les Bijoux de la Castafiore (*The Castafiore Emerald*)
Page 59
First published in *Tintin*, 1961–62
Casterman, 1963
Indian ink and gouache
47.8 × 35.6 cm
Fondation Hergé
[repr. p. 193]

Les Bijoux de la Castafiore (*The Castafiore Emerald*)
1962
Blueline proof for page 59 for *Tintin* magazine
Watercolour on printed proof
Approx. 30 × 21 cm
Fondation Hergé

Les Bijoux de la Castafiore (*The Castafiore Emerald*)
1962
Pencil outline for page 59
Graphite pencil
Approx. 55 × 36.5 cm
Fondation Hergé

Camille Jourdy
born 1979, France

Rosalie Blum, vol. 1: *Une impression de déjà-vu*
Pages 38, 39, 41, 42, 43
Actes Sud, 2007
Indian ink and watercolour
Approx. 29 × 20 cm each
Camille Jourdy Collection
[repr. p. 204]

André Juillard
born 1948, Paris

Le Cahier bleu (*The Blue Notebook*), vol. 1
Cover art
Casterman, 1994
Indian ink and watercolour
33 × 49 cm
9ᵉ Art Références Collection, Paris

Le Long Voyage de Léna (*Lena's Odyssey*)
Written by Pierre Christin
Page 13
Éd. Dargaud, 2006
Indian ink and watercolour
45 × 34.2 cm
Private collection, Courtesy MEL Publisher
[repr. p. 205]

Richard McGuire
born 1957, USA

Here
Pantheon, New York, 2014
Digital artwork
Video presenting the entire work
[repr. pp. 198–199]

David Prudhomme
born 1969, France
Pascal Rabaté
born 1961, France

Vive la marée!
Cover art and page 42
Futuropolis, 2015
Graphite pencil and Indian ink
42 × 29.7 cm each
Private collection, Courtesy MEL Publisher
[repr. p. 207]

Vive la marée!
Page 10
Futuropolis, 2015
Graphite pencil and Indian ink
42 × 29.7 cm
Pascal Rabaté Collection

Anna Sommer
born 1968, Switzerland

Damen Dramen
'Die Frau aus der Zoohandlung', pages 5 to 9
L'Association, 1996
Indian ink and white gouache
42 × 29.7 cm each
Anna Sommer Collection
[repr. p. 206]

Yū Takita
1932–90, Japan

View over a Rainy Backstreet
c. 1970
Indian ink and watercolour
30.2 × 24.2 cm
Private collection, Courtesy MEL Publisher

Untitled
c. 1970
Indian ink and watercolour
37.5 × 21 cm
Private collection, Courtesy MEL Publisher

Untitled
c. 1970
Indian ink
40.5 × 33 cm
Private collection, Courtesy MEL Publisher

Somehow Sumeko Is 17 Years Old
Between 1970 and 1975
Title page artwork for the magazine *Myojo*
Indian ink and watercolour
37 × 26 cm
Private collection, Courtesy MEL Publisher

Kiyoshi
c. 1980
Indian ink
40.5 × 33 cm
Private collection, Courtesy MEL Publisher

Kiyoshi and his Mother
c. 1980
Indian ink
36 × 28 cm
Private collection, Courtesy MEL Publisher

Jirō Taniguchi
1947–2017, Japan

Aruku Hito (*The Walking Man*)
Chapter 8, page 11
First published in *Bang*, no. 3
Casterman, 2003
Indian ink and screentones
36.5 × 26.5 cm
Private collection
[repr. p. 196]

Inu wo Kau (*Land of Dreams*), 1991
'The View of the Garden', p. 12 & 13

Casterman, 2005
Indian ink and screentones
39.1 × 27 cm each
Furari Co., Ltd.
[repr. p. 197]

Yoshihiro Tatsumi
1935–2015, Japan

Untitled
c. 1970
Indian ink, gouache and watercolour
36.2 × 52.5 cm
Private collection,
Courtesy MEL Publisher
[repr. pp. 194–195]

Chris Ware
born 1967, USA

Jimmy Corrigan: The Smartest Kid on Earth
First published in *Acme Novelty Library*
Pantheon Books, 2000
Indian ink and blue pencil
60.5 × 38.1 cm
Private collection,
Courtesy MEL Publisher

Building Stories
'Spring', 'Summer', 'Fall', 'Winter'
2003
Ink, non-photo pencil, white gouache
Pantheon Books, 2012
Indian ink
69.9 × 50.8 cm each
Chris Ware Collection, courtesy Galerie Martel

Building Stories
'Actual Size'
Pantheon Books, 2012
Ink, graphite pencil and gouache on Bristol board
74 × 101.5 cm
Chris Ware Collection, courtesy Galerie Martel
[repr. pp. 200–201]

Rusty Brown
First published in *Acme Novelty Library*
Pantheon Books, New York, 2019
Indian ink, white gouache and blue pencil
71.5 × 51 cm
Private collection,
Courtesy MEL Publisher

LITERATURE

Pénélope Bagieu
born 1982, France

Sacrées sorcières (*The Witches*)
Based on the novel by Roald Dahl (1983)
Pages 141 to 152
Gallimard Jeunesse, 2020
Digital artwork
Courtesy David Highams Associates Ltd and Roald Dahl Story Company
[repr. p. 227]

Dino Battaglia
1923–83, Italy

La caduta della casa degli Usher (*The Fall of the House of Usher*)
Based on the story by Edgar Allan Poe (1839)
Page I
Published in *Linus*, no. 50, 1969
Indian ink
37.2 × 26.7 cm
Pietro Alligo Collection
[repr. p. 214]

Il Golem (*The Golem*)
Based on the novel by Gustav Meyrink (1915)
Page I
Published in *Linus*, no. 74, 1971
Reprinted in *Totentanz*, Milano Libri, 1972
Indian ink
36.5 × 25.2 cm
Pietro Alligo Collection

Lo strano caso del Dottor Jekyll e del Signor Hyde (*The Strange Case of Dr Jekyll and Mr Hyde*)
Written by Dino and Laura Battaglia
Based on the novel by Robert Louis Stevenson (1886)
Page I
Published in *Linus*, no. 106, January 1974
Indian ink
36.7 × 25.8 cm
Pietro Alligo Collection

La Signorina Fifi (*Mademoiselle Fifi*)
Based on the short story by Guy de Maupassant (1882)
Page I
Published in *Linus*, no. 150, 1977
Reprinted in *Battaglia raconta Maupassant*, Milano Libri, 1978
Indian ink
35.5 × 26.2 cm
Pietro Alligo Collection

Alberto Breccia
1919, Uruguay–1993, Argentina

Caperucita roja (*Little Red Riding Hood*)
1980
Based on the tale by the Brothers Grimm (c. 1857)
Pages 2 to 4
Published in *Hurra*, undated
Reprinted in *Qui a peur des contes de fées?*, Revival, 2019
Coloured paper cut and pasted on cardboard, gouache
40 × 29.5 cm each
Deposit by the rights holders of Alberto Breccia at the Musée de la Bande Dessinée, CIBDI, Angoulême
[repr. p. 216]

Dracula
Freely based on the novel by Bram Stoker (1897)
Chapter 3, pages 4 & 6
Les Humanoïdes Associés, 1993; repr. Rackham, 2006
Gouache on paper mounted on cardboard, varnish
47.7 × 33.1 cm each
Deposit by the rights holders of Alberto Breccia at the Musée de la Bande Dessinée, CIBDI, Angoulême

Dracula
Freely based on the novel by Bram Stoker (1897)
Chapter 3, page 5
Les Humanoïdes Associés, 1993; repr. Rackham, 2006
Gouache on paper mounted on cardboard, varnish
48 × 33.5 cm
Private collection,
Courtesy MEL Publisher
[repr. p. 217]

Informe sobre ciegos (*Report on the Blind*)
based on the novel *On Heroes and Tombs* by Ernesto Sabato (1961)
Page 27
French ed.: Vertige Graphic, 1993
Indian ink, white gouache and collage
50.4 × 36.5 cm
Private collection,
Courtesy MEL Publisher
[repr. p. 215]

Informe sobre ciegos (*Report on the Blind*)
based on the novel *On Heroes and Tombs* by Ernesto Sabato (1961)
Pages 26 & 28
French ed.: Vertige Graphic, 1993
Indian ink, white gouache and collage
50.4 × 36.5 cm each
Deposit by the rights holders of Alberto Breccia at the Musée de la Bande Dessinée, CIBDI, Angoulême

Rébecca Dautremer
born 1971, France

Des souris et des hommes (*Of Mice and Men*)
Based on the novel by John Steinbeck (1937)
Chapter 4, pages 27 to 34
Éd. Tishina, 2020
Acrylic, gouache and coloured pencil
42 × 63 cm each
Rébecca Dautremer Collection, Courtesy Éditions Tishina / Galerie Robillard
[repr. pp. 222–223]

Luz (Renald Luzier)
born 1972, France

Vernon Subutex, vol. 1
Based on the novel by Virginie Despentes (2015 & 2017)
Pages 249 to 252
Éd. Albin Michel, 2020
Indian ink and gouache, collages
38 × 27.8 cm
Private collection,
Courtesy MEL Publisher
With the kind permission of Luz and Virginie Despentes
[repr. p. 225]

Gary Panter
born 1950, USA

Jimbo in Purgatory
Based on *The Divine Comedy* by Dante Alighieri (14th century)
Pages 15, 19 & 32
Fantagraphics Books, Seattle, 2004
Indian ink
58.4 × 41.9 cm each
Collection of KAWS
[repr. p. 224]

Posy Simmonds
born 1945, UK

Gemma Bovery
Freely inspired by the novel *Madame Bovary* by Gustave Flaubert (1857)
'Normandy', pages 4, 5, 6, 51 & 64
First published in *The Guardian*, 1997
Jonathan Cape, 1999
42 × 29.7 cm each
Indian ink, coloured inks, graphite pencil and felt-tip
Posy Simmonds Collection
[repr. p. 226]

Jacques Tardi
born 1946, France

Brouillard au pont de Tolbiac (*Fog over Tolbiac Bridge*)
Based on the novel by Léo Malet (1956)
Cover art for *(À suivre)*, no. 40, 1981
Casterman, 1982
Indian ink
29.5 × 25 cm
Bernadette Bienfait Collection

Brouillard au pont de Tolbiac (*Fog over Tolbiac Bridge*)
Based on the novel by Léo Malet (1956)
Pages 60 & 64

First published in *(À suivre)*,
no. 40, 1981
Casterman, 1982
Indian ink and white gouache
44.2 × 32.5 cm each
Private collection,
Courtesy MEL Publisher
[repr. p. 218]

Casse-pipe à la Nation
(Death of a Marseilles Man)
Based on the novel by Léo Malet
(1957)
Cover art for *(À suivre)*, no. 217, 1996
Indian ink and coloured inks
39 × 32.3 cm
Private collection,
Courtesy MEL Publisher
[repr. p. 219]

Winshluss
(Vincent Paronnaud)
born 1970, France

Pinocchio
Freely inspired by the novel
by Carlo Collodi (1881)
'Tattoo'
2003
Unpublished
Indian ink, gouache and
coloured ink
32 × 25 cm
Private collection, Courtesy Galerie
Georges-Philippe & Nathalie Vallois

Pinocchio
Freely inspired by the novel
by Carlo Collodi (1881)
Unused cover art sketch
2008
Graphite pencil
40 × 29.5 cm
Private collection, Courtesy Galerie
Georges-Philippe & Nathalie Vallois
[repr. p. 221]

Pinocchio
Freely inspired by the novel
by Carlo Collodi (1881)
'Natural Born', pages 58 to 61
Les Requins Marteaux, 2008
Indian ink, white gouache and
wax pencil
40.2 × 29.7 cm
Private collection,
Courtesy MEL Publisher

Pinocchio
Freely inspired by the novel
by Carlo Collodi (1881)
Page 130
Les Requins Marteaux, 2008
Indian ink and gouache
42 × 29.5 cm
Private collection, Courtesy Galerie
Georges-Philippe & Nathalie Vallois

Pinocchio
Freely inspired by the novel
by Carlo Collodi (1881)
Page 148
Les Requins Marteaux, 2008
Watercolour, ink and correction fluid
32 × 22 cm
Private collection, Courtesy Galerie
Georges-Philippe & Nathalie Vallois
[repr.p. 220]

The 'Literature' room hosts a
sound installation by Sébastien
Gaxie, composer in residence
at Ircam, with support from
the composers in residence
programme of SACEM,
for the year 2024
'Echoes of Words and Drawings'
May 2024
A commission for Ircam – Centre
Pompidou
Spatial electro-acoustic soundtrack
60 mins.
With the voices of Geoffrey Carey,
Adèle Dessard, La FAME Lyon,
Sébastien Gaxie, Frédéric Gustaedt,
Hugues Jourdain, Carlo Laurenzi,
Deborah Lopatin, Paola Palumbo,
Iris Tripodi and Emmanuelle Zoll
Musician: Yom
Digital music producer: Manuel
Poletti
Sound engineers: Jérémie Henrot
& Ryo Baldet

SCIENCE FICTION

Neal Adams
1941–2022, USA

Superman, no. 204
Cover art, inked by Mike Esposito
DC Comics, New York,
February 1968
Indian ink, white gouache and
collage
44.4 × 28.7 cm
Private collection
[repr. p. 240]

John Buscema
1927–2002, USA

Marvel Calendar: The Silver Surfer
Cover art, inked by Sal Buscema
Marvel Comics Group, New York,
1981
Indian ink, white gouache
and collage
52.6 × 36 cm
Private collection

Prince Namor, the Sub-Mariner,
no. 2: 'Cry… Triton!'
Cover art, inked by Frank Giacoia
Marvel Comics Group, New York,
June 1968
Indian ink, white gouache
and collage
58.6 × 44.5 cm
Private collection

Gene Colan
1926–2011, USA

Daredevil, no. 44: 'I, Murderer!'
Cover art, inked by Jim Steranko
Marvel Comics Group, New York,
September 1968
Character created in 1964
by Stan Lee & Bill Everett
Indian ink, white gouache and
collage
44 × 28 cm
9ᵉ Art Références Collection, Paris
[repr. p. 239]

Philippe Druillet
born 1944, France

Yragaël ou la fin des temps
Written by Michel Demuth
Page 26
Published in *Pilote*, no. 727,
11 October 1973
Éd. Dargaud, 1974
Indian ink and white gouache
78.5 × 60 cm
Private collection,
Courtesy MEL Publisher

Yragaël ou la fin des temps
Written by Michel Demuth
Page 39
Published in *Pilote*, no. 727,
11 October 1973
Éd. Dargaud, 1974
Indian ink and white gouache
88 × 66 cm
Private collection,
Courtesy MEL Publisher

Lone Sloane, vol. 1: *Salammbô*
Freely based on the novel by
Gustave Flaubert (1862)
Page 8
Published in *Métal hurlant*, no. 48,
February 1980
Éd. Dargaud, 1982
Indian ink and white gouache
95 × 75 cm
Private collection,
Courtesy MEL Publisher

Lone Sloane, vol. 4: *Gail*
Pages 8–9
Self-published, 1978; repr.
Les Humanoïdes Associés, 1982
Indian ink and white gouache
102 × 66.5 cm
Private collection,
Courtesy MEL Publisher
[repr. p. 230]

Lone Sloane, vol. 4: *Gail*
Pages 10–11
Self-published, 1978; repr.
Les Humanoïdes Associés, 1982
Indian ink and white gouache
103 × 67.5 cm
Private collection,
Courtesy MEL Publisher
[repr. p. 231]

Dave Gibbons
born 1949, UK

Watchmen
Written by Alan Moore
Chapter 7, page 28
DC Comics, New York, 1986
Indian ink and collage
47 × 30.3 cm
Private collection – Fondation Boon
[repr. p. 242]

Watchmen
Written by Alan Moore
Chapter 10, page 28
DC Comics, New York, 1986
Indian ink and collage
46 × 30 cm
Private collection – Fondation Boon
[repr. p. 243]

Gil Kane (Eli Katz)
1926, Latvia–2000, USA

Marvel Treasury Edition, no. 14:
The Sensational Spider-Man
Unpublished cover art, inked by
Franck Giacoia
Marvel Comics Group, March 1977
Indian ink
44.5 × 29.1 cm
Private collection

Jack Kirby (Jacob Kurtzberg)
1917–94, USA

Fantastic Four, no. 95:
'Tomorrow – World War Three!'
Cover art, inked by Joe Sinnott
Marvel Comics Group, New York,
February 1970
Characters created in 1961
Indian ink, white gouache and
collage
44 × 29 cm
9ᵉ Art Références Collection, Paris
[repr. p. 236]

Thor, no. 257: 'Death, Thou Shalt
Die!'
Cover art, inked by Joe Sinnott
Marvel Comics Group, New York,
March 1977
Character created in 1962
Indian ink and collage
43 × 28 cm
9ᵉ Art Références Collection, Paris
[repr. p. 237]

Frank Miller
born 1957, USA

The Dark Knight Returns
Titan Books, London, 1997
Cover art
Indian ink and graphite pencil
48 × 30 cm
[repr. p. 241]

Mœbius (Jean Giraud)
1938–2012, France

Le Garage hermétique de Jerry Cornélius (The Airtight Garage)
Page 71
First published in *Métal hurlant*, 1976
Reprinted in *Major fatal*, Les Humanoïdes Associés, 1979
Indian ink
32 × 24 cm
Private collection,
Courtesy MEL Publisher

Starwatcher
Published in *Starwatcher*, Aedena, 1986; repr.: Casterman, 1992
Indian ink and watercolour
15.9 × 12.3 cm
Private collection,
Courtesy MEL Publisher
[repr. p. 234]

Upon a Star
Cover art
US edition of *Sur l'étoile*,
Epic Comics, 1987
Reprinted in the new edition of *Le monde d'Edena*, vol. 1, *Sur l'étoile*, Casterman, 2001
Indian ink and coloured inks on cardboard
32.5 × 24.9 cm
Private collection,
Courtesy MEL Publisher
[repr. p. 233]

Untitled
1988
Published in the artbook *Chroniques métalliques*
Les Humanoïdes Associés, 1992
Indian ink and coloured inks
79.5 × 59.5 cm
Private collection,
Courtesy MEL Publisher

Le Monde d'Edena (The World of Edena), vol. 3: *La Déesse (The Goddess)*
Page 35
First published in *(À suivre)*
Casterman, 1990
Indian ink and white gouache
43.8 × 32.5 cm
Private collection,
Courtesy MEL Publisher
[repr. p. 232]

Frederik Peeters
born 1974, Switzerland

Aâma, vol. 4: *Tu seras merveilleuse, ma fille (You Will Be Glorious, My Daughter)*
Pages 4, 5, 6 & 7
Éd. Gallimard, 2014
51 × 37.5 cm each
Private collection,
Courtesy MEL Publisher
[repr. p. 235]

Marie Severin
1929–2018, USA

Captain America, no. 124
Cover art, inked by Joe Sinnott
Marvel Comics Group, New York, April 1971
Character created in 1940 by Joe Simon and Jack Kirby
Indian ink and collage
44.4 × 29.3 cm
Private collection
[repr. p. 238]

Osamu Tezuka
1928–89, Japan

Astro Boy
Title page artwork
Kobunsha, 1956
Character created in 1952
Indian ink
38.6 × 27.3 cm
Private collection,
Courtesy MEL Publisher
[repr. p. 244]

Astro Boy
'Robio and Robiette'
Title page artwork
Published in *Shonen Magazine*, May 1965
Reprinted in *Astro Boy*, vol. 14, Kōdansha
Character created in 1952
Indian ink, coloured ink, gouache and graphite pencil
36.6 × 25.6 cm
Private collection,
Courtesy MEL Publisher
[repr. p. 245]

CITIES

Nicolas de Crécy
born 1966, France

Le Bibendum céleste (The Celestial Bibendum), vol. 3
Page 35
Les Humanoïdes Associés, 2001
Indian ink, gouache and acrylic
32.5 × 23.6 cm
Private collection,
Courtesy MEL Publisher
[repr. p. 253]

Archi & BD, la ville dessinée
(eds. Jean-Marc Thévenet & Francis Rambert)
Cover art
Monografik / Cité de l'Architecture et du Patrimoine, 2010
Indian ink, gouache and watercolour
39.3 × 30 cm
Private collection,
Courtesy MEL Publisher

Kawabata Dori
Published in *Carnets de Kyoto*, Éditions du Chêne, 2012
Charcoal
50 × 71 cm
Private collection,
Courtesy MEL Publisher

The Cathedral, version 2
Unpublished art created for this exhibition
2023
Inks, watercolour and acrylic
93 × 138 cm
Nicolas de Crécy Collection
[repr. pp. 254–255]

Will Eisner (William Erwin Eisner)
1917–2005, USA

A Contract with God
Back cover art
Kitchen Sink Press, 1985
Indian ink, white gouache, pencil and wax pencil
25 × 32 cm
Peter Janda Collection
[repr. p. 248]

City People Notebook
'Empty Street'
Comics USA, 1989
Unpublished illustration
Indian ink
35.5 × 28 cm
Peter Janda Collection
[repr. p. 249]

Big City, vol. 1: *New York*
1984
Cover art
Kitchen Sink Press, 1986
Indian ink and coloured inks
30 × 42 cm
Peter Janda Collection

Marc-Antoine Mathieu
born 1959, France

Julius Corentin Acquefacques, vol. 3: *Le Processus*
Page 29
Éd. Delcourt, 1993
Indian ink
35.5 × 26 cm
Private collection,
Courtesy MEL Publisher

Julius Corentin Acquefacques, vol. 4: *L'Épaisseur du miroir*
'1. Le début de la fin', pages 21 & 22
Éd. Delcourt, 1995
Indian ink
35.5 × 26.2 cm
Private collection,
Courtesy MEL Publisher
[repr. p. 259]

Julius Corentin Acquefacques, vol. 4: *L'Épaisseur du miroir*
'2. La fin du début', page 7
Éd. Delcourt, 1995
Indian ink
35.3 × 26 cm
Private collection,
Courtesy MEL Publisher

Julius Corentin Acquefacques, vol. 4: *L'Épaisseur du miroir*
'2. La fin du début', page 17
Éd. Delcourt, 1995
Indian ink
35.5 × 26.2 cm
Private collection,
Courtesy MEL Publisher

Julius Corentin Acquefacques, vol. 4: *L'Épaisseur du miroir*
'2. La fin du début', page 18
Éd. Delcourt, 1995
Indian ink
35.5 × 26.2 cm
Private collection,
Courtesy MEL Publisher
[repr. p. 258]

François Schuiten
born 1956, Belgium

Les Cités obscures, with Benoît Peeters
L'Archiviste
Page 6: 'Brüsel, dernière sortie du tram 81'
Casterman, 1987
Indian ink and acrylic
50.6 × 36.3 cm
François Schuiten Collection

Les Cités obscures, with Benoît Peeters, vol. 3: *La Tour*
Pages 2 & 3
Casterman, 1987
Indian ink
50 × 36.5 cm each
Bibliothèque Nationale de France, Rare Books Archive
[repr. p. 251]

Les Cités obscures, with Benoît Peeters, vol. 4: *La Route d'Armilia*
Page 29
Casterman, 1988
Indian ink and acrylic
53.5 × 44 cm
François Schuiten Collection
[repr. p. 252]

Les Cités obscures, with Benoît Peeters, vol. 4: *La Route d'Armilia*
Page 30
Casterman, 1988
Indian ink and acrylic
49.7 × 36.6 cm
Private collection,
Courtesy MEL Publisher

Les Cités obscures, with Benoît Peeters, vol. 6: *L'Enfant penchée*
Pages 8 & 9
Casterman, 1996
Indian ink
61.5 × 44.2 cm each
Bibliothèque Nationale de France, Rare Books Archive

La Barbarie (novel by
Jacques Abeille)
Cover art
Le Tripode, Paris, 2011
Indian ink
61 × 44 cm
Private collection

Revoir Paris, vol. 2: *La Nuit des constellations*
Written by Benoît Peeters
Pages 98 & 99
Casterman, 2016
Ink, acrylic, graphite pencil
59.8 × 43 cm each
François Schuiten Collection
[repr. p. 250]

Seth (Gregory Gallant)
born 1962, Canada

Clyde Fans
Drawn & Quarterly, Montreal, 2019
Published in *Palookaville*, no. 23, 2017
Part 5: '1957'
Pages 27 to 33
Indian ink, white gouache and collage
48.3 × 34.3 cm each
Seth Collection
[repr. pp. 256–257]

Dominion (fragment)
c. 2014
Painted cardboard
Seth Collection

GEOMETRY

Guido Crepax
1933–2003, Italy

Bianca. La casa matta
1969
Page 28
Bianca. Una storia eccessiva,
Éd. Morgan, 1972
Indian ink
51 × 36.8 cm
Private collection,
Courtesy MEL Publisher
[repr. p. 266]

Valentina nel metro
Published in *Il Corriere d'informazione*, 1975
Charlie Mensuel, no. 92,
September 1976
Reprinted in *Valentina assassina?*,
Milano Libri, 1977
Indian ink
70 × 43 cm
Private collection,
Courtesy MEL Publisher

Valentina: 'Anthropology'
Published in *Linus*, 1977–78
Reprinted in *Il Ritratto di Valentina*,
Milano Libri, 1979
Page 51
Indian ink
51 × 36.8 cm
Private collection,
Courtesy MEL Publisher
[repr. p. 267]

Valentina: *Dixie Dugan*
Inspired by the work of
J. P. McEvoy
Page 6
Published in *Glamour International Magazine*, no. 4, 1982
Indian ink
51 × 36.8 cm
Private collection,
Courtesy MEL Publisher

Jochen Gerner
born 1970, France

RG
'Mégacycle'
2013–15
Pages 1 to 12
(from a full set of 34 pages)
L'Association, 2016
Indian ink
27 × 21 cm each
Private collection,
Courtesy MEL Publisher
[repr. p. 269]

RG
'Ectoplasme'
2013–15
Pages 1 to 6 and 8 to 13
(from a full set of 22 pages)
L'Association, 2016
Indian ink
27 × 21 cm each
Private collection,
Courtesy MEL Publisher
[repr. p. 268]

Martin Panchaud
born 1982, Switzerland

Die Farbe der Dinge
(*La Couleur des choses*)
Pages 20 to 29
Ça et Là, 2022
Digital artwork
[repr. pp. 270–271]

Chris Ware
born 1967, USA

Supermouse
2019
Ink, non-photo pencil and white gouache
51 × 74 cm
Chris Ware Collection,
Courtesy Galerie Martel

Pedantry & Pedagogy – Mother
2020
Ink, non-photo pencil and white gouache
50 × 71 cm
Chris Ware Collection,
Courtesy Galerie Martel

Poster art for the 49th Angoulême International Comics Festival
2022
Ink, non-photo pencil and white gouache
76.2 × 101.6 cm
Chris Ware Collection,
Courtesy Galerie Martel
[repr. pp. 272–273]

Yūichi Yokoyama
born 1967, Japan

Doboku (*Public Works*)
c. 2005
Pages 1 to 6
Indian ink
32 × 26.7 cm each
Private collection,
Courtesy MEL Publisher
[repr. pp. 264–265]

Blutch
(Christian Hincker)
born 1967, France

'She looks just like you', based on *Hypocrite and the Loch Ness Monster* by Jean-Claude Forest
2024
Wall art created for this exhibition
Original illustration: Indian ink, coloured inks and gouache
65 × 80 cm
[repr. pp. 26–27]

Chris Ware
born 1967, USA

Drawing Table
2024
Wall art created for this exhibition
Original artwork: ink, blue pencil and white gouache on Bristol board, digital colour
76.2 × 101.6 cm
[repr. pp. 274–275]

EXHIBITION

Curators
Anne Lemonnier
Emmanuèle Payen

Scientific curators
Thierry Groensteen
Lucas Hureau

Project director
Mathilde Tissot
Assisted by
Apolline Michel Garcia

Architect and scenographer
Laurence Le Bris

Registrar
Margot Giusiano

Exhibition space manager
Pierre Dusaussoy

Lighting
Arnaud Jung

Installation and hanging
Philippe Chagnon, manager
Lucas Chol
Carlos Contreras
Philippe Delapierre
Pierre Herman
Jérôme Tillaud

Layout of documents
James Caritey
Lucia Varas

Electricians
Jonathan Faustin Girault
Marc Mameaux
Rémi Navarro

Carpenters
Léo Garion
Quentin Hascoat
Patrice Richard
Pierre Roncier

Painters
Lamri Bouaoune
Elsa Noual
Orion Papleka
Sofiane Saal
Philippe Stricher

Audiovisual production manager
Rebecca Edou

Head of audiovisual production
Alexandre Lebugle

Head of audiovisual storage
Mourade Rennou

Audiovisual technicians
Christophe Bechter
Éric Hagopian
Emmanuel Rodoreda

Image and sound processing
Jacques-Yves Renaud
Anouck Schmidt

Head of video
Nicolas Gendrault

Directors
Astrid de Cazalet
Lucia Barahona

Editing/graphics
Yann Bellet
Michaël Mallart

Sound engineers
Ivan Gariel
Bastien Pigeon

Video technician
Cyril Lecomte-Languerand

Head of photography
Alice Tremblais

Photography technician
Brunot Descout

Health and safety
David Martin

Heads of cultural outreach
Célia Crétien
Clara Gouraud
Annick Liot

Soundscape in 'Literature' room
Emmanuelle Zoll
Margot Fuchst

Reading rooms
Émilie Fissier
Barbara Arellano
Marc Guillemot

Communications officer
Marie Joly

Public relations officer
Claire Mayran

Press officers
Céline Janvier
Marine Prévot

Assistant sponsorship officer
Ysé Collomb

Graphic design
Studio Matters

Signage
Œil de Lynx

Musée national d'art moderne-Centre de création industrielle

Director
Xavier Rey

Deputy directors
Jeanne Brun (collections)
Frédéric Migayrou (industrial design)
Didier Ottinger (cultural programming)

Administrator
Xavier Bredin

Bibliothèque Kandinsky Curator and head of department
Nicolas Liucci-Goutnikov

Head of collections
Alexia Szumigala

Head of hospitality
Stéphanie Elarbi

Culture and creation department

Director
Mathieu Potte-Bonneville

Deputy director
Nicolas Larnaudie

Head of the talks programme
Jean-Max Colard

Head of art and society events
Caroline Ferreira

Head of cinemas
Judith Revault d'Allonnes

Head of live shows
Chloé Siganos

Production department

Director
Claire Garnier

Deputy director, head of adminstration and finance
Florence Masson

Head of exhibitions management
Mina Bellemou

Head of artworks management
Sandrine Beaujard-Vallet

Head of performance venues
Grégory Mortelette

Head of scenography and museography
Gaëlle Seltzer

Head of workshops and technical resources
Nathalie Weitz

Head of audiovisual production
Sylvain Wolff

Public programmes department

Director
David Cascaro

Deputy director, head of cultural outreach
Selma Toprak-Denis

Deputy director, head of public development
Cécile Venot

Head of public reception
Laurence Nida

Head of administration
Vincent Brico

Communications and digital department

Director
Geneviève Paire

Deputy director for digital
Paul Mourey

Head of public relations
Valentine Dolla

Head of visual identity
Muriel Gombert

Head of administration and finance
Léa Touchaleaume

Economic and international development department

Director
Gaële de Medeiros

Sponsorship
Anaïs Izard

International philanthropy
Marie-Claire Groeninck

CATALOGUE

General editors
Thierry Groensteen
Lucas Hureau
Anne Lemonnier
Emmanuèle Payen

Copyeditors
Audrey Klébaner
Irène Tsuji

Picture research
Léa Vicente
Lucile Boutin, intern

Translator
Jean-François Cornu

Graphic design
Romain Hisquin

Head of production
Benoît Cochet

Photography
Audrey Laurans
Janeth Rodriguez-Garcia

Publications department

Director
Guillaume Grandgeorge

Head of publishing
Chloé Demey

Head of marketing and sales
Élise Albenque

Marketing and e-commerce manager
Margot Boyer

Rights manager
Charlotte Lassansàa

Merchandising manager
Lauriane Pigot

Sales manager
Thomas Savary

Administrative and finance manager
Hélène Pérignon

Administrative assistants
Violaine Ho-Kchen-Fong
Philippe Léonard
Faïza Noirot

Art credits

© Adagp, Paris, 2024: Olivia Clavel, Georges Pichard, Roland Topor, Bernie Wrightson

Zeina Abirached, *Le Piano oriental*, © Casterman

Cover artwork from *Superman* #204 (Feb. 1968). © and ™ DC. Art by Neal Adams. Used with permission.

Charlie Adlard: © 2024 Robert Kirkman, LLC

© Fujio Akatsuka

David B., *L'Ascension du Haut Mal*, vol. 1 © David B. & L'Association, 1996

David B., *L'Ascension du Haut Mal*, vol. 5 © David B. & L'Association, 2000

David B., *L'Ascension du Haut Mal*, vol. 6 © David B. & L'Association, 2003

David B., *Les Complots nocturnes* © David B. & L'Association

Pénélope Bagieu, *Sacrées sorcières* © The Roald Dahl Story Company Limited, 1983, 2020. Licensed Adaptation by Pénélope Bagieu © Éditions Gallimard Jeunesse, 2020. ROALD DAHL is a registered trademark of The Roald Dahl Story Company Ltd.

Alex Barbier, *Comme un poulet sans tête* © Éditions DELCOURT, 1994

Dino Battaglia: © Lo Scarabeo 2023, Italia

© Edmond Baudoin & L'Association, 2004

From *Fun Home: A Family Tragicomic* by Alison Bechdel. Copyright © 2006 by Alison Bechdel. Used by permission of HarperCollins Publishers.

Enki Bilal, *Le Cycle du monstre*, vol. 3: *Rendez-vous à Paris* © Casterman

Enki Bilal, *La Femme piège* © Casterman

Enki Bilal, *Partie de chasse* © Casterman

Blain, Lanzac © Dargaud, 2024

© Stéphane Blanquet

© Blutch

Blutch, *La Volupté* © Futuropolis / Dist. LA COLLECTION

Bravo © Dupuis, 2024

© Herederos de Alberto Breccia. For *Caperucita roja* also: © Herederos de Carlos Trillo All Rights Reserved

Bretécher © Dargaud Benelux (Dargaud-Lombard s.a.), 2024

Claire Bretécher, *Madame et le bonheur* © Dargaud, 2024

© Nina Bunjevac

© Charles Burns

Graphic Novel Excerpt from BLACK HOLE: A GRAPHIC NOVEL by Charles Burns, copyright © 2005 by Charles Burns. Used by permission of Pantheon Books, an imprint of the Knopf Doubleday Publishing Group, a division of Penguin Random House LLC. All rights reserved.

© Caza. With the permission of Passenger Press, Italy 2021-2024

Cestac © Dargaud, 2024

Nicole Claveloux & Édith Zha, *La Main verte* © Cornélius, 2019

© Daniel Clowes (Courtesy Fantagraphics Books)

Comès, *Silence* © Casterman

© Nicolas de Crécy

Nicolas de Crécy, *Le Bibendum céleste*, vol. 2 © 2024 Humanoids, Inc. Los Angeles.

Nicolas de Crécy, *Le Bibendum céleste*, vol. 3 © 2024 Humanoids, Inc. Los Angeles.

© Archivio Crepax and Guido Crepax

Robert Crumb, *Fritz the Cat*, Copyright © Robert Crumb, 1965

Yellow Dog, vol. 2, nos. 9 & 10, 1969, Copyright © Robert Crumb, 1969

Robert Crumb, *Your Hytone Comix*, 'Stoned Agin!', Copyright © Robert Crumb, 1971

Zap Comix, no. 8, August 1975, Copyright © Robert Crumb, 1975

Robert Crumb & Aline Kominsky-Crumb, *Aline and Bob's Dirty Laundry Comics*, Copyright © Robert Crumb and Aline Kominsky-Crumb, 1974

Rébecca Dautremer: © éditions Tishina

Étienne Davodeau, *Le Droit du sol. Journal d'un vertige* © Futuropolis / Dist. LA COLLECTION

Ludovic Debeurme, *Le Grand Autre* © Cornélius, 2007

© Nicolas Deville

© Julie Doucet

Philippe Druillet, *Lone Sloane: Gail* © Éditions Glénat, 1978

'Illustrations From *A Contract With God*'. Copyright © 1978, 1985, 1989, 1995, 1996 by Will Eisner. Copyright © 2006 by Will Eisner Studios, Inc., from THE CONTRACT WITH GOD TRILOGY: LIFE ON DROPSIE AVENUE by Will Eisner. Used by permission of W. W. Norton & Company, Inc.

'Illustrations from *City People Notebook*'. Copyright © 1989 by Will Eisner. Copyright © 2006 by Will Eisner Studios, Inc., from WILL EISNER'S NEW YORK: LIFE IN THE BIG CITY by Will Eisner. Used by permission of W. W. Norton & Company, Inc.

© Brecht Evens

© La Maison Nue, Marion Fayolle, Magnani 2022

F'Murrr © Dargaud, 2024

© Emil Ferris & Monsieur Toussaint Louverture

Copyright © Katrin de Vries – Anke Feuchtenberger – Reprodukt

© Succession Jean-Claude Forest

Jean-Claude Forest, *Barbarella*, page 45 © 2024 Humanoids, Inc. Los Angeles.

André Franquin, *Idées noires* © Franquin / Fluide Glacial

André Franquin, *Gaston Lagaffe* © Dupuis, 2024

© Succession Fred

Fred, *Philémon*, vol. 14: *L'Enfer des épouvantails* © Dargaud, 2024

Fred, *Le Petit Cirque* © Dargaud, 2024

© Fujiko-Pro

Gébé: © Éditions Les Cahiers dessinés, Paris, 2016

© Jochen Gerner & Emmanuel Rabu & L'Association, 2016

Excerpt from *Watchmen* #7 (Mar. 1987). © and ™ DC. Written by Alan Moore. Art by Dave Gibbons. Used with permission.

Excerpt from *Watchmen* #10 (Jul. 1987). © and ™ DC. Written by Alan Moore. Art by Dave Gibbons. Used with permission

Gotlib © Dargaud, 2024

© Dominique Goblet & L'Association, 2007

© Emmanuel Guibert & L'Association, 2012

Joanna Hellgren: © Éditions Cambourakis, 2017

© Hergé//Tintinimaginatio – 2024

'Kyofu Jigoku Shojo' © Hideshi Hino, 1982

© Jacovitti

Fables paniques, Alejandro Jodorowsky © Translated by Benoît Mitaine © Actes Sud – L'An 2, 2017 & © Alejandro Jodorowsky 2003

© Camille Jourdy

Juillard, Christin © Dargaud, 2024

© Killoffer

Copyright © Aline Kominsky-Crumb, 1976

Harvey Kurtzman, *Hey Look!* © 1948 Harvey Kurtzman Estate

Harvey Kurtzman, *Jungle Book* © 1959 Harvey Kurtzman Estate

Jacques de Loustal, *Barney et la note bleue* © Casterman

Ulli Lust, *Trop n'est pas assez* © 2010 Éditions çà et là

© Albin Michel, 2020. With the kind agreement of Luz and Virginie Despentes

Jay Lynch: © The Ohio State University Foundation, Billy Ireland Cartoon Library & Museum. Used with permission.

© Suehiro Maruo

Marc-Antoine Mathieu, *Julius Corentin Acquefaques*, vol. 4, *L'Épaisseur du miroir* © Éditions DELCOURT, 1995

Lorenzo Mattotti, *Feux* © Casterman

Lorenzo Mattotti, *Stigmates* © Casterman

Lorenzo Mattotti: Collectif, *Bob Dylan Revisited* © Éditions DELCOURT, 2008 © Sony ATV Music Publishing France

Graphic Novel Excerpt from HERE by Richard McGuire, copyright © 2014 by Richard McGuire. Used by permission of Pantheon Books, an imprint of the Knopf Doubleday Publishing Group, a division of Penguin Random House LLC. All rights reserved and French translation by Isabelle Troin, *Ici* © Éditions Gallimard Jeunesse

Meurisse © Dargaud, 2024

Fanny Michaëlis, *Le Lait noir* © Cornélius, 2016

Hellboy™: The Storm and the Fury © 2010, 2011, 2024 Mike Mignola

© Frank Miller ink

Cover artwork from *The Dark Knight Returns Tenth Anniversary Edition* (Feb. 1997). © and ™ DC. Art by Frank Miller. Used with permission

© Keizo Miyanishi

© Mœbius Production - Jean Giraud Mœbius

© Chantal Montellier

Morris: © Lucky Comics, 2024

José Muñoz, *Alack Sinner* © Casterman

HADASHI NO GEN © 1973 Nakazawa Keiji. Used by permission of Nakazawa Misayo c/o Project Gen through Japan UNI Agency, Inc., Tokyo

Fabrice Neaud, *Esthétique des brutes - Journal*, vols. 1 & 2 © Éditions DELCOURT, 2022

© Thomas Ott, Edition Moderne

Martin Panchaud, *La Couleur des choses* © 2022 Éditions çà et là

© 2004 Gary Panter (Courtesy Fantagraphics Books)

Frederik Peeters, *Aâma*, vol. 4: *Tu seras merveilleuse, ma fille* © Éditions Gallimard Jeunesse

© Kiki Picasso, Loulou Picasso, 1978

Hugo Pratt, *Corto Maltese: Les Éthiopiques* © 1973 Cong S.A., Switzerland. All rights reserved.

Hugo Pratt, *La Macumba du gringo* © 1977 Cong S.A.,

Photo credits

On the cover:
Mœbius, *Starwatcher*, 1986 (detail)
Private collection, courtesy MEL Publisher

On the paperback:
(front) Mœbius, *Starwatcher*, 1986 (detail)
Private collection, courtesy MEL Publisher
(back) Jean-Claude Forest, *Barbarella*, 1964 (detail)
Bibliothèque Patrimoniale de la Cité Internationale
de la Bande Dessinée et de l'Image, Angoulême

Cover designed by Steve O Connell

Translated from the French *Bande dessinée 1964–2024* by Bethany Wright

First published in the United Kingdom in 2024 by Thames & Hudson Ltd,
181A High Holborn, London WC1V 7QX

First published in the United States of America in 2024 by Thames & Hudson Inc.,
500 Fifth Avenue, New York, New York 10110

British Library Cataloguing-in-Publication Data
A catalogue record for this book is available from the British Library

Library of Congress Cataloging-in-Publication data available on request

Hardback ISBN 978-0-500-02886-5

Paperback ISBN 978-0-500-02840-7

Printed in Spain